AF592780

CHINA'S STRATEGIC BEHAVIOUR

CHINA'S STRATEGIC BEHAVIOUR

Sanjeev Chauhan

UNITED SERVICE INSTITUTION OF INDIA
NEW DELHI

PENTAGON PRESS LLP

CHINA'S STRATEGIC BEHAVIOUR

By Sanjeev Chauhan

First Published in 2019

Copyright © United Service Institution of India, New Delhi

ISBN 978-81-941634-8-0

All rights reserved. No part of this publication may be reproduced, stored in a retrieval system, or transmitted, in any form or by any means, electronic, mechanical, photocopying, recording, or otherwise, without first obtaining written permission of the copyright owner.

Disclaimer: The views and opinions expressed in the book are the individual assertion of the Author in his personal capacity and do not have any offices endorsement. Moreover the Publisher does not take any responsibility for the same in any manner whatsoever. Attributability of the contents lies purely with Author.

Published by
PENTAGON PRESS LLP
206, Peacock Lane, Shahpur Jat
New Delhi-110049
Phones: 011-64706243, 26491568
Telefax: 011-26490600
email: rajan@pentagonpress.in
website: www.pentagonpress.in

Printed at Aegean Offset Printers, Greater Noida, U.P.

Contents

Foreword

Culture influences the way strategists think about state-craft and national security. China, with an ancient civilization and strategic tradition dating back to thousands of years, has a distinctive culture of its own. It prides itself as the 'Middle Kingdom' with its 'Emperor' lording over 'All Under Heaven'. They strongly believe in their Cultural Superiority and Civilisational Depth. While gradually integrating with the rest of the world, China's latent and demonstrated desire to accomplish its objective, on its own terms, and shape the global order continues to be strong. As China continues its inexorable rise, there are enough reasons to be concerned of its strategic behaviour. Now that China has regained its position of strength as a result of its incredible economic rise over the last four decades, it feels justified in asserting its 'rightful place' in the new world order. This is starkly visible in the recent spate of incidents in the South China Sea, Senkaku Islands, and along the China-India/Bhutan borders.

Strategic behaviour is nothing but a reflection of the eternal core values and beliefs of a nation. Not only do these values and beliefs directly affect the strategic decision making process, collectively, but they also find an expression in the strategic guidance, policy and doctrinal articulations of a country. The author uses the rubric of strategic behaviour to assess China's strategic disposition—of increased belligerence and assertiveness—as compared to the way China is usually portrayed, which is as a culturally predisposed nation that seeks nonviolent solutions to problems of state craft and has a defensive mindset, favoring sturdy fortification over expansionism and invasion.

The book traces the art and science of China's strategic behaviour in a handy format designed to enhance the reader's literacy by stimulating reflection on how to decipher the Chinese strategy in order to address the many key themes and challenges which lie ahead in the increasingly complex, rapidly changing and inevitably interconnected world of future. The book also aims to inspire further reading and research into the subject as well as work as base material to encourage the birth of effective strategies to successfully compete with China. The book is an essential resource in terms of its exhaustiveness and analytical insight on understanding Chinese strategic behaviour and is an indispensable compendium for every researcher who wants to study China in a holistic manner.

I compliment the author for this seminal work and wish him success in all his future endeavors.

New Delhi
August 2019

Lt Gen PK Singh, PVSM, AVSM (Retd)
Director, USI of India, New Delhi

Acknowledgements

As a child back from hostel during vacation, I found myself deeply curious about China—it's history and its place in the world. So, my parents brought me all the resource material about China that they could find that was within their means. Interestingly, my childhood conversations with my father, about China, have kept my fascination about the country in a perpetual state of spell. As a professional soldier, I felt no shame in approaching my colleagues and seniors, some of them numerous times, with requests for information. I have benefitted immeasurably from their wisdom, generosity and encouragement. I truly thank them to tolerating my request with good humour and grace. I apologise for not listing them all here.

But circumstances conspired in such a manner to make me write a book on China. For me initially it was a leap of wild optimism to attempt a book and it was then that Henaa Mall motivated me and guided me to give the book the right direction and structure. I want to thank Thaman Paija for providing invaluable assistance in hunting down facts that seemed impossible to find and tracking down stray reference, and Parul Gandhi for checking the semicolons and dashes in the book.

The book bears the unmistakeable mark of the United Service of India (USI) where I was fortunate enough to research on China for a year. Mentors and guides are not expected to tutor their faculty but both BK Sharma and SL Narasimhan agreed to counsel and have been more than generous with their editorial advice and enviable erudition that feature in this book. As I wrote, I found myself drawn often into insights forged in conversation with GS Katoch, Rajiv Narayanan, RPS Bhadauraia, PK Goswami, SB Asthana, Narender Kumar, Roshan Khaniejo, Rajiv Chauhan and Vivek Verma. My family, has shared in more of this process than I have usually asked of them, with humour and resilience and it was their belief in the book when it was still just the glimmer, which gave me space to work out my thoughts. I am quite certain that more adventures await us in China.

Acronyms

3Ws	Three Warfares
5G	Fifth Generation
AI	Artificial Intelligence
AIIB	Asian Infrastructure Investment Bank
ASAT	Anti Satellite
ASEAN	Association of Southeast Asian Nations
ATDCS	Agricultural Technology Demonstration Centres
BAT	Baidu Alibaba Tencent
BC	British Council
BCEG	Beijing Construction Engineering Group
BNCC	Beijing North Computing Centre
BRI	Belt and Road Initiative
CBMs	Confidence Building Measures
CCCC	China Communications Construction Company
CCDI	Central Commission for Discipline Inspection
CCG	China Coast Guard
CCP	Chinese Community Party
CCTV	China Central Television
CD	Conference on Disarmament
CESEC	China Electronic Systems Engineering
CFA	Compact of Free Association
CGTN	China Global Television Network
CLEP	China's Lunar Exploration Program
CMC	Central Military Commission
CNMI	Commonwealth of the Northern Mariana Islands
CNP	Comprehensive National Power
CO_2	Carbon Dioxide
COFA	Compacts of Free Association
COPUOS	United Nations Committee on the Peaceful Uses of Outer Space

CPC	Communist Party China
CPEC	China-Pakistan Economic Corridor
CPV	Chinese People's Volunteers
CRI	China Radio International
CSC	China Study Centers
CSE	China's Standard of English Language
CSF	Community of Shared Future for Mankind
CSR	Corporate Social Responsibility
CSSA	Chinese Students and Scholars Association
DNT	Druk Nyamrup Tshogpa
ECS	East China Sea
EEZ	Exclusive Economic Zone
ELINT	Electronic Intelligence
EM	Electo Magnetic
EO	Electro Optical
EW	Electronic Warfare
EXIM	Export Import Bank of China
FDI	Foreign Direct Investment
FONOPs	Freedom of Navigation Operations
FSM	Federated States of Micronesia
FTA	Free Trade Agreement
GAD	General Armaments Department
GANs	Generative Adversarial Networks
GDP	Gross Domestic Product
GLD	General Logistics Department
GMD	Guomindang
GSD	General Staff Department
HGV	Hypersonic Glide Vehicle
IELTS	International English Language Testing System
IP	Internet Protocol
ISL	International Shipping Lanes
JVs	Joint Ventures
KRR	Kathamandu Ring Road
LAC	Latin America and the Caribbean
LEO	Low Earth Orbit
LNG	Liquefied Natural Gas

M&As	Mergers and Acquisitions
MaRVs	Manoeuvrable Re-entry Vehicles
MEP	Ministry of Ecological Protection
MIIT	Ministry of Industry and Information Technology
MIRVs	Multiple Independently targetable Re-entry Vehicles
MDP	Maldivian Democratic Party
MOS	Ministry of Supervision
MOU	Memorandum of Understanding
MRBM	Medium Range Ballistic Missile
NAC	Nepal Airlines Corporation
NASA	National Aeronautics and Space Administration
NATO	North Atlantic Treaty Organization
NBCP	National Bureau of Corruption Prevention
NDPG	National Defense Program Guidelines
NEEA	National Education Examinations Authority
NGO	Non Governmental Organization
NISEC	National Information Security Engineering Technology Centre
NOAA	National Oceanic and Atmospheric Administration
NPC	National People's Congress
NSA	National Security Agency
NSC	National Supervision Commission
NSR	Northern Sea Route
PLA	People's Liberation Army
PLAAF	People's Liberation Army Air Force
PLAN	People's Liberation Army Navy
PLASSF	People's Liberation Army Strategic Support Force
PML	People's Mediation Law
PPP	Purchasing Power Parity
PNG	Papua New Guinea
PPWT	Prevention of the Placement of Weapons in Outer Space
PRC	People's Republic of China
PRIA	Pokhara Regional International Airport
PSR	Polar Silk Route
QTR	Qinghai Tibet Railway
R&D	Research and Development

RAT	Remote Access Tool
RPO	Rendezvous and Proximity Operations
SAR	Synthetic Aperture Radar
SARA	State Administration for Religious Affairs
SCO	Shanghai Cooperation Organisation
SCS	South China Sea
SEATO	South East Asia Treaty Organisation
SEZ	Special Economic Zone
SIDS	Small Island Developing States
SJ-17	Shijian 17
SLBM	Submarine Launched Ballistic Missile
SLOC	Sea Lines of Communication
SOE	State Owned Enterprise
SPC	Supreme People's Court
SPP	Supreme People's Procuratorate
TAR	Tibet Autonomous Region
THAAD	Terminal High Altitude Area Defense
TJS-3	Tongxin Jishu Shiyan 3
TTA	Transit and Transport Agreement
UAE	United Arab Emirates
UAV	Unmanned Aerial Vehicle
UFWD	United Front Work Department
UN	United Nations
UNCLCS	United Nations Commission for Limits of the Continental Shelf
UNCLOS	United Nations Convention on the Law of the Sea
UNESCO	United Nations Economic and Social Council
UNOOSA	United Nations Office for Outer Space Affairs
US	United States
USSR	Union of Soviet Socialist Republics
UUV	Unmanned Underwater Vehicle
WG	Working Group
WTO	World Trade Organization
XUAR	Xinjiang Uygur Autonomous Region
YREB	Yangtze River Economic Belt
ZTE	Zhongxing Telecommunication Equipment

Introduction

World is what we observe around us. On most occasions, our world is limited to its geographical expanse in terms of territory and the mundane realities which confront us on a day-to-day basis. However, there are times when unknowingly and unintentionally, we live through experiences which force us to go beyond what is around us.

As a child who was sent to a hostel at a very young age, I had the opportunity of meeting people from across the world. It was a world which, until then, had been hidden from me, only to be uncloaked and unravelled at the time when I was ready for it—a vividly vibrant atmosphere which were to later shape me as an individual and the choices I made in future. Interaction with children from all over the world, particularly the South-East Asian countries, left a lasting impression on me. What was intriguing was the root of my surname being traced to the Chinese—language. 'Chou' and 'Han'—two of the most formidable Chinese dynasties constituted my surname. It was this dizzy realisation which made me obsess over everything to do with that country. I was and I am, and I guess shall continue to remain obsessed with China. With time I had the most serendipitous interactions and encounters with China and the Chinese. I was itching to spend a year of my life dwelling deep into the mystery and magic surrounding our neighbour. What makes it tick? What motivates the leviathan? What is the most accurate label for it—a hermit or a territorial heavyweight or both? This book is a discovery of the answers to all these questions and more.

Written through the lens of an Indian who has had the privilege of serving with the Indian Army, this is my attempt to provide an understanding of my brothers across the border. There was a time in the history of this subcontinent when '*Hindi-Chini Bhai Bhai*' was a slogan people lived by. With time, the emptiness and the hollowness of this slogan could be felt by the millions on both sides of the border. However, given the manner in which the two have risen over the last couple of decades, one will not be entirely wrong to assume and state vociferously that the Dragon and the Elephant will have to befriend each other in order to survive in this increasingly intricate and complicated ecosystem. Two of the largest nations which by nature's design are juxtaposed territorially yet are as different as chalk and cheese need to provide space to each other to stay alive and thrive. While the proponents of the survival of the fittest might sneer at me for being overly optimistic, the realists know better. The idea behind this book is to provide an insight into the way China is, and at this juncture I would take the liberty of saying 'China is What China Does Not Say'. From being covert about its ambition to being overt with its modus operandi to achieve the same, China's growth has been fascinating and bewitching for an Indian who has always believed in the moral of the Aesop's Fable *The Tortoise and the Hare* that slow and steady wins the race. I am bewitched and seduced by China and the Chinese and it is this reason among others which has propelled me to undertake this journey. The book traces the trajectory of how China has evolved from the autocratic Han to the monolithic Xi. An exciting year was spent in taking a dip into China and at the end what I am left with are more questions for it is not possible in one lifetime to encapsulate its essence in a few hundred pages.

1

Being China

"When two emperors appear simultaneously, one must be destroyed...struggling and yielding is not the way of a person endowed with humanity.... I hear that two heroes cannot appear together, that two sages cannot exist in the same generation."[1]

—That is Being China.

In the debate of genetics versus environment, culture is the subtext for whichever side wins. In other words, culture plays a central character in the interpretation of our identity. It is the thread which keeps an individual and a nation intact when it comes to self-expression. After all, what is history but a saga of identity clashes and the consequent control which follows therefrom. Thus, the importance of cultural conditioning in determining the fate of any nation cannot be overemphasised. One cannot afford to overlook the role which culture plays in shaping the individual and consequently shaping the nation. Although culture is always in a state of gradual evolution, however, for any profound change in behavioural norms to take roots and associate with the society an external shock may be mandatory. It has been rightly said that, "...all cultures condition their members to think in certain ways, while at the same time providing pre-set responses to given situations. Thus, culture bounds our perceptions and the range of options we have for responding to events."[2]

The womb and the pinnacle of every civilisation is the culture which it develops after strife and struggles both within and without. In one of his candid moments, Robert McNamara, the father of policy analysis and a former United States Secretary of Defence, confessed that "...he and his colleagues in the Kennedy and Johnson administrations were unaware of the history, culture and politics of South-East Asia"[3] and it was this ignorance which gave birth to an incomplete, incoherent and insufficient policy-making process thereby leading to the commission of fundamental errors in the attitude of the United States. Understanding the strategic dimension of culture of friends and foe facilitates a better understanding of their options and helps to evolve a strategic direction while finally leading us to determine the way ahead. After all, it is different strokes for different folks.

Asia is infamous for being the hotbed for power struggles giving rise to countries where people are intoxicated on traditions, value systems and cultural megalomania. India, China and Iraq (former Mesopotamia) are all built on the love for their culture and apparently glorious past, particularly China, which is one of the oldest civilisations with archaeological evidence backing its narrative of glory and gore. In order to preserve this cultural and political supremacy, China feeds its people with a phobia of Thucydides Trap. It is this imagined and feared displacement and loss of honour which reflects in the strategic behaviour of China. However, this 'obsession' of staying perpetually predominant has resulted in the development of a 'strategic narrative' which has been successfully transmitted from generation to generation due to the longevity of the civilisation, pre-dominance in their neighbourhood, the 'continental' extent of their land mass and the isolation from the rest of the world. The four major cultural factors which have influenced the 'persistent and continual strategic narrative' are as follows: firstly, a "loose and distant brand of indirect rule by China over a considerable slice of humanity",[4] since feudal times; secondly, the deep seated fear amongst the Chinese elites that a dynasty meets its end when virtues are lost leading to internal chaos; thirdly, the legacy of ancient thinkers and their philosophies which continue to influence due to their enduring relevance; and fourthly, the tradition of writing the prolific history of over five thousand years which has led to an orientation towards classical security strategies and stratagems.

CHINESE WORLD ORDER

The Chinese World Order can be summed up in one word 'Sinocentrism', that is, China is the pivot and the rest of the world is the periphery. This notion has remained intact for over five thousand years. It is beyond debate and doubt that for China and the Chinese, their legacy is the unshakeable and deep-rooted belief that theirs is one of the most remarkable civilisations which deserves to receive allegiance from the surrounding countries in order to prevent the firm treatment which they are likely to receive should they refuse. However, to opine whether their belief is unfounded is to undermine the complexity involved in their thought and the centuries-old conditioning. One can witness the underpinnings of this superiority as it gets reflected in every interaction which China has had with the rest of the world. From its plan to 'sinicise Islam' to its tacit and paradoxically obvious pressure to establish superiority among its oriental neighbours—everything carries a stamp of the belief that China and Chinese are worthy of the supremacy they have enjoyed. So much so that the Chinese labelled their golden age "Pax Sinica"[5] which literally means 'Chinese Peace'—a feat which can only be established when there is absolute Chinese hegemony. In other words, "Pax Sinica" reiterated the sentiment—"Accept our superiority and we will confer upon you political legitimacy, develop a trade partnership and provide a range of what are known in the language of modern international affairs as public goods."[6] The sphere of influence which China cast on its neighbours has remained intact ever since the days of the Han dynasty. What is surprising though is a revival of the concept of "Pax Sinica" given the manner in which Xi Jinping has been conducting the affairs of China of late. "The great rejuvenation of China"—is an assertion, action and aspiration all rolled into one.

China has never seen itself as equal to other states, but regarded itself as a civilised beacon amidst the other uncivilised barbarians. It was this megalomania that gave rise to a condescending foreign policy by the name of "barbarian management". As per Lien-sheng Yang, this policy was designed with the aim "...to control the barbarians, the sage rulers punished and resisted them when they came (to invade China), and prepared and guarded against them when they left." However, "...if attracted by China's civilisation, they came to offer tribute; they would be treated with courtesy, and kept under loose rein without severing the relationship, so that the blame of being crooked would always be on them."[7]

For the ancient Chinese empire, Central Asia, Southeast Asia and East Asia were crucial in order to establish its 'tributaries'. The centre of power was unsteady and owed its volatility to the propinquity between the Chinese emperor and neighbouring rulers on its west and northwest. It was this constant shift in power which was responsible for nebulous dimensions of the 'Central Kingdom'.

The fabric and authority, which sustained the Emperor, the Son of Heaven (Tian Zi) to influence 'All under heaven' (Tian Xia) with the Mandate of Heaven (Tian Ming) was the texture which sustained the Chinese. Tian Xia meant different things to different people. For the Japanese, the earliest references of this term appear during the Kofun[8] period when Chinese immigrants were welcomed with open arms owing to their prowess in language and culture. For the Chinese, it had a more geographical connotation for it referred to the world as such. The idea behind this term can be summed up as, "under heaven's canopy there is nowhere that is not the king's land; up to the sea's shores, there are none who are not the king's servants' illustrates that the contention for the power of Son of Heaven was from another point of view, a contention for world-leadership."[9] Takeshi Hamashita, a Japanese scholar articulated this by writing, "Like any hegemonic order (the tribute system) was backed by military force, but when the system functioned well, principles of reciprocity involving politics and economics permitted long periods of peaceful interaction."[10]

Tian Xia was all encompassing for the Chinese. It knew no boundaries and therefore, when Britain sent a mission to China in order to initiate a relationship with the Qing dynasty, the same was accepted by the Emperor on the basis that it would enhance the power and the position of his throne. His subjects were informed that it was the yearning of the British to be civilised which led them to undertake the journey. It was, thus, an attempt to prevail further and deeper than the Emperor already had, both within and without.

The essence of the Chinese concept of power in its backyard and working of geopolitics down to present day can be understood by examining its historical relationship with a Pacified South (now Vietnam) and Island Barbarians (now Japan).

The relations between China and Vietnam have been rocky despite their common 'sinospheric' and socialist background and the only time the region to the South of China (*Dai Viet*, now Vietnam) had peace with China for nearly a thousand years was after the defeat of the Tang by the Cham Pa. The same lasted until the nineteenth century takeover by the French. This millennia of peace was the outcome of an absolute submission to the Chinese Emperor and acknowledgment of Chinese position of authority and dominance under Tian Xia. The same was intercepted in 1406 when under the Ming dynasty China attacked Vietnam.

While the brutality of the attack cannot be underplayed, it is the psychological and cultural impact of the same which was more damaging—Chinese in place of vernacular language as the medium of instruction, ban on chewing of betel nut, sacrifices before the Chinese deities, suppression of the local cults and syncretic traditions, confiscation and destruction of the national literature and imposition of the Chinese attire. These were some of the ways in which Vietnam was psychologically subjugated and was once again reduced to a tributary state.

Nearly a decade later after the Chinese invasion, a resistance movement was launched in 1418 by Le Loi, a wealthy farmer, who laid siege on Hanoi and managed to establish a new dynasty in 1428. It was during this period that the Vietnamese desired to be vindictive but were counselled against it given the futility of war and the destruction caused as a result of the same. Describing this episode Nayan Chanda wrote, "In the present circumstances it is not difficult to attack the enemy and to quench our thirst with his blood.... For the good of our two nations it is better to take advantage of this situation when the enemy is at the end of its tether to make peace with him."[11] On the contrary, Vietnamese gained China's support when Le Loi explained his desire of a full-scale invasion of Champa.

From the foregoing, it was natural to assume that Vietnam wanted to remain under the overarching shadow of China. However, the assumption was demolished when the Vietnamese ruler proclaimed himself 'Emperor' and sought investiture as 'King'. Furthermore, a major challenge for the Le dynasty (1428–1788), the strongest and most enduring regime of Vietnam, was finding the right vocabulary in its dealings with China now that Vietnam was morphing into a regional hegemon, with an increasingly imperial manner of its own toward its neighbours.

The dichotomy of the situation compelled the ruler of Vietnam to resort to a kind of play-acting on both sides. "The Vietnamese world vision contradicted the Chinese world view at a crucial point. In the Chinese view, the Chinese emperor was the universal ruler. He alone ruled the entire world in heaven's name, and 'nobody else could claim the title of emperor'. The Vietnamese, however, asserted that the world was naturally divided into north and south and each domain was ruled by its own emperor. According to the Vietnamese view, the Vietnamese emperor was the legitimate ruler of the south, while the Chinese emperor the legitimate ruler of the north."[12] Amidst this, it was not difficult to observe the constant exchange of culture between the two countries. One cannot turn oblivious to the influence of the Chinese on Vietnam. It was this influence which led to leaders such as Phan Boi Chau to seek help from the Kuomintang in order to overthrow the French.

China's waterloo was Japan. "The main driver of the change that definitively closed the curtains on the two-millennia-old Sinocentric order in the region was without doubt imperial Japan. It defeated its much larger neighbour in 1895 in the Sino-Japanese war and thereafter surged ahead of it according to almost every measure of national power over the next half century, only to be driven out of China and defeated in World War II."[13]

China's debacle in the war with Japan was a milestone in the continuing relevance of the 'Tian Xia' system in Chinese mind and spirit allowing them finally to see beyond their long-held superiority and aloofness, and abandon, if only temporarily, their traditional hierarchical view of the world whose default mode called for dealing with foreigners on their terms or not at all. Writing about the Chinese loss in the Sino-Japanese War, Liang Qichao, wrote the war "awakened my country from the long dream of four thousand years."[14]

The hangover of the humiliation suffered due to this defeat to Japan did not leave China for long. In fact, the cultural superiority and the military might, which was once believed to be invincible, was no more. It was this crack in their belief which fuelled the Chinese and unleashed their energy to resume their position in the East. The aftereffects of the defeat continue to get reflected in the modern day Chinese attitude towards Japan.

From 'Pax Americana' to 'Pax Sinica'

China's liberation in 1949 gave it teething issues. It had to re-adjust, re-orient, re-think and re-strategise so that it could work towards its old dream of Pax Sinica – Tian Xia. Modern China had to go back to the drawing board in order to impress upon the world and more importantly its neighbours that the "cutting of the Chinese melon" had not cut its spirit to rule. It was this obsession with Sino-centricism which surfaces in the manner China conducts itself even today. Howard French aptly captures the sentiments and situation of China when the world was changing gears. He writes, "China was plummeting towards a historical nadir in its relative regional power and influence. The norm for it had long been an unshakable conviction in the enduring universality of its values and ethics, its own culture, and its unquestioned centrality. The new, western form of global universality was based not on a presumed natural hierarchy in the world, with China at the apex, but rather on the presumed equality of clearly defined nations on a raft of Judeo-Christian ideas and institutions, on spreading principles of electoral democracy, on open trade instead of managed tributary exchanges, and finally on a fast-emerging regime of international law. Underwriting all of these fine sounding notions was, of course, Western power and, in the twentieth century, American power."[15]

It was this disconnect between the notions and the reality which led to the disruption of the old Chinese world order. The West exploited this very gap between the self-image which China had about itself and the geopolitical reality. The aggression of the West and by the West was a cakewalk due to the chimerical ideas of China about itself, the price of which had to be borne by East Asia.

However, it was only after the humiliation of being imperialised by powers in the continent that China realised how feeble and fragile it was. It was malnourished and needed to concentrate on regaining its lost glory through accumulation of wealth and exerting itself first in its own backyard and then later on the world in order to prevail in an all-pervasive and all-encompassing manner. It had to prove to the world that it had arrived as a country and was ready to take its rightful place; that it was no longer Washington, but Beijing which called the shots.

INTERNAL ORDER

Imperial China could have avoided its fate had it been pushed towards soul searching before it was devoured by the colonialists. From nurturing the dream of becoming "a world colonizer", it had to face the reality of being snubbed into "a world colony" for every single imperialist had a share in it. The invincible, infallible and imperial China collapsed because it did not have the power to withstand foreign attacks with its falling immunity levels. This frailty was given a romantic expression by Charles Henry Brewitt-Taylor in his translated work of the *Romance of the Three Kingdoms.*[16] He wrote, "Domains under heaven, after a long period of division, tend to unite; after a long period of union, tend to divide. This has been so since antiquity."[17]

History does not repeat itself for those who learn from it. Given that the Chinese dynasties fell prey to the same cause each time is indicative of the subtext which has hitherto been overlooked, which was their inability (back then) to learn lessons for posterity. The Xia (2205–1766 BC) met his nemesis in Shang (1554–1045 BC) who lost his authority to Zhou (1122–221 BC) who finally met his match in the Hans (202 BC–220 AD). The Yuan Dynasty (1276–1368 AD) lost its sheen when the 'Red Turban Revolts'[18] decided to put an end to it. The Mings were overthrown by a peasant rebellion and the Qing replaced them in 1644. With the downfall of the Qing in 1912, monarchy took its last breath in China. This has been summed up by John King Fairbank, "Most dynasties collapsed under the twin blows of 'inside disorder and outside calamity' (nei-luan wai-huan), that is, domestic rebellion and foreign invasion, every regime was therefore under pressure to make the facts of its foreign relations and internal governance fit the theory and so confirm its claim to rule China."[19]

China emerged from this stronger, sharper and shrewder. Post-independence, it was acutely aware of the importance of maintaining political stability. The reconstruction of China began on this very plinth—complete, absolute and unequivocal control by the CCP. It was sensitive to both the forces and while it was able to achieve stability in the international arena, it couldn't stabilize itself internally. For the Chinese "stability overrides everything"[20] but how does one ensure stability in a country which is inherently ridden with contradictions? The rhetoric might seem offensive but there are no grounds to doubt its veracity. Susan L Shirk, an expert on Chinese politics took the liberty of summing up the reality of China by selecting some of the most honest adjectives—"Fragile superpower—economically dynamic and internationally secure and confident, but domestically fragile and insecure."[21] The subjugation of Tibetans and Uighurs, the glaring economic inequalities and the constant churning of socio-economic movements further corroborate her statement. Can one forget the impact of 1989 Tiananmen Square Protests, also known as the June Fourth Incident, which led to the declaration of the martial law in China, set against post-Mao Zedong reforms?

The biggest challenge which is staring into the eyes of the Chinese political class is the economic inequality, absence of social security, severe corruption, rising unemployment, falling faith in the party governance and rural-urban divide. These challenges have led to an increase in mass demonstrations, riots, strikes, etc. Near absence of a grievance redressal mechanism further rubbed salt on the raw wounds of the masses. The situation with time only seems to have worsened with mass protests increasing by over a hundred percent in less than three decades. While the leadership was expected to display maturity given their past experience, it once again displayed lack of skill in dealing with public outrage.

When suppression substitutes solution for over centuries, you know that there exists a pathological problem in the manner the state has been structured and time and again, one is pushed to come to this conclusion. China in its new avatar is nothing more than old wine in new bottle. Acquisition of wealth, military might, violation of human rights and absence of basic entitlements give a glimpse into the insides of a country which can be driven to collapse under this own weight.

The lines separating the government from the state often appear blurred to the masses and this is especially true for a country where state is synonymous with the party. In such a situation, while people might still love their country, there is no love lost for the government.

"Wu Xinbo, the Executive Dean, Institute of International Studies at Fudan University, argued that in the post-Mao Chinese security practice, state and regime are the 'key referents of security' and that ethnic groups, mainly Tibetans, Uyghur and Mongols, constitute one of the chief threats to the state and regime security because they neither identify with the state nor with the regime."[22]

Socio-Economic Demeanour

Instability in China is like an illegitimate child whose 'real father' cannot be traced. It is a scourge that China has to deal with; more like Frankenstein. When Deng Xiaoping equated richness with glory, he did not desire aggrandisement at the cost of stability. Instead he saw wealth as an instrument to achieve glory, control and supremacy. It is this perverted misinterpretation of his statement which led to skyrocketing corruption, moral degeneration, social and economic extremities and ultimately siphoning of the national wealth.

Half-hearted measures by the political elite only gave a verisimilitude of action but did not repair any damage caused by the very same class. Hu Jintao, while addressing the delegates of 18th CPC National Congress said, "If we fail to handle this issue (corruption) well, it could prove fatal to the party, and even cause the collapse of the party and the fall of the state."[23]

China's remarkable economic development has drawn migration of workers from rural areas to town and cities in search of work. The migrant population has not only increased over the years but has also continued to face disparity in terms of the access to public services and discrimination due to household registration system (Hukou). The migrants at the beginning of the 'opening and reform' period were children of the cultural revolution who had worked on the field in the rural area, had a childhood reminiscent of hunger, stagnation and suffering, had very basic needs and were determined to succeed in spite of adversity. As compared to this, the migrants of today are products of Deng's one-child policy, have never tilled the land, have greater aspirations and are more emotionally demonstrative of their needs and are reluctant to endure in silence. However, their dreams of shaping up a future have been shattered by the high cost of living today and change in nature of job from secure manufacturing or a construction job to insecure service sector jobs such as cleaning and parcel delivery. Moreover, preference of male child in the one-child policy period has resulted in a skewed sex ratio implying men facing a more competitive marriage market and leading to more dissatisfied 'bare branches'. It is this sight which can be a source of worry for the Chinese leadership in the future, for this generation is aspirational and desires more out of life. If the economy, therefore, stagnates, it is this class of migrants which will be a source of truancy.

Xinjiang Uighur Autonomous Region: Waiting to Explode

China's relationship with one-sixth of its land is fairly complicated. Xinjiang Uighur Autonomous Region (also known as XUAR) has a population of twenty million which comprises thirteen different ethnicity, majority of whom belong to an Islamic community called Uighurs. Given their religious affinities, they consider their land (also known as East Turkistan) as a part of Central Asia. The influx of the Han Chinese into XUAR is responsible for destabilising the demography which can conflagrate into a full-fledged conflict. The rise of religious fundamentalism has the potential of emboldening the secession struggles by separatist groups like the East Turkistan Islamic Movement and Turkistan Islamic Party. China is acutely aware of the magnitude this problem can assume and has therefore initiated infrastructural development in Xinjiang just to keep the area under its firm control.

The strategy that the Chinese have adopted in order to deal with Uighur opposition is similar to the one it has adopted to deal with the Tibetan Plateau but the difference lies in the backlash and the ostracism it will receive from the international community. While it may alienate the Islamic diaspora when it comes to the former, the treatment in case of the latter will not lead to severe ramifications.

The fate of the ambitious Belt and Road Initiative (BRI) lies in the manner China deals with this community. Even though it has undertaken serious measures to ensure peace and security in this region by ensuring constant surveillance and severe crackdown of the terrorist activities,[24] it has not been able to quell the rising voices from this territory. The recent demolishing of a Hui mosque in Ningxia did not convey the right measure to the international community.[25]

China does need to tread carefully and tactfully. In the words of President Xi, "Xinjiang's security is vital to the whole country's reform, development and stability, as well as to national unity, ethnic harmony and national security"[26] and while this statement is encouraging, behind it is the Orwellian reality of Xinjiang where concentration camps are being set up which aim at 'transformation through education'.[27] The situation has worsened since 2017 when the decimation of Uighurs began. The region has turned into 'information vacuum' where journalists are under strict watch, business is scarce and political marginalisation is at its peak. The extent to which China has tried to subjugate this region is evident from number of deletions WeChat has witnessed in the last one year.

What China hopes to achieve is peace and stability in a region where Uighurs are reduced to an insignificant pliant minority without any identity of their own. Unfortunately, it is far from accomplishing the same and the severity of its measures has made Xinjiang in its original full-bloom form yoq (gone).

Tibet: Achilles Heel

Chinese may not be overtly driven by emotions, but China surely has its sore point in Tibet. While the Tibetans have held on to their status of an independent country which shared a rich historical past and religious exchange with China, the Chinese assert that Tibet has always been a protectorate of theirs and even though distortion of historical facts is not a new and novel veil to justify invasions, the Chinese chose to do so in a manner most ensanguined. "The history of People's Republic of China and rule over Tibet can be analysed in four phases: 17 Point Agreement (1951–1959) [where the two grudgingly tried to co-exist]; Democratic Reforms (1959–1965) and Cultural Revolution (1966–1976); Reform, Cultural Revival, Uprising & Martial Law (1978–1989); and Integration, Development & Uprising (1989–present)."[28]

Tibet became independent in 1911, with the collapse of Qing dynasty and with the government of Dalai Lama taking over the country. The British considered Tibet a buffer state and did not exert any influence in the region till an attempt was made to delineate the border between Tibet and British India in 1914, also known as the McMahon Line, the status of which as an international border is disputed by China.

Tibet has witnessed some of the most ghastly attacks[29] and resulted in India giving political asylum to the 14th Dalai Lama after entering into the Panchsheel Pact with China in 1955, crux of which was recognition of political sovereignty and non-interference in each other's affairs. What was seen a pact to cement friendship and bonhomie laid the very foundation of the Indo-Chinese war of 1962?

The eighties witnessed a severe crackdown of the religious freedom by seizing control of all monasteries, declaring Dalai Lama an enemy of the state and forbidding even possession of an image of the Dalai Lama. The self-immolation by monks prior to the 2008 Beijing Olympics led to a further clamping down and deploying of security forces and the Communist Party Workers in rural areas to control the Tibetan propaganda. The symbolic measures were backed by actual, active steps being taken on the ground in order to 'demonise' the religious head. The intent behind ensuring greater connectivity and accessibility along with putting in place the infrastructure to strengthen its control over the 'Roof of the World' was to strip its dignity in the most undignified manner. This was further accentuated by the Chinese asserting the exclusive right of China to select the reincarnated 15th Dalai Lama. Coupled with these was the resettlement drive orchestrated by the Han Chinese with the aim of Hanisation of Tibet.

The present dynamics of the Insecurity Dilemma in Tibet is due to repetitive 'action-reaction syndrome' due to the strategic use of repression by Chinese Party-State and persistent insecurity of the Tibetan with their Identic. Apparently, the Chinese could have snubbed this conflict even before it assumed the proportion it has today; however, it is pertinent to understand the root cause of this conflict. This is more of an image and an identity clash arising out of deep rooted insecurity of the Tibetan nation. "Tibetan positions and activities are nationalistic and the Chinese policies and practices are security and stability-driven."[30] What the Chinese views as a security and stability issue, Tibet sees as a nationalist identity issue thereby leading to a perception mismatch. "The identity insecurity at the heart of the Tibetan grievances is a product of the hard-line policies pursued by the Chinese after 1989. The hardening of Chinese policies in response to the uprising, which in turn heightens insecurity and strengthens identity on the Tibetan side, creating the conditions for another Tibetan upheaval, bringing the insecurity dilemma full-circle."[31]

BELIEF SYSTEMS

With time, 'Classics' grow in appeal. However, more often than not, they lose their relevance. The Chinese here too have displayed an exception. The value system, the strategic thinking, the outward display of strength and the internal lack of immunity are all derivatives. Their doctrines have basis in religion and their society is an expression of the tight control which classical thinkers continue to exert. However, at this juncture it is necessary to clarify that one must never make the mistake of reducing complex and ancient philosophical wisdom and tradition to a handful of concepts. These concepts originated in the same country but in a different world and therefore, to find meaning in them in the present day context is not simple. They were a product of another era and require interpretation through integration with the present socio-economic and political milieu. Viewing them in isolation and evaluating their impact will be foolhardy and amateurish. The Chinese have hence steered clear from a literal translation of these philosophies and chosen excerpts which can fit their popular sensibilities without distorting their pre-existing notions of the state, government, rights, duties, liberties, privileges, entitlements, etc. The confluence, cultural borrowing and coexistence between Confucianism, Buddhism and Taoism are what has today become a hallmark of the Chinese Culture.

Confucianism

The philosopher who continues to influence China the most is Confucius. Regarded as the 'first teacher',[32] his thoughts and ideas find meaning and relevance in life of a modern day Chinese even after his demise in 479 BC. "The Six Classics"[33] attributed to the ancient holy sages were analysed through the prism of morals and ethics by Confucius. Confucius' teachings focussed on self-control and self-preservation, the interpretation of which was presented in "Lun Yu" (*Analects of Confucius*: compiled and written by his followers). The entire paraphernalia of what and who an ideal Chinese should be is based on the knowledge he imparted. It is this hypnotic quality of Confucianism which has mystified and demystified it in an equal measure. Its offshoots led by Mencius and Xun Kuang (Xunzi) were polar opposites. While the former stood against war and denounced it as a crime against people, the latter upheld the realistic and materialistic aspect of the Confucian thought based upon his reading and understanding of the complex human behaviour. Xun Kuang wrote a book *Xunzi* which was a marriage between Confucianism and Legalism, focusing on state control by law and was adopted by the Han Dynasty as state doctrine. However, it was "Wang Aushi"[34] who imbided the Confucian Concepts as tenets for societal structure (Baojia).

Humanism lies at the essence and crux of Confucianism. Confucianism is distinguished by five 'constants' which go along with classical sizi with four virtues. The five "Constants" are "Ren" (Benevolence), "Yi" (Righteousness), "Li" (Rites), "Zhi" (Knowledge), "Xin" (Integrity),[35] and the four "Virtues" are "Zhong", (Loyalty), "Xiao", (Filial Piety), "Jie" (Continence) and "Yi" (Righteousness)", which have been procured from the Confucian texts of *Analects* and *The Book of Mencius*. "Ren (Benevolence) is the first and most important 'Constant' among the five 'Constants'. It manifests itself on the inner mind, in love and comparison for people and in avoiding harm or envy towards anyone. However, the younger generation today seems to have "...lost our humanity, our kindness and spirit. Confucianism is our only hope for becoming a great nation."[36] The bedrock of the societal norms both at the family and society level is filial piety which inoculates a reverence dutifulness, deep allegiance and esteem for one's parents, family and elders. Filial piety values devotion, selflessness and obedience, all of which are of great significance for promoting the social morality. "Filial piety, which had an exceptionally high salience in traditional Chinese society, continues to be significant in contemporary China. Although some researches argue that due to 'individualisation' in Chinese society, family obligations and filial sentiments have substantially weakened."[37]

Confucianism has been the flavour of the Chinese in the contemporary world. Coupled with shades from Buddhism and Taoism, it is being promoted as one of the best guiding philosophy embedded in it the tenets of obedience, obsequious and omnipotence. The Cultural Revolution of Mao treated the principles and the expressions of Confucianism with much condescension and disdain.[38] However, the economic reforms unleased by Deng Xiaoping tried to bring within their folds nationalism, cultural nobility and soft power. The reforms were meant to plug the ideological gaps created by Mao and end the confusion following thereafter. Xi Jinping in the keynote address at the 2565th birthday of Confucius on 24 September 2014, said "Confucianism, along with other philosophies and cultures taking shape and growing within China are records of spiritual experiences, rational thinking and culture achievement of the nation to build its home... These cultures have nourished the flourishing Chinese nation."[39] The heady cocktail of Buddhist, Taoists and Confucian philosophy serves as the bedrock for the Chinese philosophy today. The Chinese being fervently religious throng the temple establishments in order to pay homage or offer respects. It is imperative that in the modern day China the teachings of these religions are seen as the values to live by. Amidst volatility, the principles of filial piety and harmony serve as an anchorage for the people and the political class alike. Over the recent years, Confucius has emerged not just as a religious figure but also as a hero whose philosophy transcends the barriers of time. The 'revival of Confucius'[40] is more of a strategic move by the Chinese leadership such that the bottled up anger, discontentment and disconnect of the masses finds a healthy outlet instead of a rebellion. The idea is to not let the lava accumulate for a volcanic eruption, given the present spiritual health of the country.

Buddhism

Buddhism has been assimilated into all levels of Chinese culture. The interaction between Buddhism and the Chinese culture, which has spanned over two hundred years, has had a far reaching impact in areas such as arts, literature, philosophy, medicine and architecture. Today the three forces that shape the Chinese belief system can be understood as a blend of Confucianism at middle of the road, with Taoism and Buddhism supporting from the edges.

Buddhism is a philosophy which originated in India but travelled far and wide[41] due to the patronage it received from the Indian monarchs, craftsmen, the mercantile class, artisans, etc. Buddhism has seen multiple transformations arising due to the forces of assimilation in some areas and exclusion in another. Buddhism became the rice to every curry—Tibetan, Thai, Chinese, Central Asian, Nepalese, Sri Lankan, Japanese, etc. The spread took place without coercion and it continued till the Arab attacks began in Bactria.[42] The devastation caused by the nomadic tribes led to a steep downfall of the trade and hence the channel through which Buddhism spread was blocked, brutalised and broken. With time, the Chinese made Buddhism their own and with local influence and mainstream merging, it became the single most revered philosophy which the country would see in the future and made inroads into arenas where no other philosophy had reached.

With a population of over two hundred and five million,[43] China houses the largest number of Buddhists from across its schools. It is this number that China uses to claim its exclusive right on the process of 'reincarnation of Dalai lama' with the hope that it will be able to subvert the Dalai Lama and turn him into a tool of politicking. Contrary to the Chinese stand, the Dalai Lama is not a position which can be chosen by design. It is through reincarnation and as long as the single most unifying factor fails to be remain independent and sans any political interference, it will cease to remain effective.[44] The Chinese, in order to impress upon their take on the issue, have formulated a law which excludes "any foreign organization or individual from the reincarnation selection process in an attempt to legitimize China's authority and exclude all others in the selection of the next Dalai Lama."[45] For China it is crucial to be in the ultimate control of Buddhism because it uses the religion as a tool to reach out to Southeast Asia countries. It desires to control the agency of Buddhism in order to keep 1.6 billion people[46] who practise Buddhism under it passive control. Furthermore, it wishes to emerge as the sole keeper of the identity of 22 per cent of Asians by establishing emotional bonding, connectivity and patronage. It wishes to go back in time and this time productises Buddhism as its very own. It is the instrument of Buddhism which China wants to use in its Tibetan cause.

Promoting a China-centric discourse and emerging as the main centre of Buddhist learning and texts[47] and the consequent exercise of control, China knows what and how it wants to do with Buddhism. In order to help conciliate the misperceptions of 'Peaceful Rise' Jiang Zemin and Hu Jintao inertly backed Buddhism.

The ancient classical philosophy which had its roots in India and stressed on simplicity has now turned into one of the most prominent tools to gain recognition and validation. Through translations of the old classical texts it wishes to control the narrative and legacy of Buddhism while concurrently diluting and underplaying the role of the Tibetan monks.

How China embodies the tenets of Buddhism in the future is a question that can only give us speculative answers because with China expediency is the key solution to every problem. But to say that it will try to use it as much as possible to accomplish what it has set out to achieve is definitely not conjecture.

Taoism

An ancient traditional philosophy which traces back its origin to 6th century BC, Taoism finds its traces in the Chinese culture, customs and conduct. Literal translation of the word 'Tao' means 'the way'. It is the religion of unity and opposites which essentially talks about the energy of the polar opposites—Yin and Yang. With time these energies found manifestation in stark contradictions such as complete subjugation and revolt; victory and defeat and stability and instability. Flashes of the Taoist philosophy can be seen in the manner in which China tackled with its neighbour Vietnam. Absolute peace followed by absolute destruction. One can also not ignore the Taoist influence in the image China projects to the international community. While China talks about stability, security and peace in Xinjiang, it clearly demonstrates a diametrically opposite behaviour in that territory. Similarly the unleashing of economic reforms was meant to ensure an evenly distributed economic development but what has transpired is a deeper economic stratification. One can label these as an outcome of intention-action mismatch but one cannot deny the strong shades of Taoism in the aforementioned measures of the Chinese. The core concept of Taoism is 'Wu Wei' which is often translated as 'governing by doing nothing'. However, in Taoism it implies "pure effectiveness and creative quietude."[48] Huston Smith attributes "the individual who manages the concept as one who acts without strain, persuades without argument, is eloquent without flourish, and achieves results without violence, coercion, or pressure."[49] The resultant harmonious ecosystem must not be inferred as not acting at all but as an adaptability of the desired conditions of effortless and agreeable ways while maintaining harmony. The understanding of the concept gains importance in strategic thinking as it offer a more nuanced understanding of the self-reflexivity of a decision maker in terms of flow, self-preservation and contingency planning in case of failure.

Educated elite in China through history have read Taoist classics and laid considerable emphasis to them. Taoists are characterised by sensitivity to the 'way of nature'—they could be associated with rejecting unnatural assertiveness, violence and aggression. Since the followers have generally been intelligentsia and the elite, its tenets are factored more into the macro level and strategic decision making is significant.

Beliefs in Contemporary China: 'Sinicisation' and Active Guidance

Sinicisation of belief in China has been upheld by the party leadership so as to promote ethnic solidarity and religious harmony and guard against infiltration of religious extremism. China has issued two white papers on policies on freedom of belief. The first white paper one was issued in October 1997 titled, "Freedom of Religious belief in China."[50] The second white paper was issued in April 2018 and is titled "China's Policies and Practices on Protecting Freedom of Religious Belief."[51] "The release of the second white paper coincides with what some see as reaching an agreement with the Vatican on the nomination and appointment of bishops, as well as improving Vatican-China ties."[52] The presentation of the white paper came few days after the abolition of the sixty years old regulatory body—State Administration of Religious Affairs (SARA) and absorption into the United Front Work Department (UFWD) allowing for a closer control by the Chinese Community Party (CCP) of religious affairs. The white paper states that China maintains the principle that, "religion must be Chinese in orientation", and that, "active guidance", is required to be provided to them, in order that they, "can adapt to socialist society." The 'Active Guidance'[53] is a slogan of Xi Jinping, reiterated at the CPC Congress in October 2017 and at the National People Congress in March 2018."[54] The white paper firmly maintains that all religion need to conform to socialist norms and uphold the Communist Party leadership which can be construed as 'sinicisation of all religions'. This entails CPC is seeking to mould religion in China to its own image—offering it as individual right but hedging against it becoming an inconvenient excuse for mass mobilisation. A semantic policy change proceeding from the white paper is the acceptance of freedom of religious belief as a basic policy of the CPC. Previously, religion was merely a pragmatic government policy that the CPC could turn a blind eye to, and still retain its ideological purity. Such a change might be an early indicator of intent to remove the taboo associated with illegal adherence to religion.

CHINESE CLASSICS ALL TIME RELEVANCE

The Chinese have had the wisdom and the benefit thereof of recording history and documenting it which has facilitated a journey into the reconstruction of their past accurately sans ambiguity. The Chinese military—its traditions, its fodder, its training and its mind-set, are all a derivation of what was prevalent five thousand years ago and expressed in the famous eight military classics. The formal expression of a military encyclopaedia and a War College[55] back in the initial years of the first millennia is indicative of the importance accorded to the military might. These accomplishments are not isolated incidents of the Chinese but a manifestation of the Chinese thought and their attitude of resilience. It is this past which they dig into in order to back the national security thinking and prevalent doctrines.

The Eight Military Classics of Ancient China

China boasts of rich literature when it comes to military writings. The military philosophers laid down the foundation upon which the Chinese military strategy, tact, vision and discipline are modelled. While is it enthralling to see the fervour with which the Chinese have documented their thought, it is also disconcerting to witness the emotion and reverence with which they treat them for they continue to underline the modern military. Although Sun Tzu's 'Art of War' is the most celebrated, compelling and philosophical warfare treatise, however Chinese military writings are much more comprehensive. The Seven Military Classics[56] of Ancient China written between 500 BC and 700 AD were an omnibus covering all the aspects of strategy with special importance on deceiving ones opponent by covertness, outmanoeuvre and flexibility. The English translation of the Seven Military Classics was first published in 1993 by Ralph D Sawyer and subsequently in 1995 Alastair Iain Johnston in his book *Cultural Realism Strategic Culture and Grand Strategy in Chinese History*. Johnston's book combines and compares the derived strategic culture and preferences from the Seven Military Classics with the effect of these on the Ming Dynasty (1368–1644) towards the Mongol threat.

A study of the ascertainment in the classics brings on the views that 'offence is the best of defence', vis-à-vis the accommodative or defensive strategies.

Therefore, one can see China's pugnacious and offensive attitude in the light of the same. China's offensive attitude can be seen as a means to secure the borders. It is also interesting to witness the manner in which even the finer nuances of the modern defence strategy is influenced by and juxtaposed with the traditional classics which continue to direct the motives and measures which the military takes in order to emerge invincible. However, something has changed over the last few decades in the manner in which China has chosen to fight its battles. The aim is not just military might but also solid political gains, resource conservation, use of irregular force and pressure tactics so that a war can be won without the brawl. China took to these measures like a fish to water owing to the years of conditioning and psychological control in which to fight is the way to survive.

The relevance of the Eight Military Classics can be appreciated from the fact that President Xi Jinping has frequently used the following idioms from the *Method of Sima*, "Thus even though a state may be vast, those who love warfare will inevitably perish." Although Xi has been emphasising China's peaceful rise in his speeches, his actions make us believe that he is well aware of another phrase in *Methods of the Sima* which advocates peace with military preparedness—"Even though calm may prevail under Heaven, those who forget warfare will certainly be endangered."[57]

Sun Tzu

Sun Tzu, a sage and a military general during the Zhou Dynasty who lived approximately around the 4th century BC is the foremost amongst Chinese strategists. Sima Qian (206 BC–220 AD), in his book records of the Grand Historian (Shiji), gave a biographical account of Sun Tzu. Sun Tzu proposed his services to the Wu State a small state at the mouth of the Yongze River and later led Wu's forces to defeat the far bigger forces of the state of Zhu, Qi and Qin.[58] In the later years, Sun Tzu found his appreciation in the writings of eminent military leaders such as Sun Bin, Cao and Li Quan. Sun Tzu's work *Art of War*, a treatise on how warfare is intertwined with politics, diplomacy, economic, geography, etc. is "considered the oldest and greatest extant Chinese military work"[59] and has influenced the world in a manner it discerns China. "Sun Tzu lived in an age when different states vied for hegemony and fought endless bloody wars."[60] The number of wars fought in a span of about 500 years, for instance, according to one estimate, was between about 1,211 between

722 and 464 BC and about 468 in about 242 years between 463–222 BC.[61] However, Sun Tzu said the best strategy is the one that delivers victory without fighting. He said, "Generally in war the best policy is to take a state intact: to ruin it is inferior to this. To capture the enemy's army is better than to destroy: to take intact a battalion, a company or a five-man squad is better than to destroy them. To win one hundred victories in one hundred battles is not the acme of skill. To subdue the enemy without fighting is the acme of skill." To achieve the objective without fighting means that a state's response in negotiations and military campaign should align in such a manner that they improve the chances of victory and in the future leads to the state's survival and prosperity. Also, it brings out the fact that it lacks merit to gain a victory if troops are completely worn out and all resources at the disposal of state have been exhausted. The Haiti Crisis (1994) and the Cuban Missile Crisis (1962) are contemporary examples where all elements of national power were used to achieve national objectives without getting into a state of endless war.

When war is unavoidable it is best to attack the strategy of the enemy. After strategy it is the enemy's alliances which need to be attacked, as Sun Tzu stated in *Art of War*. He said, "Alliances are a double edged sword. There are times when they are needed but they also create a potential opening for opponents. The basic approach is to only create alliances when they are needed for a specific situation and not get entangled in them." In Chapter 3, titled "Planning Offensive", Sun Tzu describes how life energy (Qi) constitutes the basis for the kingdom's forces (Li) and he explains in detail how long drawn-out operations will consume Qi and bring down the military general's Li. In actual practice, most of Mao's military operations presented examples of limited war, even though formally his doctrine of People's War expounded a vision of mass-mobilisation and total war. And now, as China's leaders formally pronounce limited war as being their formal post-Cold War national security doctrine, there has been a much greater attempt at emphasising its linkage with Sun Tzu's writings. From its estimates on possible difficulties in sustaining high levels of expenditures and their impact on the morale of troops, the Art of War concludes, "Thus the army values victories; it does not value prolonged warfare." In fact, the entire Chapter 2 of *Art of War* titled "Waging War" is devoted to the single idea of how protracted warfare is not only inimical to the state but may also doom it to defeat at the hands of third parties not involved in the immediate conflict.[62] Sun Tzu even seems to suggest that in case there is a choice, "blundering swiftness" is always better than "fancy and clever prolongation."[63]

The centrality of the armed forces in civil society represents another unique feature of contemporary China. What particularly differentiates Sun Tzu's *Art of War* from the military classics relates power to militarist vigour. This significance of the military as an instrument to sustain national power has endured in Chinese thinking. Its reflection can even be seen in contemporary times. In addition to preservation of the centrality of the conventional armed forces, the centrality of the militaristic culture is also most visible in China's nuclear theologies where the entire effort since 1955 had clearly been geared towards using this as an instrument of warfighting. For the first three decades, the idea of developing civilian nuclear technology was not even on the agenda of China's leaders. Similarly, the doctrinal discussions on China's nuclear battlefields clearly reflect an even stronger and more peculiar Chinese obsession with their past where, amongst others, Sun Tzu has remained the most preferred reference point for purposes of credibility in both tactical and strategic arguments about modern nuclear warfare.[64] At the strategic level as well, China's posture of ambiguity can be directly traced to Sun Tzu's chronicle.[65]

Sun Tzu's concept of deception has been repeatedly highlighted to represent one such unique feature. Undoubtedly, the use of deception to achieve surprise has always been universally applied, yet it is said that the Chinese use of deception seems not only quantitatively more frequent but also qualitatively much more widespread and complicated.[66] But most of all, what makes the Chinese conception of deception so unique is the use of ambiguity by the administrating of adversaries perceptions, something that would usually by regarded as "outright cheating". Sun Tzu's dictum, "Attack where they are unprepared, go forth where they will not expect" has, over the centuries, become the watchword of Chinese stratagem.

The decisive argument of *Art of War* is "Shih". Shih attempts to devise circumstances which are favourable to success or leverage its own interests to a position of ascendancy. The Chinese aim of conceptualising and operationalising strategy is to achieve Shih by "combination of men's hearts, military weapons, and natural conditions".[67] Moreover, in contemporary times when the realms of security have gone much beyond the military, Shih would mean "acting according to situation"[68] so as to provide the external setting to create an advantageous situation.

Apart from being so central to China's own scholastic traditions, Sun Tzu's appeal has transcended the borders of China and found takers in various other countries. "In Japan Hayashi Razan (1583–1657 AD) becomes the first Japanese to write a critical commentary on the Art of War"[69] and Komiyama Yasusuki (1829–1896 AD), a professor of 'Chinese Classics' and expositor of Sun Tzu, "influenced the military thinking of many of Japan's great heroes, including General Nogi and Admiral Toga."[70] There have been studies that have linked Sun Tzu's influence in Japan's later war operations, including its surprise attack on Pearl Harbour. Sun Tzu's Art of War was popularised in the west by Father JJM Amiot, whose summary translation was published in Paris in 1772. The first English translation of Sun Zi's *Art of War*, by Lionel Giles to be noticed in the west, was published in London in 1910. Growing interests in asymmetric warfare and non-kinetic means has rejuvenated Sun Tzu's findings which are studied in military academies globally. Moreover, today *Art of War* has been co-opted by legions of all types of competitive endeavours as the universal nuggets of wisdom offered by Sun Tzu can be applied to life's conflicts and obstacles.

Sun Tzu's importance in the present day world cannot be undermined in his impact on China. His role and legacy have influenced the Chinese in an all-encompassing manner and the bridge between what China is and what China hopes to become can be built through the instrumentality of his philosophy. His presence is strong and so is his place in the minds of those who seek to obtain legitimacy.

Historical memory built around nationalist exercises a critical function in deciding who we end up being. 'Being China' is not easy and while as a country, China is definitely aspirational for the countries which received independence around the same time, it is not a feat to be achieved for by the ordinary, from Sun Tzu's meditative warfare to Pax Sinica, and from using barbarian management as the nomenclature for foreign policy to maintaining the reverence for its classics, China encompasses it all. 'Being China' requires absolute dedication to the ambition of Chinese supremacy. However, what is truly an uphill task is to 'Stay China'. Making a commitment is easy but fulfilling is not. 'Staying China' is that difficult aspect of commitment which warrants something much greater than lip service.

NOTES

1 Mark Mancall, "The Ch'ing Tribute System: An Interpretive Essay," *The Chinese World Order: Traditional China's Foreign Relations*, 1968, pp. 64-66, https://doi.org/10.4159/harvard.9780674333482.c6

2 Jeannie L. Johnson, Kerry M. Kartchner, and Jeffrey A. Larsen, Strategic Culture and Weapons of Mass Destruction: Culturally Based Insights into Comparative National Security Policymaking (London: Macmillan, 2009), pp. 5-6.

3 Lawrence Sondhaus, Strategic Culture and Ways of War (London: Routledge, 2006), p. 130.

4 Howard W. French, Everything Under the Heavens: How the Past Helps Shape China's Push for Global Power (New York: Vintage, 2018), p. 5.

5 Different ages experienced different world orders. In the ancient times, there was Pax-Romana, during the medieval times, Pax-Britannica and in the modern times, Pax-Americana. Today, Pax-Sinica is threatening to upend Pax-Americana. But this time, the forces of rise and fall of empires have changed in varying degrees of statecraft of geo-economics, geo-politics, geo-strategy, diplomacy, warfare and technology which could lead to a new system with new rules or new system with old rules.

6 French, Everything Under the Heavens, p. 6.

7 Lien-sheng Yang, "Historical Notes on the Chinese World Order," *The Chinese World Order: Traditional China's Foreign Relations*, 1968, p. 23, https://doi.org/10.4159/harvard. 9780674333482.c4.

8 Kofun period (300-538 AD) is a period in the history of Japan named after the style of burial mounds built for the ruling class. Moreover the period is famous for cultural imports such as blue–gray clay pottery called Sueki from Korean Peninsula and Buddhism and writing styles from China.

9 Yan Xuetong, Ancient *Chinese Thought, Modern Chinese Power* (Princeton: Princeton University Press, 2013), p. 218.

10 Giovanni Arrighi, Takeshi Hamashita, and Mark Selden, The Resurgence of East Asia: 500, 150 and 50 Year Perspectives (London: Routledge, 2004), p. 20.

11 Nayan Chanda, Brother Enemy: The War After The War (San Diego: Harcourt, 1986), p. 115.

12 Anthony Reid and Yangwen Zheng, Negotiating Asymmetry: China's Place in Asia (Honolulu: University of Hawaii Press, 2009), pp. 79-80.

13 French, Everything Under the Heavens, p. 9.

14 Zheng Wang, Never Forget National Humiliation: Historical Memory in Chinese Politics and Foreign Relations (New York: Columbia University Press, 2012), p. 74. Liang Qichao (1873–1929) was an influential author and thinker of late Qing and early Republican China.

15 French, Everything Under the Heavens, p. 8.

16 The *Romance of Three Kingdoms* is considered to be one of the four 'Great Classical Novels' of China. The other three novels are: *Water Margin*, *Journey to the West* and *Dream of the Red Chamber.*

17 Guanzhong, Luo, and Brewitt-Taylor, C.H. *Romance of the Three Kingdoms / Luo Guanzhong; Translated by C.H. Brewitt-Taylor*. EBooks @ Adelaide. Adelaide: University of Adelaide Library, 2012. https://adelaide.hosted.exlibrisgroup.com/permalink/f/k1i7is/ALMA51155047770001811

18 Hook, Brian. *The Cambridge Encyclopedia of China*. Cambridge: Cambridge University Press, 2nd Edition, 1991.

19 Fairbank and Chen, The Chinese World Order, p. 4.
20 Xinhua, March 6, 1997, Deng Xiaoping's dictum was that 'Stability Overrides Everything", but he also argued that the leadership needed to "keep a cool head and enhance its political flair and acuity in handling contradictions among the people."
21 Shirk, Susan L. *China: Fragile Superpower*. New York: Oxford University Press, USA, 2007.
22 Xinbo Wu, "Security Practice of a Modernizing and Ascending Power," in Asian Security Practice, (Ed.) Material and Ideational Influences (Stanford: Stanford University Press, 1998), pp. 123-24.
23 Xinhua News Agency, "CPC Pledges Unremitting Efforts to Combat Corruption—Beijing Review," *Beijing Review*, November 9, 2012, http://www.bjreview.com/Cover_Stories_Series_2013/2012-11/09/content_511215.htm.
24 China considers situation in XUAR as a potential trouble spot, which if not addressed in time, will translate into a major ethno-religious conflict. It has declared to curtail the three evil forces of "separatism, extremism and terrorism". The strong arm tactics to brow beat the Uyghurs involves a massive highly controlled surveillance apparatus where activities of users on instant social messaging app such as WeChat is monitored, installation of a comprehensive biometric picture of the population by collection of facial recognition, DNA, blood and voice recognition samples and installation of around 170 million cameras to keep public localities in urban areas under continuous video coverage.
25 Hui, a Muslim Minority of China has a population of 10 million people. The Weizhou Grand Mosque in Ningxia, in August 2018, came under altercation as Chinese official wanted to demolish the mosque. The issue conveyed an expansion in girth and breath of repressive measures against Muslim minorities.
26 Xinhua News Agency, "President Xi Stresses Xinjiang's Stability Vital to Whole Nation," *Global Times*, May 1, 2014, http://www.globaltimes.cn/content/857756.shtml.
27 It is believed that over one million Uighur Muslims have been held in 'reeducation camps' with a charter to 'carry out anti extremist education' have been legalised as 'vocational skill training centres' on October 10, 2018.
28 Tsering Topgyal, The Insecurity Dilemma and the Sino-Tibetan Conflict (London: London School of Economics and Political Science, 2011), pp. 98-99, http://etheses.lse.ac.uk/237/1/Topgyal_The_Insecurity_Dilemma_and_the_Sino-Tibetan_Conflict.pdf.
29 In 1950, the Mao-se-Tung army invaded Tibet and in 1959, after the Chinese suppressed a rebellion in Tibet, the 14th Dalai Lama and a few of his followers took asylum in India.
30 Dawa Norbu, China's Tibet Policy (London: Psychology Press, 2001), p. 333.
31 Tsering Topgyal, China and Tibet: The Perils of Insecurity (London: Hurst & Company, 2016), pp. 38-39.
32 Huston Smith, The World's Religions, Revised and Updated: A Concise Introduction (New York: HarperCollins, 1991), p. 154.
33 "The Six Classics" define the Confucian tradition of China. "The Six Classics" are *Book of Changes*, *Book of Documents*, *Book of Odes*, *Book of Rites*, *Spring and Autumn Annals* and *Classic of Music*.
34 Wang Aushi (1021-1086) an economist, statesmen, chancellor and poet of the Song Dynasty who attempted major socioeconomic reforms known as the New Policies.
35 Dagobert D. Runes, The Dictionary of Philosophy (New York: Philosophical Library, 2006), p. 338.

36 Andrew Jacobs, "Confucius Statue Vanishes Near Tiananmen Square," *The New York Times*, April 23, 2011, http://www.nytimes.com/2011/04/23/world/asia/23confucius.html.

37 Xiaoying Qi, "Filial Obligation in Contemporary China: Evolution of the Culture-System," *Journal for the Theory of Social Behaviour*, 45, no. 1 (2014): p. 141, doi:10.1111/jtsb.12052.

38 "Mao branded Confucius as feudal and backward influence and during the 'Cultural Revolution', young radicals destroyed and defaced Confucian temples and artifacts", Peter Ford, "The Mystery of Confucius' Disappearance from Tiananmen Square," *The Christian Science Monitor*, April 25, 2011, https://www.csmonitor.com/World/Global-News/2011/0425/The-mystery-of-Confucius-disappearance-from-Tiananmen-Square.

39 Xinhua News Agency, "China Commemorates Confucius with High-profile Ceremony," *Global Times*, September 25, 2014, http://www.globaltimes.cn/content/883335.shtml.

40 Since 2004, the communist authorities have rehabilitated Confucius by adopting him as a brand for Confucius Institute world over. In 2010, timed to the sixtieth anniversary of communist party in power was the release of state-sponsored film "Confucius". On 1 Dec 2011, a seismic step was made in the rehabilitation of Confucius with the installation of a 31-foot bronze statue of Confucius overlooking the East Side of Tiananmen Square, however even before one hundred days could be completed the statue disappeared on 21 April 2011 night, may be proving that the left wing had won the debate for the time being.

41 "According to Sir Edwin Arnold's book The Light of Asia (1879), Buddhism influenced millions for over 26 centuries and the spatial dimension of its dominions extended 'from Nepal and Ceylon cover the whole Eastern Peninsula to China, Japan, Tibet, Central Asia, Siberia, and even Swedish Lapland."

42 Bactria is an ancient region of central Asia between Hindu Kush Mountain Ranges and Amu Darya River where the imperial areas of China, India, Persia and Mediterranean meet. Now it is divided among the 'Stans' (Turkmenistan, Afghanistan, Uzbekistan, Tajikistan, and Pakistan) and holds a key position as it is astride the BRI and also due to its vast reserves of hydrocarbon.

43 China has the largest population of Buddhists in the world (250 million) which is 18.2% the total population of China. The Buddhists in China belong to the Theravada, Mahayana and Tibetan school. Tibetan Buddhist is closer to Vajrayana School with high stress on rituals. The Tibetan school has four major sects Nyingma, Karma Kagyu, Sakya and Gelug.

44 The present 14th Dalai Lama has expressed on 24 September 2011 that China has no legitimacy to decide the 15th Dalai Lama and a message on his website states "When I am about ninety, I will consult the high Lamas of the Tibetan Buddhist traditions, the Tibetan public, and other concerned people who follow Tibetan Buddhism, and re-evaluate whether the institution of the Dalai Lama should continue or not. If it is decided that the reincarnation of the Dalai Lama should continue and there is a need for the Fifteenth Dalai Lama to be recognized, responsibility for doing so will primarily rest on the concerned officers of the Dalai Lama's Gaden Phodrang Trust. Bear in mind that, apart from the reincarnation recognized through such legitimate methods, no recognition or acceptance should be given to a candidate chosen for political ends by anyone, including those in the People's Republic of China." The Dalai Lama during various press interviews has also alluded that the next Dalai Lama could be born in India or could even be a girl.

45 State Religious Affairs Bureau Order No. 5: "Measures on the Management of the Reincarnation of Living Buddha's" is an order dated 03 August 2007 from the State Administration for Religious Affair which states that "all the reincarnations of tulkus of Tibetan Buddhism must

get government approval; otherwise they are illegal or invalid."

46 "Buddhist Population 1.6 Billion According to Some Experts," *Buddha Weekly*, February 12, 2016, https://buddhaweekly.com/buddhism-now-2nd-largest-spiritual-path-1-6-billion-22-worlds-population-according-recent-studies/.

47 The common Buddhist Text: Guidance and Insight from Buddha a project undertaken by International Council of Vesak under the stewardship of the Mahachulalongkorn-Rajavidyalaya University (MCU), Thailand proposes one text of selected translations from Pali, Sanskrit, Chinese and Tibetan into English. This project commenced in 2012. In this project the participation of Tibetan influence has been eased out.

48 Smith, The World's Religions, Revised and Updated, p. 198.

49 Ibid., p. 210.

50 White Paper, "Freedom of Religious Belief in China," Embassy of People's Republic of China in the United States of America, Beijing, October 1997, http://www.china-embassy.org/eng/zt/zjxy/t36492.htm.

51 White Paper, "China's Policies and Practices on Protecting Freedom of Religious Belief," *Protecting Freedom of Religious Belief*, April 4, 2018, http://english.gov.cn/archive/white_paper/2018/04/04/content_281476100999028.htm.

52 Sang Pu, "China's Religious Freedom White Paper Is Doublespeak," *Ucanews.com*, April 19, 2018. https://www.ucanews.com/news/chinas-religious-freedom-white-paper-is-doublespeak/82097.

53 Xinhua News Agency, "Full Text of Xi Jinping's Report at 19th CPC National Congress," *China Daily*, November 4, 2017. http://www.chinadaily.com.cn/china/19thcpcnational congress/2017-11/04/content_34115212.htm

54 Bernardo Cervellera, "White Paper on Religions: Beijing Defends Itself." *AsiaNews.it*, March 4, 2018. http://asianews.it/news-en/White-Paper-on-Religions:-Beijing-defends-itself-43516.html.

55 Song Dynasty (960-1126AD) compiled the world's first military encyclopaedia (*Wuqing Zongyao*) in 1041 AD and established the first war college in 1043 AD.

56 The Seven Military Classics are *T'ai Kung's Six Secret Teachings*, *Methods of Sima*, *Sun Tzu's Art of War*, *Wu Qi's Wuzi*, *Three Strategies of Huang Shih-kung* (Weo-Liaozi) and *Questions and Replies between T'ang T'ai-tsung and Li Wei-kung*. The eighth Military Classic which has been added to list is *Sun Bin's Military Classics*.

57 Ralph D. Sawyer, One Hundred Unorthodox Strategies: Battle and Tactics of Chinese Warfare, (Boulder: Westview Press, 1996).

58 Michael Loewe. "Selections from Records of the Historian. Written by Ssu-Ma Chien, Translated by Yang Hsien-Yi and Gladys Yang," *The China Quarterly*, 83 (1980): 588. doi:10.1017/s0305741000013047.

59 Sawyer, One Hundred Unorthodox Strategies: Battle and Tactics of Chinese Warfare.

60 Herrlee G. Creel, The Origins of Statecraft in China: Volume One; The Western Chou Empire (Chicago: University of Chicago Press, 1970), pp. 242-316.

61 Cho-yun Hsu, "Wars and Warriors," in Ancient China in Transition: Analysis of Social Mobility, 722-222 B.C. (Stanford: Stanford University Press, 1965), pp. 53-77.

62 Sun Tzu and Sun Pin, "The Complete Art of War", Translated by Ralph D. Sawyer, (Boulder, Colo: Westview Press, 1996), p. 48.

63 Sun zi and Samuel B. Griffith, "The Art of War" (London: Oxford University Press, 1963), p.73.

64 Chong-Pin Lin, China's Nuclear Weapons Strategy: Tradition Within Evolution (Toronto: Lexington Books, 1998), p. 88.

65 V.R. Raghavan, "*Arthashastra and Sun Zi's Binfa,*", in Tan Chung ed., Across the Himalayan Gap: An Indian Quest for understanding China (New Delhi: Gyan Publishing House, 1998), p. 126. Writing about the ambiguity of China's Posture in Modern Nuclear Warfare "Transplanted into contemporary times, in the vernacular of China's theologies of nuclear deterrence, counter-value targeting would be considered by Sun Zi as the least desirable; counter-force targeting would only slightly better: counter-control targeting, though without exact correspondence, would be still better by virtue of its proximity to the mind; and the highest form of targeting would be counter-strategy."

66 Lin, China's Nuclear Weapons Strategy, p. 21.

67 William H. Mott IV and Jae Chang Kim, The Philosophy of Chinese Military Culture: Shih vs. Li, (US: Palgrave Macmillan, 2006), p. 11.

68 At the 6th International Symposium on Sun Tzu's Art of War Li Rulong explained Shih as "acting according to the situation."

69 Zhao Shunanlong, *"The Initial Battle is Decisive Battle and Preparations for Military Struggle in the New Period."* Jiefangjun Bao. August 18, 1998, p. 6.

70 Ibid., p. 176.

2

Staying China

"The winter solstice has always been special to me as a barren darkness that gives birth to a verdant future beyond imagination, a time of pain and withdrawal that produces something joyfully inconceivable, like a monarch butterfly masterfully extracting itself from the cocoon, bursting forth into unexpected glory...",[1] when Zukav dipped his pen in the ink of 'despondence and hope' little did he know, that he was giving poetic expression to the story of a country which swears by its past, builds on its present for a future which holds the promise of reviving its past.

China is nothing if not a resilient and self-inspiring nation. A country which could feed its masses on about a hundred years of humiliation in recorded two thousand year old historical past deserves to be acknowledged for the manner in which it has used history to ignite its pace in the present. China is what China does and it is here that one needs to pierce its veil to see what lies beneath it. What does it mean to 'Stay China'? While to the world it might mean emerging as an icon for the countries who got independence in the 20th century, for China it means keeping alive its nationalistic sentiments, spirit of revolution, well thought through strategy and giving rise to a leadership who has understood the pulse of the Chinese.

Evolution of strategic thought is all about keeping pace with times in terms of economy and technology with a strong underpinning of emotion. What now needs to be understood are the factors which feature in charting out the Chinese political and social-economic history over the years. One cannot undermine any of these factors because the absence of even one of them will only give us fragments of China and not what it is today.

It might seem preposterous for a country as large as China to only rely on its historical past to give inspiration for its neighbours, such as India, which have often turned to the developments in the West to seek inspiration and strength. 'If they can, could do it, so can we' became the slogan for the reform movement in India in the late 18th and the early 19th century. The same, however, was not applicable to China which looked at colonial rule as a distortion of its glorious past and a dent on its identity.

We all have different takeaways from our experiences and while the takeaway for a country like India was to keep up with times, Chinese decided to shun the control by the West and the influence thereof by labelling it as 'national humiliation'.

NATIONALISM

Nationalism has been defined by Benedict Anderson in his book *Imagined Communities* "as a socially constructed community, imagined by the people who perceive themselves as part of that group."[2] Emperor Qin Shi Huang who was the founder of the Qin dynasty not only territorially united China by successful military campaigns both in South and Central Asia, but also carried out large number of reforms in fields as diverse as measurement, writing and transportation to standardise procedures and lay the foundation for a unified system of governance. In spite of subsequent disunity there has always been an inherent urge in nearly all subsequent dynasties for grand unification as Dong Zhongshu[3] claimed, "The grand unification of China, a paramount law of eternality, is the universal tenet of all ages."[4] However, the Chinese nationalism is a recent occurrence been shaped on the sensitivity of the colonial era and its resultant humiliation.

In the history of every country, there comes a point which serves as the beginning of an end and the end of a beginning. In case of China, the opium trade served as the dawn of the 'century of humiliation' and the end of its claim of being the pinnacle of invincibility and civilisation. The breakdown of negotiations with the Qings over the opium trade resulted in the annexation of Canton (now Guangzhou) which further led to the British gaining foothold in Central China. Subsequent naval clashes between the two led to beginning of the First Opium War (1839–1844) and ended with the British taming the Dragon and obtaining concessions pursuant to the "Treaty of Nanjing".[5] Control of Hong Kong, extraterritoriality for British subjects in China and expansion of trade with unilateral gains for the British jolted the Chinese from their slumber. While for the British this meant huge monetary gains, for

China it implied a brutal crushing of their pride and ego. In the history of China, the period hereon is labelled as 'Bǎinián guóchǐ'. This period, however, came to an end when Mao Zedong seized the moment on 01 October 1949 by declaring the formation of People's Republic of China (PRC). These one hundred and nine years became an indelible part of China's psychology as a nation, something that is has been trying to forget and yet not trying to forget to keep alive the fire in the belly of the Dragon.

It is pertinent to understand it was not just the subversion at the hands of the British which China had to withstand during its century of humiliation. Boxer rebellion of 1901, the Japanese onslaught, the Treaty of Wangxia signed by the United States and China in 1844, forcible relinquishment of North East China to Russia and cession of ports to Germany were events which rubbed salts on the wounds of the Chinese. Matt Schiavenza rightly captured the chronology and the emotion of China when he wrote, "This was the most tumultuous century in the China's history, one that featured an incessant series of wars, occupations, and revolutions and one that did not end until the victory of the Communist Party in China's 1945–1949 civil war."[6]

The continuous defeat in wars and colonial dynamics led to a patriotic fervour among the people. May Fourth Movement, a hundred years ago (1919), was a student protest against imperialism with a core spirit of patriotism and nationalism. The May Fourth Movement needs to be viewed not in isolation but as a culmination of betrayal which the Chinese felt after their promises were not kept. Under the garb of promising to return Shandong Peninsula, all the allies had done was seek the Chinese support with no intention of living up to what was promised to it. The Chinese had looked at the First World War to finally get rid of the extraterritoriality of foreign powers, reversal of the '21 Japanese Demands' and the ceding of the previously controlled German territories. The Treaty of Versailles had not only spelt disaster for the Germans but also for the Chinese. The humiliation which the Chinese faced, however, did not end here. The previously held German territories were handed over to Japan—a country which had rubbed the Chinese the wrong way every single time. The Chinese outcry came in the form of severe protests in Tiananmen Square and spread like wildfire to the other parts of the country where students, school children, workers and the mercantile class organised strikes and claw back of the Treaty which was talked of peace in its letter but created discord in its spirit. But the same could not be undone.

The May Fourth Movement is a watershed event in the Chinese nation building. It lead to reflection by people on Confucian values, initiated a vernacular style of writing, promoted science and lead to activism of the people in public affairs. This people activism in public affairs leads to the creation of communist party in 1921 by a few of the protest leaders. Moreover, during the May Fourth Movement, intellectuals such as Hu Shi and Lu Xun promoted new ideas and opposed the traditional idea and thus, liberation of thought began. The non-restoration of Shandong and the complete ignorance of China's interests lead to a feeling of suspicion and disbelief towards the West and in some respect deforms Chinese attitudes and tenor of relations with other states to this day. Disillusioned with the West and undermined in the equity of the Allies, founders of the Communist Party of China (Chen Duxiu and Li Dazhao) altered their course to reflect on writing of democrats or federal and instead turned to writing of Soviet Union. This led to the popular saying among the Chinese revolutionaries—'No Sun rises in the West for China'. Although the movement was primarily a patriotic protest movement, it lead to a significant promotion of science and experimentation and could be called as the initiator of the "Chinese Renaissance". Mao Zedong described the May Fourth Movement as a "new stage in China's bourgeois-democratic revolution against imperialism and feudalism."[7]

The May Fourth Movement was not an event in the Chinese history. It became a tradition and a manifestation of student activism. The impact of the May Fourth Movement was livid as it came to be that landmark which divided the Chinese timeline into 'prior May Fourth' and 'post May Fourth'. A society as fractured, as that of China was seen as a united force against the unfair Treaty. One can see how the incident is fresh in minds of the youth and how they continue to draw inspiration from it.

Humiliation is not an empty experience which passes with time. Its remnants and after effects can be severe and when all you have is your pride, a public event can be both damaging and demoralising. It has been established beyond doubt that manipulation of memories through deconstruction and reconstruction of the narratives of the victims is one of the most common ways to sway the popular sentiment in any direction the manipulator chooses.

The historical memory of modern China is shaped by the puncturing of the national identity during the century of humiliation and is used today to stir nationalistic sensibility and provide an expression to strengthen the nation so that it is not in any way humiliated again. The Chinese not only accept this as an inextricable part of its psychology but also resonate with the resolve of not being subjugated ever again. Andreas Forsby attributes this period of humiliation by imperialist powers for the creation of a unique sense of victimisation and insecurity by inscribing "on the Chinese soul an inferiority complex that has mostly manifested itself as a revanchist directed at the Western powers and in particular Japan."[8] It is this century of humiliation that gives China a sense of purpose along with a sense of entitlement to reclaim their true position in the world affairs.

Even though China tries to ride on its past humiliation to justify almost everything it does to prevent it from ever happening again. One needs to acknowledge that it was not the Chinese who wrote the history this time. This time the narrative was in the hands of the British whose vainglory shone further when they attacked Beijing's Summer Palace after the murder of several British and French troops. The purpose of the attack on the Summer Palace was summed up by Orville Schell and John Delury when they wrote, "The destruction of Yuanming Yuan was to be a 'solemn act of retribution', said the British commander Lord Elgin, in which no blood would be spilled, but an emperor's 'pride as well as his feelings,' would be crushed."[9] The point of this attack was to psychologically damage the Chinese in a way that their faith in the Emperor was shaken and their confidence destabilised. However, the opprobrium of the Chinese sowed the seeds of revenge and cemented their resolve to never forget the disgrace which was brought to them. Even today, the ruins of the Summer Palace stand as a bitter memory to fuel their sentiment of 'never again'. Wars are won in the mind of the soldiers while the British believed in it, the Chinese live by it till today.

Since the opening of the economy the CCP has used nationalism as a value to cement its relation with the Chinese society and to vent out anger, criticise and denunciate foreign power. The CCP has fallen back on nationalism in the May 1999 bombing of the Chinese Belgrade embassy against American, EP3 incident in April 2001, outrage over 2005 Japanese history textbook and visit of the Japanese Prime Minister to Yasukuni Shrine.

At this juncture it is imperative to understand the mechanics in which the Communist Party draws its legitimacy. The CCP was responsible for reviving China by finally bringing its nemesis to an end. On 1 October 1949, Mao Zedong established the Proclaimed People's Republic of China he declared that the Chinese exile has come to an end. The country not only looked at him as its hero but he was seen as the architect of 'New China' and back then the CCP was given legitimacy on a platter. However, it could not afford to lose the support and the sentiment of the people which it had garnered over time and therefore it had to go beyond the obvious measures to retain the same. For CCP democratic elections were not on cards because of the inherent unpredictability of democracy and hence had to succumb to measures which could sway public opinion and sympathy in its favour without making it conspicuous. It was then that the Party decided to seize control of what and how history would be taught in schools. The narrative surrounding the century of humiliation became the defence of the Tiananmen movement in 1989. What the world labelled as a struggle for democracy, the Party painted as foreign interference and a strong education system with patriotic underpinnings that was expected to wipe out the taints. It was essential to reorient the youth such that any signs of protest could be redirected outwards. A part of this strategy involved taking absolute control of the literature in order to ensure that what was retained in the public memory was the humiliation. Literature, however, did not limit itself to the books but went beyond it. Pictures and strong visuals of the Chinese soldiers were displayed and soon the emotion found its way in the Chinese calendar as the 'National Humiliation Day'. From history books to literature, the Party gradually controlled the mental and the emotional makeup of the masses. The People's Liberation Army played its part in incorporating it as a symbol of the brutal fate suffered by an once upon a time an opulent palace during the Second Opium War and the same was imparted as National Defence Education's Law to the students.

The date of the National Humiliation Day was fixed as 9 May because on that day the Chinese President in 1915 was forced to accept the Japanese ultimatum of 'Twenty One Demands', and the same was commemorated on an annual basis by the National Teachers' Association. Ever since (1915), 9 May has been celebrated as the day to remember. The couplet of "V for Vendetta"[10] can be used to best describe this situation—"Remember, remember the fifth of November of gunpowder treason and plot. I know of no reason why the gunpowder treason should ever be forgot."[11]

William Callahan penned down that, "In the early twenty-first century, there is no sovereignty crisis as there was in the early twentieth century when imperialists were busy dividing up China. Rather with the Tiananmen crisis and the disintegration of communism in the Soviet bloc, the CCP was facing a non-traditional security threat: regime security, ideological security, and cultural security. Thus after 1989, there was a shift from primarily producing nationalism, as in the 1920s, to concentrate on containing nationalism. To contain the nation, it is necessary to construe insecurities such as National Humiliation Day in order to limit the expression of identity to approved activities and feelings. As the National Defence Education Day poster told us identity not only marks the border between us and them, but also contains 'us' in China."[12] It is this comparison of the twentieth century China and the twenty-first century China which the Party chose to underplay to keep the feeling of humiliation alive and the fire lit. It is this narrative which was exploited differently at different times by different leaders for the same purpose. To protect China from the winds of democracy and capitalism, to keep the ulterior motives intact and to seek perpetuity for the Party.

Will the present theme of 'humiliation' continue as part of nationalism as China rises to become a great power under President Xi Jinping? When China feels it has reached equivalence or even pre-eminence related to Great Powers. There would be a case in point to discard this humiliation as a theme of low status or weakness and adopt a more dynamic theme. However, the CCP has invested deeply in the theme of being bullied by the West and how it has struggled to slowly but steadily drag and nurture the nation to wealth and power. The CCP would always aim to ensure that its revolutionary sacrifices remain fresh and in the sharper focus of the population. Moreover, the CCP could always hobble with the fact that it could once again plunge into humiliation. It comes out, that national humiliation is too beneficial a shared emotion to be laid off at present.

UNINTERRUPTED REVOLUTIONS

In the modern history of humanity, revolution has directly affected or influenced every country of the world. Revolution can be defined as "an event that used irregular procedures aimed at forcing political change within a society and that had lasting effects on the system of the society in which it occurred".[13] In any revolution it is important to understand the causes, themes, influences and outcomes. The opening lines of Beatles famous song "Revolution", "You say you want a revolution, Well you know, We all want to change the world,

You tell me that its evolution, Well you know, We all want to change the world"[14] very aptly brings out dynamics of an revolution. Theda Skocpol interpreted the three revolutions—French (1789), Russian (1971) and Chinese (1911)—in her book *State and Social Revolution* and according to her Social revolution is "rapid basic transformation of the society's state and class structures...in part carried through by class-based revolts from below."[15]

The theme of revolution provides the focus for political history of China. The Chinese revolution is comparatively difficult to figure out due to protracted period and the large number of issues. There are four distinct eras of Chinese revolution in its political history—Republican Revolution, Nationalist Revolution, Communist Revolution and Reform and Opening up Revolution. One general feature that has characterised all the four eras of revolution is the search for a modern state which could take its rightful place in the global order.

In the first era, the 'Republican Revolution' (1885–1922), foreign encroachment had increased, China's internal strength had decreased, and there was a population explosion coupled with complete torpidity in the industrial, commercial and scientific know-how. Attempts to reform the imperial system from within the system failed. In the early part of twentieth century there was a growing feeling among the students of disenchantment and intellectual despair against the imperial system. This was followed by a turbulent period of ineffective Republican governance and chaotic decade in which ideas swung between capitalism, constitutionalism and anarchy. The public space was dominated by Dr Sun Yat-Sen and intellectual arena by Lu Xun during this revolutionary period.

Dr Sun Yat-Sen devoted his complete life to the cause of revolution. He was born when China was still reeling under the aftermath of the failure of the Taiping Uprising. It was his exposure to the outside world which propelled him to work incessantly towards upgrading China in terms of technology and economy. His earliest stint with revolution was in 1894 when he organised the 'China Revival Society' (Xing Zhong Hui) which was based on the very foundation of putting an end to the Qings, national rejuvenation, and establishment of a federal government. The constitution of the society was to prevent subjugation of China at the hands of western imperialist for the plunder and loot of its resources. The message it sent led to an upsurge in the nationalistic sentiment of the people and proliferated their abhorrence towards the foreign rule.

Sun Yat-Sen's protest against the unpalatable and one-sided Treaty of Shimonoseki with Japan invited him to a sixteen-year exile during which he travelled across the world and started China Revolutionary League with inroads in many European countries. His political programme, his publication by the name of *Min Bao* all aimed at elaborating upon his 'San Min Chu I' (Three Principles of the People)—nationalism, democracy and livelihood. In these three principles the essence of modern China was captured. In 'Nationalism' was embedded the revival of the spiritual principles of China; in 'Democracy', was embedded the seed of political revolution which would overthrow the Qings; and in 'Livelihood', was embedded the ambition for solving the socioeconomic problems which China was battling against. It was the principle of 'Livelihood' which contained the ideals of socialism. Equipped with these three, Sun Yat-Sen, set out to create a utopian society—an anti-bourgeoisie, anti-feudal, anti-landowning social setup.

On 10 October 1911, Republic of China was established after a two-thousand-year Imperial rule of the Manchus was brought to an end through a military uprising in Wuchang. Li Yuan-hung and Sun were elected as Vice President and President respectively. In early 1912, Sun Yat-Sen took over as the Provisional President. However, he later relinquished the same in favour of Yuan Shin Kai. Soon after his relinquishment, Yuan proved to be a monarchist and after his death, Sun Yat-Sen turned to establishing Kuomintang at Canton. He also turned to the Bolsheviks to draw inspiration and accepted their hand of amity and friendship. Later, it was the Soviets who help Sun Yat-Sen in revamping the Nationalist Party and sought the support of the peasantry. Till he breathed his last, Sun Yat-Sen worked towards reconstructing, remodelling and rebuilding China and its political system on the ideals of democracy and socialism. For China, Sun Yat-Sen was its hero but for Sun Yat-Sen, China was his life. He has often been labelled as the Confucius of New China. However, to attach any tag to his contribution would be undermining his effort. There are distinct differences between the two and it is best if no parallels are drawn between them for both are great in their own right.

Lu Xun is not a writer and neither is he a revolutionary. Lu Xun is more of cult figure whom China gave birth to in circumstances which coincided with societal upheaval, political imperialism, economic suffering and psychological damage. Lu Xun was one of those rare Chinese who had the benefit of wealth, foreign education and English learning. His works criticised the gender discrimination which was accepted as a norm in the Chinese society and made an attempt to purge the society of the dogma and tradition. He glanced at Chinese society thought the spectrum of the West but his spectacles were made of nationalism. The most celebrated literature—*The True Story of Ah-Q* (A-Q zhengzhuan), *Diary of a Madman* (Kuangren riji), and *My Old Hometown* (Guxiang)—continue to charm the Chinese masses. His endorsement of the reform of the Chinese script as a tool for survival revolutionised the Chinese writing and his satire of the Chinese revolution unravelled the glaring yet perfectly hidden discrepancies between the goals of the revolutionaries and those of a common man. His championing of revolution was based on his idea that revolution was embedded in evolution and hence needed to be accepted as an integral part and manifestation of growth. Lu Xun sympathized with the Party and critiqued Chiang Kai Shek. It was this sympathy which earned him his stature of a Chinese hero and gave him a place in Mao's speeches. However, his stories were withdrawn from the curriculum in 2007 in order to replace the dark introspection with the confidence exuded in Kung-Fu stories such that the young impressionable minds could adapt to the changing milieu and develop an attitude which was imperative to be nurtured in the twenty-first century. The brand of nationalism had to change in the wake of the Chinese resurgence. But his popularity despite these measures continues to capture the propensities of the Chinese youth. His traces were prevalent in the manner the 2008 Olympics were received by the Chinese masses, albeit the Party's effort of making it all about the resounding victory of China over its internal issues and towering economic might. Lu Xun brought about a certain degree of freshness and intellectual independence. He was a recipe of the West prepared with Chinese ingredients and therefore deserves the place and following he enjoys till today.

In the second era of 'Nationalist Revolution' there was a considerable upswing in mid 1920s in revolutionary upsurge which resulted in an accord between the Nationalists and the Communists. The accord aimed to achieve the elimination of warlords and foreign imperialists and the establishment of a strong central government. However, the accord broke in April 1927 after Chiang Kai-shek began his bloody elimination of the Communists, the trade unions and the peasant associations. Chiang tried to establish a national government since the Revolution of 1911, which turned out to an incompetent, brutal and corrupt and could not achieve the aim of unity and independence.

In the third era of Chinese Revolutions (1949–1976), Mao Zedong "stressed the need for continuous revolution, which resulted in an internal situation of sustained turmoil in which Chinese Communist Party (CCP) leaders emphasized the threat of ideological enemies and traitors inside China being controlled or orchestrated by outside forces. This produced a mix of heightened social paranoia and political and economic chaos, which at times plunged the country into widespread famine and at other times erupted into civil war-like violence".[16] Mao in 1927 wrote about revolution, "A revolution is not a dinner party, or writing an essay, or painting a picture, or doing embroidery; it cannot be so refined, so leisurely and gentle, so temperate, kind, courteous, restrained and magnanimous...The rural areas need a revolutionary upsurge, for it alone can rouse the people in their millions to become a powerful force."[17]

"The Chinese Revolution was a genuinely popular revolution, not a coup d'état carried out by a small group of conspirators. It was massive in terms of the numbers of people who were directly involved in the revolutionary movement and the even greater numbers whose lives were crucially changed by the outcome of the struggle. The revolution was largely made by peasants, who inaugurated a long-term process of development that is reducing the peasantry to an increasingly small minority of the population. Peasants were both the beneficiaries and the victims of the revolution they made. The human costs of the Chinese Revolution have been considerable—not only the many millions who perished in the long revolutionary struggle but in the many more millions who were persecuted politically after the revolutionaries came to power, not to speak of the tens of millions who perished as a result of the political misadventures of the Great Leap Forward and the Cultural Revolution."[18]

In the fourth era of 'Reform and Opening up' Deng Xiaoping initiated the most decisive changes in the history of Modern China. Deng felt that unless China could expand and modernise its economy it would remain poor, weak and vulnerable. Thus a sustained, meaningful improvement in the quality of life of the Chinese people was essential both for national survival and regime security.

Another, issue which manifested in this era was student activism. Because students have played such a significant role in Chinese history, their movements are not only interesting, but also critical in determining the future stability of the regime.[19] The Tiananmen Square massacre of 1989 is an example how a country steeped in tradition never forgets to retrace its steps in the times of adversity and opposition. One may be tempted to pose pertinent questions at this stage. Why has the Tiananmen Square been silent for last thirty years? Has the incident lost its grip over the citizens of New China? Although the Chinese student community is no longer kept in a bottled atmosphere, economic growth with prolific job opportunities have ensured that the student community does not carry as many grievances against the leadership as it had harboured before.

The present student protests over formation of labour unions need to be kept in the radar to explore the dynamics and emerging grievances. On 17 November 2018, a large number of self-proclaimed Marxist labour activists (many of whom are students) were rounded up. The present crackdown on labour protests commenced in June 2018 after efforts made by Jasic workers in Shenzhen who had tried to give shape to an independent trade association, which was declared illegal. No independent trade associations are allowed in China and all trade association are required to be registered with the All-China Federation of Trade unions.

"The CCP has artfully woven an origin story romanticising its revolutionary lineage, in which it is the champion of the downtrodden and the only political force capable of transforming China into the global economic power it is today. Invocation of Marx and other communist figureheads support the Party's attempts to establish an impeccable ideological pedigree. In a speech delivered in May 2018 to celebrate Marx's 200th birthday, Party Chairman Xi Jinping said the CCP was indebted to Marx, calling him a teacher of revolution for the proletariat and working people all over the world."[20] However, the issue is that Marxism is an ideology of working class self-emancipation by revolution whereas the CCP is today a party modelled for governance and cannot afford a revolution or class struggle.

This discrepancy between the CCP communist ideological basis and the contemporary significant blending of Sinification of Marxism, leading to economic reforms based on socialist market reforms and 'control' by the party are being questioned by the labour activism.

"Although grounded in communist ideology, this latest labour movement ultimately challenges the structure of Chinese society—the structure that has enabled economic growth at breakneck speed, while simultaneously keeping the Party firmly in power. If this structure is questioned, the Party's authority will be questioned."[21] However, whether the revolutionaries will rile up in the future and demand political reforms is a question that can only be answered in retrospect.

STRATEGIC REFLECTION ON MILITARY CAMPAIGNS

The Chinese use of force has historically been flexible and dependent on their perceived power differential. "One defends when his strength is inadequate: he attacks when it is abundant."[22] The Chinese empire was at the acme during the first half of the Qing Dynasty and dropped to its lowest during the latter half of the Qing Dynasty during the century of humiliation. Whenever weak during the dynastic era, it came to the negotiation table, sought time and only gave up when there was no other way out. Chiang Kai Shek and his nationalist government with their eleven Dash Lines were not short of this imperialistic ardour either. The communists on taking over did not dither in use of force against the Americans in Korea or in asserting themselves over Tibet and Xinjiang. They did not abstain from using force as "pedagogical instruments"[23] with India and Vietnam.

A strategic reflection of the Chinese military campaigns from 1934 furnishes a framework and insight into the Chinese way of solving the dilemma—when to enter into a conflict, mid-course correction and achieving of advantageous culmination point. Moreover, it provides an effective conceptualisation of Chinese schema for warfare in the future.

Long March and Civil War: From Confusion to Awakening

"The rise of many great nations has been marked by events, which in retrospect; attain legendary, if not mythical proportions. The signing of the Magna Carta, the Battle of the Alamo, the storming of the Bastille, and the siege of the Winter Palace were of such significance that they became indelibly carved into the national characters of the respective populations. The Long March of the Chinese Communists First Front Army rivals, and in many cases exceeds, the hardships and political significance of the any other event in the world."[24] General Samuel, an eminent military historian, described the Long March as

"An even more majestic achievement than the retreat of the 10,000 Greeks from Persia to the Black Sea four centuries before Christ: The Chinese Communists repeatedly tested and confirmed man's ability to undergo indescribable hardship, to overcome every challenge placed in his path by nature determined to thwart him; to triumph over enemies equally determined to destroy him; and to reach his goal. Alike, Greeks and Chinese endured scorching heat, bitter cold, thirst and hunger. Alike, they climbed snow-covered mountains, slept in the snow, marched and fought and marched again. Alike, they reconciled internal disputes that threatened to tear them apart. Alike, they survived. But Mao's Chinese marched 6,000 miles to Xenophon's Greek's 2,000; they marched for a year, not merely four months; they were ten times more numerous than the Greeks; and their survival had infinitely more historical significance."[25]

Chiang Kai-Shek's vision of China was not one of a communist leviathan and his vision was supported with the men and the money obtained from the capitalist world of the West. The West desisted China from turning into a communist state with the value system imported from the Soviet Union and on their part provided the requisite wherewithal to accomplish the same. Ironically, Adolph Hitler provided Chiang Kai-shek with General Hans von Seeckt to devise an anti-communist plan and he was instrumental in drawing the contours of the "Blockhouse Strategy" which caused major reversal for the CCP in its self-governing region—Kiangsi Soviet.

The Long March is less about military equals claiming territory, but more about political and ideological survival. The course and event of the Long March is a story of 1,00,000 men and women fighting for their survival against the military might of a technologically advanced army and the geographical terrain of China. The three most important landmarks of the Long March which are recounted till today are—the Tsunyi Conference; the capture of the Luting Bridge; and the rough trail over the Great Snow Mountain.

Held on 15 January 1935, the Tsunyi conference can be labelled as 'coming of age' for the Chinese for it was the moment of carpe diem for the Chinese. It was this conference which led to the emergence of Mao Tse-tung as the leader of the Chinese forces, the course alteration of the Red Army, "the unshackling of the communist movement from the clutches of the leadership in Moscow"[26] and placing of the destiny of the Chinese into their own hands.

Militarily the battle for the Luting Bridge is one of the highly significant stories of Long March because the story does not begin with Luting Bridge but with Anshuchang. The original plan of capturing a crossing at Anshuchang was abandoned in favour of an alternative crossing site at Luting due to uninterrupted air interdiction by Kuomintang and the slow rate of flow at the ferry crossing. The Fourth Shock Regiment marched ninety miles in forty-eight hours to reach the Luting crossing site on 27 May 1935. The bridge was suspended between two cliffs, over two hundred and fifty feet above the ground, most of its wooden planks of the walkway had been removed and two regiment of Kuomintang were deployed astride Luting for the protection of bridge. In spite of barrage of mortar and machine gun fire the twenty two volunteers with only small arms and hand grenade launched a daring and gallant frontal attack. The defender was so overwhelmed by the courage and grit of the attacker that they fled. With the survival rate well above 80 per cent, Mao's act was touted as a glorious victory.

The last monumental event of the Long March was the trail over the Great Snow Mountains. This trail was a judgment call by Mao who was famous for taking the small road in face of uncertainty. However, this time, his judgment backfired for the First Front Army was not prepared for undertaking a journey as rough as the trail. Given the ill-preparedness of the forces, an estimated eight thousand survivors, who encamped in Shenshi Soviet of Northern China on 16 October 1935 were ravaged by the over 90 per cent casualties. There survivors were a source of inspiration for a popular revolution which brutally took over a much more massive and superior west supported military still enjoying worldwide commendation for being a part of the victory over Japan.

In 1945, at the outset of the civil war the Chinese Communist Party had to prove its mettle before an enemy which was notches higher. Despite the inherent inequality between the two forces, the communists survived the Civil War and inflicted losses on the Nationalist Forces in Manchuria. What led to this spectacular show of strength was the morale and the resolve of the Red Army and it was its tenacity which saw it through the initial years of strife and struggle. The guerrilla war that ensued was fought and won with the bravado in the stories shared by the survivors of the Long March. It was this never say die spirit which came to be known as the "Yenan spirit and was passed on as a psychological legacy."[27]

In 1948, the tide turned dramatically with Communists Forces winning over the Nationalist in Central and Northern China and as though the cosmos sided with the Communists, the Nationalist Government collapsed and turned the scales in their favour. It was finally victory for the underdogs and in its impact, the Long March continues to linger on till today and has been rightly called as "an Odyssey unequalled in modern times."[28] It is a story of a poorly fed, ill-equipped, and small but not insignificant force which defeated a large army by the sheer dint of its morale, courage and resilience.

Korean War

For a nation which had just received its self-rule and dignity, being embroiled in a war was not a very sound strategy. But the Chinese had to indulge in it and pander to the demands of the Soviet Union in order to cement its ties with the superpower and uphold the Sino-Soviet Treaty of Friendship. While Mao was cushioned due to the presence of Soviet Armed Forces and his fears of being sandwiched between two strong countries were assailed, it still was imperative for the Chinese to shield its sovereignty and protect its industrial hub in Manchuria.

Further, Mao saw his participation in the Korean conflict, as his opportunity to attack Taiwan, an integral part of its foreign policy. The United States did apprehend an aggression of this nature and engaged on both the fronts, that is, to protect Taiwan from the Chinese invasion and participate in the Korean feud. Along with open vilification of this measure, the Chinese forces were deployed heavily on the border with North Korea and along the coast adjacent to Taiwan. For China, defending its coast along with its terra firma did prove to be a tall order but it did not desist in the face of a powerful adversary.

The Chinese made it very clear that their entry into the war will not be for reasons other than their own survival and in order to indicate the same alerted Washington that crossing the 38th parallel would be their trigger. The United States' blatant ignorance of the warning led to the infiltration by the Chinese troops and a formal entry into the war.

The Chinese People Volunteers (CPV) initially, by end of 1950, succeeded to push US and Korean forces south of 38th Parallel and subsequently by January 1951, south of Han River. The UN engineered ceasefire began as "Chinese demanded of complete withdrawal of troops from Korea, Taiwan and a confirmed seat for China in the Security Council—strength makes ambition possible."[29] However, when the Chinese forces began to bleed, Mao's rigidity melted albeit for a short while. With well-crafted strategy and double the effort, Mao once again ordered an offensive in order to negotiate a settlement from a position of strength. This time, American blood was spilled and the Korean War was won by Mao and his forces.

A victory this early in its life as a nation which had seen a century-long foreign rule and subversion conveyed that China could not been taken for granted and would not hesitate in use of force even at the cost of extensive losses.

The Sino-Indian Conflict of 1962 and Doklam Standoff of 2017

No one had imagined that two countries with such rich historical exchange would end up in a conflict. Sino-Indian ties carried the stamp of '*Hindi-Chini Bhai Bhai*' (Indians and Chinese are brothers.) However, when China chose to declare war, it did so under the garb of 'courtesy emphasises reciprocity'.[30] The Chinese put the onus of the 1962 entanglement on the Indian leadership on the grounds that backing out from a fight would lead of cession to the Chinese territory.

The Chinese launched the offensive on 20 October 1962 and by 20 November 1962, China had captured all its claimed territory in the western sector and in the south-captured the area up to the Outer Line. "On November 22, 1962, Mao declared a unilateral ceasefire and the Chinese troops withdrew to 20 km from what China perceived to be the Line of Actual Control since November 07, 1959."[31]

Mao's attack on India came at a time when China was embroiled in conflicts on all the fronts—lack of success of Great Leap Forward, breakdown of the Sino-Soviet Friendship, Great Leap famine and internal turbulence in Tibet. China's international position was also in a state of quandary owing to the Americans fighting in Vietnam, Chiang Kai-shek's threats to attack the Mainland and Sino-Soviet animosity. Thus, attack against India when China was mired in a multitude of problems, both internal and external needed to be understood and analysed in a manner which uncloaks the Chinese mind-set and mentality. An offensive against India was required as a feel good factor and as a show of strength. Given that Mao's political image was at an all-time low[32] and speculations surrounding his weakness were rife, it was imperative for him to regain his apparently lost glory. His power was challenged by the then emerging leaders of China[33] and Mao needed an opportunity to make a come-back with double the fervour and strength. He desperately wanted to recapture the political spotlight and he sought to do so by adopting an attitude of disdain and aggression towards its long-time friend and neighbour. The tonality of the Chinese media towards India had changed and it had started to indicate that India might be the first one to make the move to attack China. With time, this warning had changed to a call to defend the borders of the Chinese territory and under the pretext of safeguarding its own borders; Mao launched an offensive against India.

A war which took a heavy toll on the military forces of both the countries was started purely out of personal ambition thereby indicating that even though Mao projected himself as the champion of the Chinese, in reality he had championed his own cause.

Yet another reason for the Sino-Indian conflict was the need to assert itself as a natural ally of Pakistan which had signed the South East Asian Treaty Organization (SEATO), a pact engineered by the United States against China. While with India, China adopted a more high-handed and rigid approach, with Pakistan it was willing to make concessions. This difference stemmed from the role India played as a bridge between the Washington and Beijing. However, given that China wanted to develop an independent equation with Asian countries, it chose to sacrifice its peaceful relations interspersed by border issues with India for Pakistan which assured for a quid pro quo treatment within pacts such as SEATO. Pakistan turned to China for help against India and in turn championed the Chinese cause on the global stage.

Even after five decades, China is obstinate in its attitude towards India. Chinese expect India to take the first step in bridging the trust deficit and restore peace in the conflict ridden patch. References to the same manifested even in 2017 during the Doklam standoff. Withdrawal of troops as a precondition for bilateral peace was the first step which the Chinese proposed and in doing so did not desist from making reference to the conflict of 1962. The Chinese media emphasised on the need for India to seek lessons from the past and not forget the humiliating defeat which the Chinese had inflicted. It has always been a question of tonality. With Pakistan, China has adopted a conciliatory tone with India it chooses to deal with harshness and belligerence.

The Sino-Vietnamese War, 1979

The Sino-Vietnamese Conflict of 1979 was principally one of displaying dominance against a small neighbour which had battled against the twin forces of France and the United States to gain its independence. The pugnacious Chinese attitude was a clear deviation from its 'let us talk' strategy and that could be attributed to the stationing of Vietnamese troops and recognising Khmer Rouge and Sihanouk as leaders of Cambodia.

Growing proximity between Vietnam and Soviet Union and the following Treaty of Friendship and Cooperation instilled fear and suspicion among the Chinese and they saw it as an attempt of the Soviet Union to encircle the Chinese territory. A treaty which clearly stated that in case of an attack or apprehension of attack would support each other was a cause of concern for the Chinese. The attack by the Vietnamese troops in Guangxi Province followed by the aggression towards Cambodia gave China the moral ground to retaliate. However, the Chinese were sceptical of any international wrath they might invite as a result of this attack and therefore clear instructions were issued with regard to earmarking the territory of the attack and the nomenclature of the same. China wanted to appear as a defender of its territory which is protective of its people and friends. But in 1979, the Chinese forces crossed the borders of Vietnam and reached till Hanoi in order to send a clear message that China has the wherewithal to defend itself and will not take any aggression lying low.

The three-week tussle ended with the PLA incurring severe losses in terms of men and material. The silver lining, however, was the international support China received as an ally of the West, particularly of the United States and isolation of the Soviet Union as a power hungry, ideology driven country. For the Chinese it was more of a reality check and led to massive modernisation of the military. China was looked upon as a country which could not be taken lightly and at the same time was aware of its roles and responsibility in the increasing shrinking world.

LEADERSHIP DECODED

Newly independent countries may desire to be like China. However, the wish to be like China and to stay like China is separated by a huge gorge between desire and deserving. On one hand, the political leadership struggles to maintain internal stability and keep the territory intact and on the other hand, it has to appear to be unflinching for external world in order keep its messaging right.

What appears, is usually what it is not and China is a living example of that. It has to constantly walk the tight rope of learnings from its past and make them seem relevant in the present day world such that its people can never question the measures and the motives of the Chinese leadership. Coupled with it is the struggle to deliver on the economic front to top the number game when it comes to being ranked in the category of the fastest growing economies. China cannot afford to appear weak. Neither can it afford to commit the mistake of being intoxicated by its own supremacy. It has to be on guard at all times. Complacency, misplaced trust and poor negotiations have damaged the nation in a manner that it has not yet recovered from it. China has been trying to be too many things in one go and so does the CCP.

The CCP which was initially thought of by the outside world as a "group of bandits"[34] or gang of unenlightened peasants, have remarkably endured self-inflicted hardship and have played a major role in defining, defending and cobbling China into 'statehood'. The CCP through its leaders such as Mao have helped in the resurrection of China and the Chinese. It was his call which finally led to the culmination of the century of humiliation and the CCP has exploited this very aspect of the Chinese history such that the future generations of China feel indebted to the Party and its leadership which has never belied the hopes and aspirations of its people.

In order to attain statehood it has left no stone unturned in achieving the same. It has used every single instrument and manoeuvre in order to achieve just that. From displaying excellent diplomacy skills in the international arena to ensuring economic prosperity, both backed by military might the Party has tried to deliver on all the fronts. In its own backyard, it has used war, pacified the Hans, manipulated history and the narrative of religion and used outright aggression to keep XUAR and Tibet under its firm control.

With every change in leadership, China made an attempt to send the right signals. "Mao Zedong took a broken colossus, made it whole, and stood it up on its feet. Before the Chinese Communist Party came to power, China lay broken and fragmented..."[35] due to several decades of post–Qing dynasty fragmentation, foreign occupation and civil war. "The territory China held when Mao declared the PRC on 1 October 1949, did not include vast swathes that are part of China today: coastal stretches, the island of Hainan, those mountainous holdings of Xinjiang and Tibet, large tracts of forests and hills in the southwest."[36] Mao's political and diplomatic initiatives were designed to re-establish a 'Greater China' by undertaking military adventures and misadventures to unify these lands and weave their peoples into the social fabric of China. While Mao Zedong tried to instil a sense of confidence by extolling its glorious past in the otherwise battered masses, he was not oblivious to the need to constantly evolving international milieu. He championed economic security, evoked favourable responses from the international community, won friends, defeated enemies, kept alive the threat of being subjugated again, actively engaged in dialogue and ensured that China became a force to reckon with. He did not let China and the Chinese interest get alienated for he had seen what alienation could lead to. His 'Great Leap Forward' sent the country into a frenzy of sorts but then despite the internal pressures he kept China intact.

"Deng dragged China to reason and strength."[37] He reminded CCP of the need to seek truth from facts. He focussed on economic reform and rebuilding of the Chinese economy. He never really deviated from the leanings of his predecessor but his approach was to keep pace with the times. He wanted to protect the tradition of Mao and at the same time compete with the growing economies of its neighbours. Deng's strategy of opening during the twilight of 1978 entailed abandoning the state planning model in favour of market forces such that China could integrate and emerge as a formidable player in the global economy. He had a more pragmatic and realistic way of looking at the world. His approach of omnibus reforms—reaching out to international organizations to seek assistance, establishing deep diplomatic ties during the Cold War, right sizing of the defence forces, strict check on the population growth—may sound unlike China, but were more China in essence than ever before.

After Deng, the baton was passed on to Jiang Zemin "who nurtured the still wounded giant and ensured that it continued to grow."[38] When he took over China, it had taken a severe hit when it came to GDP numbers. Arrested economic growth along with social unrest welcomed Jiang Zemin. To add fuel to the fire, there was diplomatic isolation and an imposition of economic blockade had been made by the United States in wake of Tiananmen Square. However, Jiang Zemin amidst the bedlam and boycott, emerged as a champion of the developing world. He made inroads into the markets of the countries which the West had blacklisted or ignored. He expanded the base for the procurement of raw materials, for ready markets for the Chinese products, won back Hong Kong, set up a regulatory regime to augment foreign investment, ended its enmity with Russia, forged deep connection with South Korea and tried to bring together the Oriental world in order to emerge as its leader.

Jiang Zemin's left a somewhat structured and streamlined China. But it was Hu Jintao who took over a structured China and stream rolled it to win the 2008 Olympic Games, emerge as a shop-floor of the worlds, and assume an important place in the World Trade Organization. China, under Hu Jintao, was ready to participate in trade wars, negotiate free trade agreements, establish regional trading blocs and witness a double digit growth. Hu Jintao was not oblivious to the growing economic inequality, plague of corruption and the consequent after effects. It was he who took strong measures to address these issues and gave China its new punchlines "new socialist countryside" and "harmonious society". He made full use of what was available to him and tried to gain access to that which was not available.

When Xi Jinping came to power, he had his own set of unique challenges to battle against. The world was changing and so was the demography of China for the youth could no longer be overtly subverted or kept in dark. In this rapidly changing international climate, Xi's agenda was to curb the rampant corruption, control civil liberties, tightly monitor the information flow, engage vociferously (both through words and actions) in claiming territories and indulge in somehow diminishing Japan's stature. Equipped with a well-designed strategy, a rock solid plan and clear vision, all aimed at making China great again. He made his intentions clear when in his first address he stated, "we must...push forward the great cause of socialism with Chinese characteristics and strive to achieve the Chinese dream of the great rejuvenation of the Chinese nation."[39] Xi's speeches are a clear indication of his ambitions and his ambitions are not limited to one country or one continent.

"President Xi does indeed seem to be a different kind of Chinese leader from his two predecessors, more self-assured, more decisive and more of a risk-taker. With Xi in power we see a China more confident in its global role and in what it can offer to the world. A number of decisions previously left in abeyance have been taken since Xi became China's president, such as the acceptance of a combat role for Chinese peacekeepers in UN operations, the enunciation of the major infrastructure and connectivity project known as the

Belt and Road Initiative (BRI), and the establishment of the Asian Infrastructure Investment Bank (AIIB). Beijing has also been more willing to use its veto in the UN Security Council—as it has done six times with respect to the Syrian crisis since 2011—a very unusual move for the PRC, which has used a total of only twelve vetoes since it entered the UN in 1971."[40] Xi's report to the 19th Congress affirms that China has arrived on the international arena and is ready to take its rightful leadership position, "China's international standing has risen as never before. Our Party, our country, our people, our forces, and our nation have changed in ways without precedent. The Chinese nation, with an entirely new posture, now stands tall and firm in the East."[41] The dominance which China has displayed in its foreign policy, the revamping of its military rank and file, the famous trade wars with the United States, the tacit acceptance of currency manipulation, ways of arm-twisting the weaker nations to accept the Chinese demands, resource allocation in mega infrastructure projects and growing influence in the South China Sea, make Xi one of the most powerful leaders in the world. He has offered an alternative to a unipolar world once dominated by the United States.

Xi Jinping has tackled the newer issues such as intellectual property, cyber security, the Dark Continent, naval security and maritime rights with an unmatched grasp, clarity and precision. This reveals that China shall march confidently on its way to becoming a world power. What remains to be seen though is how Xi will respond to challenges of an ageing population, intensifying trade wars and a more demanding youth.

It is pertinent not to forget that Xi needs to last long in order for China to continue to 'Stay China' and become more. Concurrently, it is also imperative that the world does not throw any black swan event to thwart the pace at which the Dragon is moving. Needless to say that 'Staying China' would involve an interplay of both internal and external factors. Internally, it demands stability, externally it desires a dependent US, a tolerant India, an ignorant Africa and an awestruck South East Asia.

NOTES

1 Gary Zukav, "Solstice Joy," *HuffPost*, February 26, 2012, https://www.huffpost.com/entry/solstice-joy_b_1171628.

2 Benedict Anderson, Imagined Communities: Reflections on the Origin and Spread of Nationalism, (Brooklyn: Verso, 2006), pp. 6-7.

3 Dong Zhongshu (179-104 BC) was a great scholar of the Han Dynasty. He is associated with the promotion of Confucianism as the official ideology of Chinese imperial state.

4 Quoted in Hanshu Dong Zhongshu Zhuan (The Book of Han: Biography of Tung Chung-shu).

5 Anglo-Chinese Treaty signed in 1842 which ended the First Opium War and gave the British unfettered access to the Chinese territory.

6 Matt Schiavenza, "How Humiliation Drove Modern Chinese History," *The Atlantic,* October 25, 2013. https://www.theatlantic.com/china/archive/2013/10/how-humiliation-drove-modern-chinese-history/280878/.

7 Ankit Panda, "The Legacy of China's May Fourth Movement," *The Diplomat,* May 05, 2015, https://thediplomat.com/2015/05/the-legacy-of-chinas-may-fourth-movement/.

8 Andreas B. Forsby, "The United States Army Signal Command: Past, Present, and Future," An End to Harmony? The Rise of a Sino-Centric China 5, no. 3 (2011): pp. 5-6, http://www.politicalperspectives.org.uk/wp-content/uploads/Introduction3.pdf.

9 Orville Schell and John Delury, Wealth and Power: Chinas Long March to the Twenty-first Century, (New York: Random House Press, 2013), p. 40.

10 V for Vendetta is a dystopian political thriller of 2005. The usage here is purely metaphorical.

11 Rhyme recited on Guy Fawkes Night, the 5th of November, when effigies of Guy Fawkes are burned. Guy Fawkes was a leader of Roman Catholic Conspirators who attempted to carry out the failed 'Gunpowder plot' to assassinate King James of England.

12 William A. Callahan, China: The Pessoptimist Nation, (Oxford: Oxford University Press, 2010), p. 83.

13 Jack A. Goldstone, The Encyclopedia of Political Revolutions, (London: Routledge, 1998), p. vii.

14 Released in 1968 by Beatles when Vietnam War was raging, Martin Luther King Jr was assassinated and anti-War protest movements were in full swing in America.

15 Theda Skocpol. States and Social Revolutions: A Comparative Analysis of France, Russia and China, (Cambridge: Cambridge University Press, 1979), p. 33.

16 Andrew Scobell et al., *At the Dawn of Belt and Road: China in the Developing World* (Santa Monica: Rand Corporation, 2018), p. 13.

17 Mao Tse-tung, "Report on an Investigation of the Peasant Movement In Hunan," Selected Works of Mao Tse-Tung, 30 March 1927, https://www.marxists.org/reference/archive/mao/selected-works/volume-1/mswv1_2.htm.

18 Maurice J. Meisner, *The Significance of the Chinese Revolution in World History,* (London: Asia Research Centre, London School of Economics and Political Science, 1999).

19 Philip G. Altbach, Student Political Activism: An International Reference Handbook, (Santa Barbara: Greenwood Publishing Group, 1989), pp. 75-89.

20 Simone V. Nieuwenhuizen, "China: a Party of Governance and Control, Not Revolution," Lowy Institute, November 23, 2018, https://www.lowyinstitute.org/the-interpreter/china-party-governance-and-control-not-revolution.

21 Ibid.

22 *Sun Tzu, Art of War, Ch IV, Verse 6,* Griffith, Samuel B, op. cit fn 44, p. 128.

23 Edward C. O'Dowd, Chinese Military Strategy in the Third Indochina War: The Last Maoist War, (London: Routledge, 2007), p. 73.

24 Charles C. Duell, "The Long March: Victory Or Defeat?," Air Command And Staff College

Air University Maxwell AFB, AL 36112, 1988, https://apps.dtic.mil/dtic/tr/fulltext/u2/a207330.pdf

25 Dick Wilson, The Long March, 1935: The Epic of Chinese Communism's Survival, (London: Hamish Hamilton, 1971), p. xiv.

26 Harrison E. Salisbury, The Long March: The Untold Story, (New York: Harper & Row, 1985), p. 130.

27 Maurice J. Meisner, Mao's China and After: A History of the People's Republic (New York: The Free Press, 1977), p. 35.

28 Random House, Red Star Over China, (New York: Random House, 1938), p. 177.

29 Sulmaan Wasif Khan, Haunted by Chaos: China's Grand Strategy from Mao Zedong to Xi Jinping, (Cambridge, MA: Harvard University Press), 2018, pp. 61-62.

30 John W. Garver, "China's Decision for War with India in 1962," Alastair Ian Johnston and Robert S. Ross eds. New Directions in the Study of China's Foreign Policy, (Stanford, CA: Stanford University Press, 2006), p. 115.

31 Hong Yuan, "China Won, but Never Wanted, Sino-Indian War," *Global Times*, last modified June 28, 2012, http://www.globaltimes.cn/content/717710.shtml.

32 Kenneth G. Liberthal and Bruce J. Dickson, A Research Guide to Central Party and government Meetings in China 1949-1986. (Armonk, NY: M. E. Sharpe, 1989), p. 87. Since the Shanghai meeting of April 1959, Mao had suffered a downfall in his political stature with his retirement from the post of the Chairman of the People's Republic, "although he still continued as Chairman of the Party and played from behind the scenes".

33 The 'Seven Thousand Cadres Conference' held in January 1962 marked the lowest in Mao's leadership position, as his power was challenged by leaders such as Liu Shaoqi and Deng Xiaoping, was emerged by leaders China. Amrita Jash, Mao Zedong's *Art of the 1962 War*: Perception of Opportunity Versus Perception of Threat, KW Publishers Pvt. Ltd, Manekshaw Paper No. 76, 2018, p. 10. https://www.researchgate.net/publication/328146395_ Mao_ Zedong's_'Art_of_the_1962_War'_Perception_of_Opportunity_Versus_Perception_of_Threat

34 Khan, Haunted by Chaos, p. 237.

35 Ibid, p. 246.

36 Ibid, pp. 5-6.

37 Ibid., p. 246.

38 Ibid.

39 Xinhua News Agency, "Xi Vows to Press Ahead with 'Chinese Dream'," *China Daily Website*, March 17, 2013, http://www.chinadaily.com.cn/china/2013npc/2013-03/17/content_16314303.htm.

40 Rosemary Foot, "Remembering the past to secure the present: Versailles legacies in a resurgent China," *International Affairs*, 95, no. 1 (2019), pp. 143-160, doi:10.1093/ia/iiy211.

41 Xinhua News Agency, "Full Text of Xi Jinping's Report at 19th CPC National Congress," *China Daily Website*, November 4, 2017, http://www.chinadaily.com.cn/china/19thcpcnationalcongress/2017-11/04/content_34115212.htm.

3

Decoding China

"The idea that Chinese are all striving for 'the American way of life' is a dangerous misconception. They are striving for 'the Chinese way of life'. As a result, Chinese development has a certain kind of prideful, internal energy that helps the nation's confidence."[1]

When Joshua Cooper Ramo, a leading journalist spoke about the existing paradox in the mind of an average Chinese, he was trying to put words to an otherwise nebulous, dichotomous thought which hitherto had not been said aloud. When one tries to decode the Dragon, one needs to understand its psychology, its ideological underpinnings, its sociological perspective on gender roles, its motivation, its ambitions and its goals. While this might be an easier task when one talks of a small, island nation which has not seen much conflict during the course of its existence, the same becomes mighty difficult when it is undertaken in the context of China.

China is complex. There is nothing simple about being China. There never was and there never will be. Decoding China is like peeling an onion—there are multiple layers and each layer has a distinct purpose and function. In order to understand China one needs to empty oneself from preconceived conceptual notions for it is an exercise that requires a teleological reorientation. The apparent clash between what one knows and what one sees is so stark that at times it is difficult to separate the reality from thought. For instance, what ideology means in one part of the world is not what it means for the Chinese. It is here that one needs to deconstruct one's notion of ideology and spend some time with the Chinese definition in order to understand what it truly stands for.

IN THE CHINESE IDEOLOGICAL TRENCHES

Policy-making process in China has a history of its own. It all began with ideology underscoring state's policy. However, with Deng's arrival, ideology lost its pedestal and was replaced by utilitarianism and pragmatism.[2]

Policy became a course of action to meet an end and not the conclusion in itself. With well-etched and well-defined goals, Deng heralded a new age of reforms. However, this came to an end when President Xi Jinping came to power. With Xi came his adulation for ideology and one finds a resurgence in ideology in policy making. President Xi tried to take ideological positions in policy and in this process gave rise to an ideological thread which ran through every single policy which the Party formulated. It was felt by Xi that given a surge in the concept of individualism and the resultant materialism, ideology had taken a backseat. In order to draw validation of his stance on ideology, he relied upon the developments especially in countries which had touted democracy as the foremost method of governance and multi-party system as an equalising force when it came to representation of aspirations of all the sections of the society. Brexit, refugee crisis, increasing popularity of rightist political parties, fractured mandates, political instability, etc.—all were seen as a culmination of flawed governance in the West.

Primarily governed by western values of liberalism, democracy, universal human rights, free markets and free trade, the countries in the West have clear allegiance to a system which shares no similarities with the Chinese model and fabric. However, given the present turmoil in Europe, it is easy to blame the liberal value system for the political, social and demographic debacle. President Xi milked this crisis to propagate his agenda and spread his concepts. His ambitions do not stop at making China reclaim its legitimate position in the world order but to give rise to a solid 'China Path' as a viable alternative to the 'American Dream'. In other words, he wishes to construct the Chinese Dream on the ashes of the American Dream and for accomplishing the same he speaks of "Four Confidences"[3] encompassing 'system, theory, path and culture'. As per the "Four Confidences", Xi's political philosophy carries forward the tradition of long numbered policies and aims at reforming the Chinese society in a manner that people take pride in their culture. This, however, does not undermine the role played by 'fear' in keeping the regime intact lest it collapses.

It will be foolish to assume that in his mission to establish an authentic Chinese society, Xi would have not factored in the power of social media in spreading the love for the Western ideology and the growing demand for democracy in traditional tyrannical countries. In fact the rate at which the dictatorial regimes are crumbling is most definitely inspirational (and to some extent even aspirational) for a common Chinese. Therefore, the need to weave an alternative narrative is even more crucial for Xi.

Since Xi became the chairman of the Party he has spoken extensively about the 'great rejuvenation'. He was acutely aware of the spell democracy casts on youth and in order to counter that, he is doing his best to make the Chinese way a convincing option for his countrymen. By projecting his ideology as a credible tool to survive in the long run, he is also trying to repair the damage caused to it. Subverting ideology to individualism needs to be overturned and China is not leaving any stone unturned to accomplish the same. The Chinese model of economic development and growth became the epitome when the economic meltdown of 2008 took place. Publicised as the failure of the free markets and thereby an extension of the Western ideology and politics, China could curb the nascent voices which spoke of deregulation and opening of markets. In fact, Xi is often seen quoting, "Never before the Chinese people been so close to realizing their dreams."[4] While the concept of the 'Chinese Dream' was popularised by Xi, it was first discussed in 2010 by Liu Mingu in his book *China Dream: Great Power Thinking and Strategic Posture in the Post-American Era*. But, the Chinese Dream is in many ways different from the American Dream. The American Dream pays priority to self-enrichment and accomplishment whereas the Chinese Dream is a combined effort that asks all citizens to devote their life for the greater national good.

The task of a unified ideology which President Xi has set himself on is not easy to accomplish given that Chinese society is not what it used to be. The 'society has changed'[5] in its constitution, colour, character, and code. The economic, regional, societal, political cleavages have deepened and consequently to give rise to one approach which is appealing and workable for all will prove to be catastrophic. Also, one cannot afford to miss the divergent opinions which have taken root and shape in the Party itself. Once an ideological block of ice, the CCP today is melting to include different voices in its folds. The cherry on the cake is however the fear of being 'overthrown' ideologically and politically which has never left the Chinese. The phobia of being seduced by Western values is real and has not left the Chinese political class since the very beginning.

To make this task easier, Xi relies on a four-fold strategy—first, rhapsodically portrayal of the ideological legacy; second, extolling the impetus given to ideology by his predecessors; third, selectively selecting western concepts which can be moulded to give a Chinese flavour; and fourth, eulogising the Chinese traditions while borrowing from them. However, the most prominent manner in which Xi is trying to accomplish this is to infuse Chinese values in Western concepts such that the 'rule of law' of the Western world is accepted as 'rule by law' by the Chinese. Xi has adopted a two-pronged approach to buttress his ambition of ideological dominance. First is known as 'ideological protectionism' and second is known as 'massification of ideology'. 'Ideological protectionism' implies weaving the policy around ideology meaning thereby that the core of the policy, that is, ideology remains shielded at all times. His measures of strengthening the social credit system, infusing discipline, a hardliner stand on corruption and a blanket ban on public debate and discourse on 'seven harmful concepts'.[6] Xi's overt support and expression of his thought did not end with altering the institutional mechanisms but extended to persecuting liberals and intellectuals under the new law. Furthermore, the corporate sector is expected to openly owe allegiance to the Party and the extent of its political loyalty determines its entitlement quotient. By classifying corporates as 'rule-confirming' and 'rule-breaking', the party keeps dissent in check.

'Massification of ideology'[7] is the second aspect of Xi's approach. Massification simply implies increasing the mass base of the ideology. While the Chinese have been subjected to such ideological hypnotism before, the manner in which it is being carried out is certainly novel. This time Xi's team is spreading the political doctrine by using tools[8] which enjoy personal interface with the masses. The lingo is free from any jingoism and is relatable. Instead of being parochial and preachy, it is about vision, dreams and aspirations. It goes beyond communication and control. It tries to give rise to the idea of a 'modern-model citizenry' which is worth emulating and whoever falls short of perfection in spreading this message is punished. Core socialist values need to be advertised at all times and every cog in the machinery has to perform up to till full potential and efficiency. In Xi's universe, those who make mistakes are not exonerated but executed.

Expanding the mass base of the ideology also requires a calculated and a well-thought through strategy for pulling down the anti-thesis of that ideology. A realistic assessment reveals that if the Party needs to be successful in selling the quintessential Chinese-style socialism along with denigrating the Western ways, it needs to establish a more direct connect with the Chinese masses. China not only seeks to do that by controlling the content over social media, electronic media and print media but also by instigating Washington to enter into trade duels, energy debates, etc. But the approach falls short in its endeavour. The 'Four Confidences' notion is not rooted in reality and the ban on discussion and debate on topics of vital importance further ostracises the ideology. The control needs to be slow and subtle for it to be effective. However, subtlety is not a trait which the Party can claim to possess.

Xi's pet project cannot be successfully delivered if the same obliterates or subverts economic growth, employment generation and environmental health. For ideology to work in the minds of the Chinese, the policy needs to work on the ground. But with growing income disparity, graft, societal imbalance, concentration of power and housing crisis, one cannot say for long Xi plans to charm the Chinese with lofty ideological ideals. No matter how strong the curb on social media is the fact that there exist multiple sources from which information can be accessed, works as a spoiler for the Xi's government. The Xi Jinping administration needs to deal on fairly even terms with growing socio-economic uncertainties. If the administration is able to boost efforts to stabilise economic growth and social well-being then the people would not resist any further control due to ideological reigning. However, disruptive event such as instability due to social, economic and political upheaval or wide spread environmental disaster could change the picture resulting in radicalisation of the society.

YIN TALKS TO YANG[9]

The clash between thesis and antithesis is not new. Scholars across the world have accepted the coexistence of diametrically opposite viewpoints, powers, energies, thoughts and forces. This peaceful juxtaposition of seemingly polar opposites in one frame indicates the ability to deal with paradox with equanimity. Chinese since the very beginning have mastered this art and have labelled this phenomenon as the 'Yin-Yang' which traces its origin in the teachings of Taoism. It is this dualism of every aspect of life which made the Chinese understand the value of balance. This philosophy and notion of balance has only cemented with time and one can safely conclude that it is the acceptance of this paradox which has made China cope with the radical transformation of its society, economic highs and lows and cultural metamorphosis.

Yet another aspect of this philosophy is that the two are not separated by any borders. The forces are self-contained and do not need any segregation to retain their respective identities. This approach found its takers in the Party leaders. From Mao to Xi, all have initiated and pushed their reforms and thoughts under the garb of Yin-Yang which needs no validation given its religious backing. Any change in social norms of a country influences its national psychology and identity. Changes in citizens' values, thoughts, orientation, relationship and linguistic features influence the leadership to adapt to changes, both directly and indirectly influencing decisions on strategy.

Six Records of Floating Life: Quintessential Chinese Confucian Family

The Family

Chinese society developed as agrarian in the expanse of Yellow River. In the villages, majority were the tillers of the land, mostly belonging to the same larger family or clan. The interdependence for labour, barter of goods and in time of frequent calamities developed a strong bond amongst them. This has made the Chinese society greatly interdependent with emphasis on family and kinship connections.

The norms of the Chinese society are responsible for inculcating the political values among the individuals. The Chinese are made to value their families as the atomic unit of the society. It is this unit which fosters harmony and keeps an individual collected and close. The roots of this thought originated during the times of Confucius who regarded an individual as a furtherance of the family lineage thereby making family the pivot around which the life of an individual is woven. It is this notion which establishes harmonic relationships within a family and between two families and ultimately the entire social conglomeration of families. Harmony is not only seen as an attribute of human relationships. It embraces relationships between the individual and environment, communities, etc. too. However, with economic independence and advancement, the element of harmony from the Chinese society is weaning away. Families are not as close knit as they used to be. The concepts of authority, order, seniority, collectivism, individualism, societal norms, etc. are being revisited in the present context and while one can see a change in these texts of these values, the subtext continues to remain the same.

In his autobiography *Six Records of Floating Life*, the Chinese scholar Shen Fu has described the look and the feel of a typical Chinese family during the Qings. Marked by rigid hierarchical structure and watertight division of roles, a typical Chinese family two centuries ago was not very different from what it is today. There are definite deviations but the same are not as stark when compared with an American family.

The relationship between parents and children is characterised by a dramatic functional shift from the 'filial piety' due to the one child and little emperor syndrome. Today it is a well-accepted norm among the young to challenge their parents regarding matters of their marriage. In ancient China, the institution of marriage was arranged by parents and elders looked for a marriage partner based on comparable societal and economic stature with the guiding rule being "matching doors and windows". In the last thirty years, the customs towards courtship and marriage have been upended from the ancient arranged marriage system to a system influenced by the West. The number of dating shows on the television has increased drastically; live-in relationships and divorces in China have skyrocketed. Moreover, for the Chinese youth, traditional value such as pure love has been replaced by pervasive materialism.

The Chinese society has radically changed overtly but the allegiances to Confucian doctrines have not. Contemporary China is not as overtly Confucius in its conduct. But covertly the notions of hierarchy, power and gender differentiation continue to constitute the reality of Chinese. The "let the ruler be a ruler, the minister be minister, the father be a father and the son be a son"[10] rule has lost its grip and charm.

"Age is revered because it is associated with wisdom. Chinese society tends to have certain contempt for immature enthusiasm; the young are taught early to hold their tongues while their elders are speaking."[11] This cultural attribute is believed to preserve 'harmony' of a society by its hierarchical structure, which is clearly demonstrated in the "Three Cardinals."[12]

The position of women in a family and society has drastically improved since Mao Zedong declared that "Women Hold up Half the Sky" which was a powerful statement which laid stress on the fact that woman need to move outside the domains of the house into the professional arena. In the family hierarchy, the wife's subordinate status of being obedient, bearing children and with a role confined to household is a thing of the past. Today nearly 40 percent of all independent companies in China are owned by women.

Beyond Society: Kinship, Guanxi and Professionalism

The traditional Chinese culture was shaped in kinship system which consisted of four categories.[13] The hierarchical system of kinship functioned as a network of support and bonding with a genetic or family connection so as to address each other properly and maintain harmony within the family. The notion of *Guanxi* is a horizontal, informal and unofficial personal connection and contacts construct which has been created "to get things done, from simple tasks to major life choices."[14]

However, the economic reforms have promoted an accepted norm of openness, competition and rewarding performance which have led to a balance between *Guanxi* and professionalism. However, unlike other global markets, in the Chinese market the governmental role is much more effective and active as a consequence the relevance of both *Guanxi* and Professionalism have got commingled to unite into a whole.

State and Society Relations

President Xi's tenure has witnessed constant strengthening of inter-linkages between society and state. While the democratic world has worked towards disentangling the two where the state is independent of the society in both existence and nature, China, under present leadership has tried to give rise to a fabric which is a culmination of both in the interest of stability and efficiency.

China does not look at stability as an outcome of strong institutions with systems of collective responsibility and checks and balances but as a result of a personal characteristic of the leader. In a system which is personality and performance driven, the legal system is not expected to deliver its most obvious functions but to protect and insulate the system from any onslaught. Rights are negotiable but rites are not, for the former destabilises the state but the latter deepens its presence.

Furthermore, it is the nature of the leader which determines the quality of leadership the Party chief lends. The bureaucracy works as a support system contrary to the steel frame it is in other countries. The leader assumes control of the body and bureaucracy of the state which can spell disaster for China if the leader is susceptible to corruption and moral contamination and the bureaucracy weak. Given the economic expanse of China and the outside influences it is subjected to, the Party is aware of the tight rope it is walking on and therefore, it is trying its best to throw up leaders who have the capability of being at the helm of a party-army fusion and can also be charismatic, dominant and inspire faith in people.

From the foregoing, one might be tempted to predict doom for the Chinese state and society. But, one needs to take a closer look to understand the sum and substance of the Chinese society which focuses on the genre of principle and performance and not on pluralism and participation.[15] It is this obvious choice of the Chinese which has given rise to a regime which comprises a structured, centralised, strong and elitist bureaucracy which focuses on order rather than quality of governance. The Chinese cannot fathom experimenting with an alternative form of governance unless they are caught in a political rigmarole. This is further accentuated by the fact that they are living under a system which has been tried and tested for centuries. Even though the potency of the western influence cannot be taken lightly coupled with the minority of the Chinese being intoxicated by the romantic version of the West, the Party is aware that the sizeable majority of the Chinese population is comfortable with the present system despite its flaws. However, to say that the Party takes the threat of the Western influence lightly will be to undermine the perpetual paranoia it is under. It is fully aware that the western winds romancing the Chinese can destabilise the existing paraphernalia and hence never underestimated the same.

Voluntary Genetic Drift

Falling fertility rate is an issue most countries are grappling with. The weight of an ageing population not being supported by a young, robust, physically and mentally agile labour force becomes unbearable for any economy, its growth notwithstanding. China is also fighting the same battle. With over a quarter of the Chinese population staring into seniority of age by 2050, Beijing is worried about the human resource management and demographic imbalance. While this imbalance was a result of multiple factors, the chief factor amongst them was the aggressive family planning and 'one-child policy' which the Chinese policymakers had pursued in order to ease out population pressure.

Today, the lion's share of the younger generation, due to international exposure has accepted small family as the reproductive norm. The forty years of family planning and the changed preferences of the younger generation has casted a demographic shadow that will impact the Chinese social development and economy as there is significant increase in the ageing population as compared to births. As a result "demographics are set to have a far-reaching and long-term impact on Chinese savings and consumption, the external balance, growth, the labour market, industrial structure, the pension system, and the public finances".[16]

Consumption Pattern: Ethical Idealism and Materialism

A change in the society is often succeeded by a change in the pattern of spending of the masses. While the Chinese society painted materialism to be a sin[17] and stressed on idealism, the expression of success was essentially the number of acquisitions thereby indicating the contradiction in the concepts of wealth and socialism. However, this essentially Confucian values are eroding with time and one finds young generation of Chinese being driven by consumerism and comfortable with the idea of being materialistic. "Such a paradoxical attitude towards saving, borrowing and spending has to arbitrate between the present and the future, and between the economic habits inherited from tradition and the hedonistic consumption mentality developed with the emerging Chinese society."[18]

Individual Thinking and Behavioural Styles

Chinese ways of thinking and behaviour have been a mystery for the world and are quite difficult to comprehend. Psychologists have often described Chinese as 'inscrutable', so much so that book *The Inscrutable Americans* requires a competition christened an 'the inscrutable Chinese'. The Chinese Individual thinking style can be characterised in terms of any of the five ways—moderation, dialecticism, holism, intuitiveness and authority, and the key Chinese behavioural dynamics which are distinct and have great social significance in interaction are 'face' and 'passive coping'.

The concept central to understanding Chinese thinking is the concept of 'Mean or moderation' (zhongyong). The concept translates into pursuing the middle ground in all actions and activities, not taking extreme positions and taking decisions only after discussing and listening to different viewpoints. Since time immemorial, the concept has been interwoven into the education system of the country and understanding of this aspect was tested in examinations conducted for civil servants in imperial China. Due to the resurgence in Confucian teachings in the contemporary educational system, students today are expected not only to be aware of the teachings but also gain understanding and proficiency. A further hallmark of Chinese thinking is the belief that things can change from one extreme to another. This 'dialectical' (Blanzheng) view of thinking is based on the Taoist Book Yi Jing (Book of Changes), which revolves around three interchanging and interrelating themes—first, the eternity of change in the universe, second, accepting the inevitability of changes, and third, the dynamism of balance between opposites. Without disturbing order and stability, seemingly contradictory theorems can be clubbed to put together a system which is vibrant form within but shaky outside. Another foundational belief in the Chinese worldview is 'Holism' (Tianren Heyi). All things, from nature to people, are interrelated parts of a unified whole, the idea being one of the basic tenets of two thousand year old Confucianism. In contemporary Chinese communication, use of 'He' (harmony based on diversity) 'Hexie' (harmony) and 'Hexie Shehui' (harmonious society) have become common currency in verbal commination. An intuitive experience (Zhijue) based form of thinking is used in a variety of settings especially in interpretation and academic tasks. The Chinese tradition of social hierarchy of experience and age is respected. Thus, in any discussion or dispute, the most senior or knowledgeable person is accorded the privilege to be the arbiter. This kind of psychological pattern what might be called authority-minded way of thinking (Quanwei) is linked with the phenomenon of citing, referring to, drawing upon and expressing respect towards the powerful, knowledgeable, and elderly.

In social interaction, aggressive behaviour and belligerent opinions are not appreciated. Therefore, dissent is the hallmark of a functional democracy. However, when it comes to China, dissent is equated with defiance. In schools and universities, the students refrain from questioning their teachers and stay silent when they do not agree with what is being taught. Disagreement is avoided and people go to great length to remain polite and courteous. A Chinese 'face' simply has greater social significance while interacting socially. An oft-repeated Chinese proverb, "A person needs face as a tree needs bark." An individual can lose face as a consequence of failure, not achieving objective, losing his cool, being hostile or failing to show appropriate respect. Inability to accord someone his due respect is a grave offence in Chinese society. If someone is made to lose face, it is not only that individual who feels aggrieved but others who are aware of that also take it as a huge transgression. An anecdote from the spring and autumn period about social significance of 'face' delineates how "The last emperor of the Sui Dynasty, Yang Di had trees bound in expensive silks and frequently treated guests to fine meals to exert his face-ness."[19] Chinese civilisational 'Passive Coping' beliefs place a greater attention to the importance of nature and character of one's inner thoughts and desires to manage stress and emotional distress rather than trying to make overt changes in the environment. Instead of interpreting stressful experiences as negative, the Confucian doctrines advocate that individuals value the negative experiences by acknowledging the personal growth and toughness and consequences brought by these experiences.

DESIGN OF STRATEGY: THINKING, GAMING, ASYMMETRY AND AMBIGUITY

The Chinese design strategy takes into account the instruments and the outcomes which China is desirous of. Since its inception, the strategy has been sweeping in its intent, objective, action and goals. The sub-themes of this strategy which play a monumental role are—thinking, gaming, asymmetry, ambiguity. All of them aim at realising the Chinese hopes and aspirations.

Way to Strategy Thinking

Strategy always implies pursuing one's interests all at once. More often than not, it requires the insight and the intelligence to rank one's interests in their order of priority. Therefore, the formulation of strategy does not begin with the goal but with choice. The formulation of strategy commences gradually as China decides to formulate those interests which need to be pursued. The formulation of strategy begins with an objective thought which can be tested against standards which are the same for any and every observer. These tests are not a result of passion but precision, and therefore, obliterate the involvement of any personal emotion. The goal setting is an objective process and the goal is, hence, a convergence of such thoughts rooted in pragmatism. The manner of pursuit is, however, subjective. The Chinese Xinhua Zidian (Xinhua Dictionary) explains the objective-subjective thought process—"Subjective refers to a person's thinking or understanding. Objective refers to the material world existing outside of a person's consciousness. The relationship between subjective and objective is a dialectical unity. Objective does not rely on subjective and exists independently, it is the source of subjective, it determines subjective; subjective reflects objective, and actively reacts with objective, under certain conditions it determines the effect of objective. The objective world is constantly developing and changing, and a person's understanding must also accordingly develop and change. There are frequent contradictions between subjective and objective. Only through practicing constantly to overcome the contradictions between subjective and objective does subjective understanding accord with objective reality, and only then can the world be effectively changed."[20]

The strategy on paper and the strategy in action are engineered by the objective-subjective dynamic between thought and policy. The same has been captured beautifully by Senior Colonel Luo Xiangde when he wrote in 2010 that the process of the evolution of the Chinese thought is "a strategic thinking activity in which subjective ideas are manifested through objective realities".[21] The objective goals and realities are exploited by the leaders to fulfil their subjective aims. Thus, the Chinese way of thinking begins with objectivity and ends with subjectivity.

Way to Gaming

To expect a watertight segregation of sports and the impact it exerts on the society in which it is played is to fool oneself. While sports are a form of recreation, the choice of sport and the manner in which it is played indicates the prowess of the players.

China has been famous for martial arts and Wei Ch'i which require both mental and physical agility. Martial arts, in fact, have been an integral part of the Chinese life and by denigrating it to the position of a sport is unfair. However, given that in the modern times, it has been classified as a sport and has lost some of its sheen, one can safely say that the sway it once had on the Chinese society has loosened up a bit.

Much has been written about the importance of martial arts in China and the emotion which surrounded it, but there has not been much discussion around its origin and the role played by it in the games of war. *Art of War* written by Sun Tzu, extensively talks about the sport and its hypnotic power. Philosophically speaking, martial arts became the source and origin of three major lessons which the Chinese have inadvertently learnt and made a part of their DNA—focus or graze, meeting the hard with softness, and hiding techniques to deceive.

Dragon's Focus or Graze: Whenever a Chinese is faced with a problem his/her perception of the issues and behaviour base, he/she first arranges his/her thoughts to see the disposition of things and then deliberates on the solution of the problem. Richard E Nisbett in his book *Geography of Thought* describes the "look at the object, attributes and category" of both Oriental and American origin people. He concludes that the "oriental mind takes the bigger picture, the disposition of things."[22] This proclivity to observe the disposition from side to side is mirrored in Chinese theorists' depiction and interpretation of strategy, which are much more extensive than the American explanation of concept. Yagyu Munenori (1571–1646), the Samurai, in his book *The book of Family Traditions on the Art of War* further elaborated on this divergent focus or 'Far Seeing' in an Oriental mind. "If you gaze at a single leaf on a single tree, you do not see the other leaves. If you face the tree with no intention and don't fix your eyes on a single leaf, then you will see all the many leaves. If your mind is preoccupied with one leaf, you don't see the others, if you don't set your attention on one, you will see hundreds and thousands of leaves."[23]

Meeting the Brute with Softness: To think of martial arts as a form of meditation is inconceivable for most. But if one were to go deeper and look at the emotions behind the same, it would come as no surprise that Tai Chi, an intense form of martial arts originated as a result of an observation whereby gentleness was used to thwart the enemy in its ambition of taking over by force. Answering force with force will lead to both the sides being fractured, fragmented, feeble and flawed. Answering force with tenderness would divert the energy of the opposition and once spent, it would be easy to redirect the same. The fact that the strategy driving this method of resistance is to look into the nature of the enemy attack and spot weakness in it such that the same can be exploited is one of the biggest learnings of the Chinese. The term used to describe this tactic was 'The King, The Fool and The Fox' strategy. The King strategy is based on the Chinese proverb "wait long, strike fast"[24] which involves concealing one's intentions and motives and attacking the enemy on his weak spot. The Fool strategy is based on the Samurai maxim "the angry man will defeat himself in battle as well as in life"[25] and revolves around misleading the enemy by constant movement and messaging without once allowing the enemy to take a glimpse at the real motive. The aim is to keep the enemy embroiled in so much signalling and interpretation that it cannot go beyond the obvious and uncloak the true intent. The Fox strategy is based on the Chinese classic Tao Te Ching written by Lao Tze, "he who is fearless in being bold will meet his death; he who is fearless in being timid will stay alive."[26]

It is the toughest of them all because it requires sending mixed signals to the enemy. In other words, the idea is to manipulate the strategy of the enemy by revealing half-truths such that its perception, plan and practice can be moulded to suit the needs of the manipulator. The enemy without his knowledge will act in a manner which is beneficial to the opposition.

Deception by Hiding Techniques: Martial art forms differ from one country to another. One major difference between the Chinese Martial art forms and Japanese and Korean Martial art forms is that the former is unclear in its movement. It is difficult to discern the meaning behind the histrionics involved in it and its combat applications. The Chinese brand of martial arts is shrouded in secrecy in its attitude and theme and the purpose behind it is to appear confusing to the enemy such that it cannot plan its defence. In Chinese martial arts schools of the past, the best fighter was one who could balance strength and skill with patience and cunningness.

This technique that truth is outside of all fixed patterns also finds place in the thirty six Chinese strategies. Stratagem number 13, 'Beat the Grass to Startle the Snakes'[27] is followed when the enemy's plan is not clear and there is a need to the judge the reaction of the enemy and therefore, as a precursor a brief and direct attack like a feint is launched to evaluate enemy reaction and create confusion in the enemy's mind. Stratagem number 20 'Trouble the Water to Catch the Fish'[28] involves creating confusion in the enemy forces so as to weaken the enemy's perception and judgment by doing something unexpected and thus making the enemy doubt his/her own thinking. Stratagem Number 7, 'Create something from nothing'[29] which involves sending false signals not once but twice or even more to create an expectation in your enemy and then change course to deceive the enemy. Deception is not only a part of any martial art competition or contest with an adversary but also in their philosophy mentioned in The Six Secret Teachings of the Jiang Taigong, "When the Sage is about to move, he will certainly display a stupid countenance."[30]

A simple board game may not seem to be of any significance in determining the behaviour of the Chinese but given its rules, it surely provides an insight into the fodder on which Chinese have been raised. Wei Ch'i shows how by maintaining constant ambiguity and smokescreen, one can confuse the enemy and paralyse any attempts made by the opponent in strategizing a counter-attack. Understanding the Chinese leadership is a tall order but understanding how Wei Ch'i is played is not, and one of the ways to reach, grasp and interpret Chinese thought is to observe and internalise the tricks involved.

The game involves searching answers for three questions before designing any strategy. First, what and how will the strategic leverage be created; second, how can things be kept in a state of perpetual haze; and third, how to achieve multiple interests and desired ends. An extension of these questions is the moves of encircling, dividing, conquering and controlling territories and the game comes to an end when the stalemate arrives. An expression of such moves in the arena of international affairs can be seen when Henry Kissinger in his book *On China* drew parallels between Wei Ch'i and the Chinese actions in the past century. China's claim in the South China Sea was seen as a typical Wei Ch'i response to the United States' action of encirclement. Shades of Wei Ch'i are also discernible in the ambition of Belt and Road Initiative (BRI) and the control of Africa—two areas which have historically been ignored by the United States but will assume importance in the future.

In one's quest for decoding China, it is necessary to go beyond the obvious and search for answers in nuances. Wei Ch'i is one such nuance that must not be missed when one tries to discover what lies beneath China's strategic behaviour.

Twist in Design: Asymmetry

Asymmetry is not a highly regarded adjective. In fact, it is often used to denote a pattern which does not 'fit in' with fine patterns and designs. However, in case of Chinese, this adjective is imported to denote the quality of their strategy and the manner of engaging one's adversary in a battle.

The concept of 'asymmetry' first found mention in Sun Tzu's *Art of War* where it referred to the type of attack which does not follow any set pattern and therefore, catches the enemy by surprise. It is this element of surprise which adds to the richness of the attack. Shashoujian (Assassin's Mace, a Chinese weapon) is known to practise the asymmetrical methods of warfare and is often portrayed as its hero and is often quoted when the discussions revolve around issues of cyber-attacks, network attacks, etc. China is extremely sensitive to the thought of these network attacks and therefore, is taking utmost care both in action and in allocation of resources to safeguard them. Additionally, it is pertinent to note that while the rest of the world is looking at strengthening the symmetrical warfare, China is heavily invested in sharpening its asymmetrical warfare.

What Happens in Ambiguity, Stays in Ambiguity

Chinese master the art of creating ambiguity. The ambiguity is not created to mislead the world but is used as a smokescreen to hide the real intention. It appears as ambiguity for the rest of the world but for the Chinese it is crystal clear. The ambiguity happens as the Chinese language has been an ideological language with its distinctive Morphophonological nature and it stays in Ambiguity due to its deliberately manufactured fallacies so as to blur its motive. Under the cloak of this whirlpool and bedlam, China clearly furthers its motives and while one may see how hungover the Chinese are on this strategic tool, let us not for a moment forget that this instrument is not recent. It traces its origin to the ancient Chinese stratagem of 'hide a dagger in a smile' and 'Battle of Pride'. The 'Hide a dagger in a smile' is to hide a strong will under a serene, unconcerned and self-satisfied appearance so as to make an adversary slack while working in secret to subdue the opponent. 'Battle of Pride' advocates a method of behaving in an obsequious manner, making the adversary who is stronger, proud of its own virility to soften its vigilance against your plan and wait until the opponent reveals his/her weak points to subdue him/her once and for all.

Given the nature of the Chinese stand on issues of global warming, nuclear proliferation, sustainable development, etc. one can clearly see how the aforementioned tactics have been used to hide the true motives and intentions. Also, in relation to its core objectives, these tactics are dropped like hot potatoes and on such issues, the true nature of the Dragon surfaces—unyielding, inflexible and proactive. It is this fearlessness which it naturally takes to dealings with its neighbours. The dynamic which China shares with the world is not homogenous. The manner in which it chooses to act and react is solely determined by the proximity it shares with the cause or the issue involved. For instance, in case of Taiwan, China initially used ballistic missiles under the garb of reintegrating and reunifying with the island. However, with time as it gained more power, strength and clout, it became more aggressive and straightforward in its approach.

From oscillating between Deng's keeping a low profile to being assertive under Xi, China has learnt to adapt to the changing dynamics of the world politics instead of coming across as a rigid nation with a definite agenda.

With Trump administration, previous penchant for non-confrontation and engagement of the US with China at any cost has been replaced by US calling China in the January 2018 National Defence Strategy as a "revisionist" nation bent on changing international norms and geostrategic status quo. Moreover, Mike Pence, Vice President of the United States, on 4 October 2018, at Hudson Institute clearly laid out the United States National Defence Strategy of 'compete, deter and win'.

In such a scenario, will China continue with its strategic ambiguity or adapt to newer strategies? An anecdote from the Zhinang Quanji is recounted to show as how China has historically been able to overcome its vulnerability by adapting to new situations by creating fresh ambiguity. "King Zhou (of the Shang dynasty) lost count of the date because of a long night of drinking. He checked with his attendants but nobody could tell him what day it was. He then sent a messenger to check with Qi Zi. Qi Zi said to his disciples: 'As the king and the whole country lost count of the date, our country is in danger. If I become known as the only person who knows the date, I'll become very vulnerable. So he told the messenger that he was also too drunk to tell the date'."[31]

CONSTITUENTS AND EXPRESSIONS OF STRATEGY: ANECDOTES, STRATAGEMS, WORDS, SLOGANS

Posterity is the biggest teacher. People preserve history in order to gain insight into their past such that they can get perspective in the present and for the future. In case of China, preservation of history, folklore and old civilisational values is a process which has continued for over five millennia and continues to inspire and influence the Chinese leaders and Chinese strategy. But it is essential to look at the other factors influencing the Chinese strategy in order to understand it in its pith and substance.

The Chinese strategy should not be seen as a sum total of what China stands for, instead, it should be seen as a culmination of anecdotes, stratagems, words and slogans. It is dynamic in its expression but static from within. It is an organic extension of ideology, struggles and thought processes that China has developed over centuries. What has transformed over the years is the increase in complexity but the core has remained unchanged and it is this core which gets reflected time and again in the political slogans which China selects as buzzwords.

The process of transformation of this ancient historical pattern or information into contemporary, relevant and actionable information is done by a metaphorical process "in which the identifying qualities of one thing are transferred in an instantaneous, almost unconscious, flash of insight to some other thing that is, by remoteness or complexity."[32]

The anecdotes, which the Chinese use are for the purpose of giving rise to role models—deeds of valour done by heroes in order to inspire future generations. Once again, it needs to be understood that not every act of valour and bravery is used. Careful selection of heroes whose actions and sacrifices can be merged with the present needs and aspirations of contemporary China is the norm. The process of deconstructing and reconstructing is simultaneous and the result is a body of symbols which can be used to influence the Chinese masses in the favour of the Party's ideology and thought. Anecdotes contain parts of history which need to be painted and projected in a manner that the same become powerful tools of political manipulation. Among the ancient written text which is most famous for containing 497 anecdotes of political manipulation and warfare during the Warring State period (453–221 BC) is Zhan Guo Ce (Strategies of the Warring States). Subsequently, in the Ming Dynasty, a compilation of anthological anecdotes was undertake. The most notable among them being the *Zhi Nang* (*Sack of Wisdom*) by Feng Menglong (1574–1646). The appeal of anecdotes and sayings in contemporary China can be judged from the fact that the book *Anecdotes and Saying of Xi Jinping* with 109 anecdotes and sayings, which Xi Jinping has mentioned in his speeches and articles while been President, has gained widespread interest from the public after its publication on 8 June 2017. The relevance of anecdotes to a contemporary Chinese strategist can be appreciated from the remarks of Feng Menglong in the preface in his book *Zhi Nang*, "Successful use of (anecdotes) depends on one's intelligence, but it is always helpful if he knows a lot of past events."[33]

If anecdotes are the consonants, then stratagems act as the vowels in the

Chinese strategy. Found in the ancient texts, these stratagems act as the instruments of developing and sharpening cognitive behaviour and channelising thoughts, perceptions and emotions. The power they exert on the minds of the Chinese is immense and it is this impact which is then utilised to make the Chinese think and react in a uniform way. These stratagems are powerful because they end up gaining control of the mind. *Sanshiliuji* (Thirty-Six Stratagems) is one of the most famous texts in ancient Chinese tradition which is divided into six parts, each part including six stratagems. The popularity of *Sanshiluji*, although it has a quasi-non-canonical stature, is due to its structure (four or three character) being akin to proverbs, universal validity (politics, military and social interaction) and oversimplified digestible sound bite-sized cryptic statements. The relevance of Chinese stratagems today was brought out in 1999, by the book *Unrestricted War* which appreciated the future war as "transcends all boundaries and limits."[34]

The third genre of 'words' refers to the strategies expressed by single or double character words due to Chinese being an ideographic script. In contemporary Chinese society, many words have become increasingly popular. Two words which have become popular are *tui* (push away) and *tuo* (delay). The tactic of Tuozijue is used to deal with complex issues that apparently do not seem to have an instant solution; therefore reducing the importance of the problem making it easier to solve the issue over a protracted period.

In China, political slogans are in fact snapshots of national strategies. In the mysterious world of Chinese politics, slogans are extremely significant. They communicate the perception and vision of the leadership to the common man. An understanding of the past rhetoric and current governing philosophy of the Chinese Communist Party gives a consolidated views of what preoccupies China's leaders in their times. The national political slogan are catchy, short, rhythmic and are just like patterns used in everyday Chinese speech to get the message across to the masses. 'Chinese People have stood up' (1949), 'Let one hundred flower bloom' (1956), 'Dare to think, dare to act' (1958) and 'Smash the four olds' (1966), were the slogans of Mao Zedong's time. During Deng Xiaoping's tenure slogans such as 'Reform and opening up' (1978), 'Seek truth from facts' (1978) and 'Have fewer children, raise more pigs' (1979) were popular. During Jiang Zemin's tenure, 'Three represent' (2000) and during Hu Jintao's tenure 'Harmonious Society' (2005) and 'Three Supremes' (2007) were the most prominent national political slogans.

The Chinese strategy is an example of a well-knit sweater in which the needles were the anecdotes, the stratagems and the words, but the wool was the political slogan which merely changed colours but not quality. The political slogans adopted by the Chinese gives an insight into the philosophy of the Party. Crisp, succinct, often hard-hitting and relevant, these slogans are such that they can be cacophonic to the ears of a democrat but melody for a communist. From Mao's 'Chinese People Have Stood Up (1949)' to Hu Jintao's 'Three Supremes (2007)', each slogan was thick with emotion and resolve. Under the present government, every slogan stands for governance either on a standalone basis or in relation to one or more of its aspects.

For the building blocks (anecdotes, stratagem, phrases and political slogans) to be translated into a successful strategy requires a skilful balance of whether a strategy can be justified ethically (normative) and whether or not it will be effective (pragmatic). In China these two skills are complementary and need to coexist in the strategy.

A bird's eye view of political slogan (buzzwords) under Xi Jinping clearly indicates a conceptual shift from 'hide and bide' to diplomacy and great revitalisation of nation.

A Dream Within A Dream (Zhongguo Meng)

While the ambition of the Chinese has always been evident much as they have attempted to keep it hidden, another aspect of China which in the recent years has gained prominence is 'the Chinese Dream'. Touted as the antithesis of 'the American Dream', the Chinese Dream encapsulated the sentiment of superiority of the Chinese in all spheres.

Coined by Liu Mingfu in 2010, the phrase first appeared as the name of the book *China Dream: Great Power Thinking and Strategic Posture in the Post American Era*. Since then, till November 2012, when President Xi was elevated to the numero uno position of the Communist Party, the phrase did not garner the attention it deserved. However, post March 2013, it became the metaphor for everything which was essentially Chinese and therefore better and worthier. 'The Chinese Dream' was also used multiple times to connote what China hopes to be in the future. When Xi spoke about the definite goals which China intends to achieve, he was signalling to the world that China can no longer be taken lightly. According to him, by 2021, China would be a "moderately well-off society" and by 2049 would have elevated itself to the position of a modernised, prosperous economy modelled on Chinese brand of socialism.[35] For Xi, achieving the Chinese Dream meant reviving, rejuvenating and resuscitating the Chinese nation such that it could be restored to its previous glory. Also, it was a reaffirmation of the goals of the Party to elevate Chinese to a position where they could dream of having a home, hearth and vocation in order to resonate with the dreams and aspirations of the young.

One needs to be mindful at this juncture and understand the audience for whom the concept of 'the Chinese Dream' was given birth to. The phrase was expected to charm the Chinese and not the world and therefore, while it received acceptance and applaud at home, it created confusion for the rest of the world for it could not grasp its true import. What 'rise' meant to the outer world, meant 'rejuvenate' for the inner core. Yet another interesting facet of this 'rejuvenation' is its chronology. Once again, the world might think it is a recent phenomenon which draws inspiration from the West, what one fails to notice is that the buzzword has remained unchanged since the times of Sun-Yet-Sen. It was used as a slogan, an aspiration and an inspiration by the political leaders to seek support from the people. The reforms were initiated with the aim that they will rejuvenate China and the humiliated Chinese spirit.

President Xi exploited this very tattered and humiliated spirit to exacerbate the impact of the post first Opium War with British in 1840[36] and offered solace to his people by extolling the Confucian principles and working aggressively towards redefining the identity of the Chinese. Embedded in this identity are the seeds of anti-western and anti-Japanese sentiments which also act as powerful motivational sources.

While the American Dream celebrates the individual and the person in the individual, the Chinese Dream celebrates personal sacrifice for the nation which is more than just an aggregation of individuals.

The contrast between the Chinese Dream and the American Dream appeared as an article in People's Daily in June 2013 when it performed the threadbare analysis of both the terms and opined that while the centre of the American Dream was the individual, the spirit of individualism and the freedom to pursue dreams and perform to one's highest potential, the Chinese Dream was centred around the nation which is unstoppable in its pursuit of power and prosperity. The glaring divide between the two indicates that behind the façade of the terms lies the strategy of its passionate pursuit. Furthermore, the picture which was painted by the Chinese for the Chinese was not one of difference in approach but a qualitative superiority of one over the other. The Chinese interpretation of the Chinese Dream was that it is the holy grail of goodness as opposed to the satanic forces which operate behind the American Dream.

Forced Serendipity and Opportunity: Strategic to Historic

China's rise was not incidental but accidental. Had the opportunity not presented itself as a result of a multitude of factors, China would have never been able to exploit the same to arrive where it has today. The Twin Towers' attack, China's entry in WTO, a severely engaged US in war of terror, an economic meltdown, an uninterrupted double-digit growth along with emergence as the manufacturing hub of the world—China used every opportunity to its advantage. The rise of China was more or less peaceful but the result of this rise has been far from it. China has taken strategic positions which appear to be counter-productive for the Americans. Chinese no longer consider themselves as a 'second fiddle' to the United States in Asia and therefore, in their view, their interests reign supreme. Given that the period of strategic opportunities is over, Chinese foreign policy has taken a historical shift particularly with regard to its stance on countries suffering due to political instability owing to their experiment with democracy and the consequent regime change.

Once Beijing realised that the on the heels of strategic opportunities has arrived a 'period of historical opportunities', it did not waste any time to posit its interests at par with those of Washington, sending a clear message that the interests of the two superpowers are irreconcilable. Washington on its part has emerged as a champion of the cause and interests of smaller Asian entities making China realise that it still has a long way to go before usurping power from the hands of the United States. The manner in which Taiwan flouted its political arrangement in 1992 and the construction of a new Senkaku patrol unit by the Japanese indicate that the Asian powers are not ready to give in and submit before the Chinese might.

Shared Future, New Model, and the Chinese Solution

President Xi's diplomacy is a fusion of three different sub-narratives each serving as a means and an end in itself. "Community of Shared Future" is a thought and a foreign policy goal; "New Model of International Relations" is an objective and a process, construction of which is underway; and the "Chinese Solution" which is embedded in the Chinese value system and philosophy to look at resolving global issues.

"Community of Shared Future"

China has done its best to assert itself in almost all arenas of global dominance. However, in the arena of political philosophy and isms, China's contribution in the 21st century even though significant has not been sizeable.

"Community of Shared Future" (CSF) is the new ism in the Chinese diplomacy. Often quoted by Xi Jinping, it holds within it an important goal of the Chinese foreign policy, so much so, that it now features in the 'XJP's Thought' in the Party's constitution. The need for this amendment to the constitution was felt when Xi decided to make CSF the pivot and purpose of China's engagement with the world.

The five elements which are essential to achieve this shared future are— 'Partnership, Security, Trade and Investment, Civilization and Ecology.'[37] Each of them need to be understood from two different, and at times diametrically opposite viewpoints, that is, what these requirements mean to China and what do they mean to the world. As per the understanding of the Chinese, 'partnership' entails mutual respect, equality treatment, rejection of Cold War mentality such that deep connections between the states can be forged with communication and engagement driving the relationship instead of alliances and mutual enemy technique. CSF necessitates all-pervasive 'security', thereby obliterating the need of an armed conflict along with putting up a united front against terrorism. 'Trade and Investment' were clubbed together to promote economic stability in a manner that globalisation becomes an inclusive process. Exclusionary approach and impact of globalisation has caused much imbalance in the world and CSF hoped to rectify by promoting trade and augmenting investment such that the fruits of the same are shared by all. Respect for and 'acceptance of diverse civilisation' was considered critical for CSF. Countries must replace alienation with reciprocation, conflict with collective learning, and dominance with harmony. Last but not the least was the stress on maintaining an ecological balance to prolong the longevity of the human race on Earth.

The Chinese view CSF as an intellectual input in the theory of international relations. However, China has been careful in not projecting CSF as an alternative to the UN-led present international order but as an addendum to the same to make the supra-national body more inclusive and broad in its target and more productive in its work.

No one has questioned the nobility of CSF but doubts were raised on the intent with which the Chinese launched it. It was seen as a part of China's plan of projecting it as the most obvious choice in selecting the next world leader and as a champion of the underdog with a definite global vision which was based on egalitarianism and fairness. Also, it was an attempt to tilt the world opinion in favour of the Chinese model of growth and development which was hitherto looked at either with disdain or with suspicion or with both.

The world is aware of the Chinese distaste for 'everything West' and by putting forth CSF, China has been able to make a case against the Western ideology by accusing it of being hegemonic, exploitative, exacting and biased. Xi in his speeches and addresses has often appealed for democratising the international system to prevent concentration of power in the hands of a few.

"New Model of International Relations"[38] (Xinxing guoji)

Initially known as the "new type of great power relations", the "new model of international relations" is an alternative that China is working towards. Based on the concept of mutual win-win, the "new model of international relations" looks at establishing relationships between nations whereby reciprocal respect for each other's interest is indispensable thereby indirectly giving legitimacy to China's pursuit of its interests without being thwarted. In establishing the same, the most obvious choice is the developmental model and the social system, and not the one propagated by the West. Furthermore, the new model shuns the concept of unipolarity and hegemonic control by one nation. However, the fallacy in this model cannot be missed, given that it indicates to the rest of the world that for China its interests are paramount and non-negotiable and the dream of 'no confrontation, no conflict' that it is trying to sell is but a utopia and hence elusive.

'Chinese Solution'

The 'Chinese solution' is essentially a Chinese way of looking at the issues. The logic behind this epithet is to revisit and relook at the issues in a novel manner, in other words, relinquishing the American smartness in the favour of Chinese wisdom. Seen as an extension of the Chinese model, the Chinese solution looks at the issues through the prism of socialist market economy and given that the United States is losing its economic supremacy, the Chinese solution, in the speeches given by the Chinese leaders, is made to appear as the most obvious choice. With a definite undertone of superiority and condescension, the Chinese solution is projected as the one-stop shop solution to the issues mankind has been battling against.

These blinkers are so typical to the Chinese that in order to understand and decode China for the rest of the world, it is imperative to wear them once to know what is befuddling for an outsider is clarity for those in the ring. One might be tempted to step inside the ring and uncloak China for the world but this process would be incomplete unless one is able to describe it in the clearest possible terms how China and the Chinese feel.

NOTES

1 Joshua C. Ramo, *The Beijing Consensus* (London: The Foreign Policy Centre, 2004), p. 32.

2 The famous Sichuan proverb quoted by Deng "No matter if it is a white cat or a black cat; so long as it can catch mice, it is a good cat." symbolises the pragmatism of the era of reform and opening up and the decline of ideology.

3 Hu Jintao's work report to 18th Party Congress laid out three Confidences—"Confident in our chosen path, Confident in our political system and Confident in our guiding theories." The "Confidence in Chinese Culture" was included by Xi Jinping as the fourth Confidence in December 2014.

4 Chris Buckley, "Xi Jinping Thought Explained: A New Ideology for a New Era," *The New York Times*, February 26, 2018, https://www.nytimes.com/2018/02/26/world/asia/xi-jinping-thought-explained-a-new-ideology-for-a-new-era.html.

5 The profile of the Chinese society, over the years has undergone economic and social diversity. A substantial difference in employment and living conditions exist to between coastal areas and region in the West and also between the rural and urban areas.

6 The seven 'harmful' concepts on which public debate are prohibited are "constitutional democracy, universal values, civil society, neoliberalism, freedom of the press, criticism of the CCP's historical achievements, questioning the reform and opening policies and their socialist nature". General Office of the Central Committee of the Chinese Communist Party, "Notice on the current state of the ideological sphere", Document No. 9, 22 April 2013, https://www.chinafile.com/document-9-chinafile-translation.

7 "People's Daily: Promoting the Popularization ofTheory using Massificaation Measures", *CCP News Net*, 27 September 2012, http://cpc.people.com.cn/pinglun/n/2012/0927/c78779-19123327.html.

8 New formats and channels such as social media and videos made by outsourced public relation companies are the tools being used by Xi.

9 Yin-Yang Philosophy views that all global circumstances are created by binary cosmic paradoxical forces called Yin and Yang. Yin is dark, negative and feminine, whereas Yang is bright, positive and masculine.

10 Selections from the Confucian Analects: On Government, Analects 12:11.

11 Lin Yutang, My Country and My People (New York: Halcyon House, 1938), p. 45.

12 The Three Cardinals are "Wives follow the order of husbands," "Ministers follow the order of the king," and " Son follows the order of fathers."

13 The four categories of kinship are "*Ben-jia*" (one's own family), "*wai-xing*" (relatives outside the household), "*nei-xi*" (wife's relatives), and "*qin-xi*" (relatives of different surnames).

14 Thomas B. Gold, "After Comradeship: Personal Relations in China Since the Cultural Revolution," *The China Quarterly* 104 (1985): pp. 657-672, doi:10.1017/s030574100003335x.

15 Michael D. Swaine, Ryan DeVries, "Chinese State-Society Relations: Why Beijing Isn't Trembling and Containment Won't Work," *Carnegie Endowment for International Peace*, March 14, 2019. https://carnegieendowment.org/2019/03/14/chinese-state-society-relations-why-beijing-isn-t-trembling-and-containment-won-t-work-pub-78596.

16 Mr. I. Lee, Mr. X. Qingjun, and Mr. M. Syed, China's Demography and its Implications, (Washington: International Monetary Fund, 2013), p. 3.

17 Confucius said "Gentleman values justice, a base person values money." Chinese traditional values regard materialism with contempt. This distaste for materialism was strengthened by Mao's slogan "We'd rather want socialist weed than capitalist grass."

18 Guy O. Faure and Tony Fang, "Changing Chinese Values: Keeping up with Paradoxes," *International Business Review* 17, no. 2 (2008): p. 200, doi:10.1016/j.ibusrev.2008.02.001.

19 "Why Are Chinese So Concerned About Saving Face?, " *Chindianet*, April 15, 2018, http://en.chindianet.com/bencandy.php?fid=67&id=3100.

20 *Xinhua Cidian* (*Xinhua Dictionary*), 1985, p. 1106

21 Luo Xiangde, "Considerations on Guidance for Information-System-Based System of Systems Operations," *China Military Science*, No. 4, 2010, pp. 51-55.

22 Richard E. Nisbett, The Geography of Thought: How Asian and Westerners Think Differently – and why (London: Hachette UK, 2011).

23 Yagyu Munenori, The Book of Family Traditions on the Art of War.

24 Stefan Verstappen, "The King, the Fool, and the Fox," *Chinastrategies.com*, http://www.chinastrategies.com/the-king-the-fool-and-the-fox/.

25 Ibid.

26 Hays, Jeffrey. "Tao Te Ching: Chapters 41 to 81." *Facts and Details*. http://factsanddetails.com/china/cat3/sub10/entry-5578.html#chapter-33.

27 Peter Taylor, The Thirty-Six Stratagems: A Modern Interpretation of a Strategy Classic (Oxford OX1 3LD: Infinite Ideas, 2013), p. 56.

28 Taylor, The Thirty-Six Stratagems, p. 79.

29 Ibid., p. 37.

30 Stefan Verstappen, "Strategy for the Street," *Chinastrategies.com*, http://www.chinastrategies.com/strategy-for-the-street/.

31 Menglong, Feng. "Zhinang Quanji" [Complete Package of Wisdom]. 2 Vols. Beijing: Huashan Wenyi Chubanshe.

32 Robert A. Nisbet, Social Change and History: Aspects of the Western Theory of Development (New York: Oxford University Press, 1969), p. 4.

33 Chien Chiao, "Strategic Behavior of Chinese Political Elites", *The Chinese University of Hong Kong*, p. 15, http://www.cuhk.edu.hk/ant/publish/workingpaper2.pdf.

34 Liang Qiao and Wang Xiangsui, Unrestricted Warfare (Beijing: PLA Literature and Arts Publishing House, 1999), p. 12.

35 Xi Jinping, "Achieving Rejuvenation Is the Dream of the Chinese People," as available in, Xi Jinping, The Governance of China, Volume I (Beijing: Foreign Languages Press Co., 2014), p. 107.

36 Qiushi, "The China Dream Brings Together Boundless Positive Energy", *Qiushi* no. 07, April 1, 2013.

37 Yang Jiechi, "Promoting the Building of a Community with a Shared Future for Mankind," *Theory China*, December 12, 2017, http://en.theorychina.org/xsqy_2477/201712/t20171212_360713.shtml.

38 China Foreign Minister Wang Yi, "Build a New Type of International Relations Featuring Win-Win Cooperation," *The Study Times*, June 20, 2016, https://www.fmprc.gov.cn/mfa_eng/wjb_663304/wjbz_663308/2461_663310/t1376908.shtml.

4

Emboldening China

Chinese behaviour, backed by its recent quotient of prosperity and influence has emerged "sooner and more assertively than was expected."[1] These changes have strained China' relationship with not only its neighbours but also the West, thereby making China "one of the loneliest rising powers in world history."[2] There are several elements that have facilitated China's behavioural change. Firstly is China's cursive belief in itself to deal with technology and issues of sovereignty on territorial disputes; secondly is China's dissatisfaction over the perceived hindrance by anti-China forces to retake its rightful place in spite of its economic rise and military strength; and thirdly is the economic slowdown, current trade wars and the ongoing domestic reforms that have brought anxiety among Chinese leaders who have resultantly adopted the twin strategy of domestic repression and foreign aggression. It is this confluent of growing belief in oneself, state of dissatisfaction and anxiety that has resulted in China's newfound boldness.

ECONOMY

Nobel Laureate José de Sousa Saramago from Portugal knew what it meant to live in a country which had once yielded and enjoyed immense economic power. Therefore, when he wrote, "...it is economic power that determines political power, and governments become the political functionaries of economic power,"[3] he knew that economic dominance precedes political dominance. China is a classic case of how a country can make itself count after being ruled over by every single imperialist nation. With economic resurgence came political rewards, and China did not waste any time in establishing the connection between the two before it set on to the path of achieving its goals.

China was cognisant of the impact it would exert on the world if it emerged as a leading economic nation. Hence, Deng in 1978 began to separate ideology from economy and opened the floodgates of economic reforms. It witnessed astounding economic growth when it jumped seven places in forty years in the nominal GDP Index.[4]

Over the years, China has taken complete control over global manufacturing and trade[5] and while the growth story seems miraculous, one cannot deny that what lay behind it was incessant hard work and sharp policy-making with a definite eye on the future. China's success was not overnight and given its perseverance, its story contains valuable lessons for all the other countries. It is a story of how investing in infrastructure and human resource can fast track the growth of a nation which was once in shambles.

The Third Plenary Session of the Communist Party in December 1978 proved to be a watershed moment for China. It was the year when the Chinese were unleashed—the farmers were allowed to tap into the potential of the local markets and there was a tectonic shift in the manner and nature of practising agriculture. From collective farming to individual responsibility, from being a closely sheltered economy to an economy which allowed free flow of foreign capital, from strict pricing restrictions to profit-oriented corporates with a self-determined waged structures—the Chinese economy witnessed a sea change. These reforms radically altered the growth rates—from six per cent in 1953–1978 to staggering nine and a half per cent in 1978–2016. Coupled with dizzy growth rates was the rapid urbanisation that changed the colour and character of the cities. Workers from all over thronged urban centres which saw massive vertical and horizontal expansion.

Another sign of a robust economy is the 'rebalancing of the economy'—descending contribution of the primary sector and rising contribution of secondary and tertiary sectors in the aggregate GDP. The performance by the Chinese stood out in this regard when modernisation not only ignited the tertiary sector but also accelerated its growth thereby resulting in 46.1 per cent of the total share in GDP in 2018. The secondary sector closely followed the tertiary sector and was responsible for contributing 45 per cent of the total GDP.[6] The pressure on the primary sector was eased out due to the constant reforms introduced by the Chinese government. At the cost of inviting controversy, let us say that the Chinese introduced their version and shade of 'glasnost' without having the same impact it did on the erstwhile USSR. The

Chinese economy opened slowly and steadily with the rate of its openness commensurate with the pace of its reforms.

While the strength of the Chinese economy cannot be questioned and neither can one be ambivalent about its visible astronomical rise, the honeymoon, however, now seems to be over for the Chinese. It is imperative that any slowdown in the second largest economy of the world would have implications for the rest of the world. The investors are eyeing the economy with much scepticism given its growth being the lowest over the last two and a half decades. The Chinese economy is losing steam despite stimulus packages and pressure on the banks to lend, and there are multitudes of factors which are at play for the same. With the onslaught of the ongoing trade wars between the United States and China and the shift of supply chains to countries with even lower manufacturing costs coupled with insipid domestic demand—China requires systemic and structural remodelling. However, given the global dependence on the Chinese economy, a slowdown is a jittery situation and therefore will require close monitoring.

Stay Connected; Stay Strong

China has been a quick and a smart learner. It has learnt the importance of 'staying connected' and its impact on the contiguity to its goals. The Chinese understanding of connectivity transcends its physical connotation and expands to include digital, economic, strategic, etc. In the new world, power is more symbolic than real and it is over here that measures such as breaking the American hegemony over the oil-finance cycle while simultaneously fostering connectivity gave China the much needed edge. However, China's failure to maintain and sustain these measures dwindled the hopes of those who were looking forward to an economically fierce and politically prevalent China. But to say that world has lost faith or stopped seeing China as a threat, as the case may be, is it to be immature and superficial. The manner in which the Chinese have held the idea of 'connectivity' close to their heart can be seen in their aggressive pursuit of their dream project, that is, the Belt and Road Initiative (BRI).[7] It is seen as the cornerstone of Xi's tenure which aims at the revival of the Chinese glory.

Touted as the Silk Route of the 21st century, BRI aims to bring together even the remotest corners of the world with China in the centre. Using infrastructure projects as a glue to bring and stick the world together along with using the Chinese funds to feed this leviathan is not only ambitious but also courageous. At the end of Second BRI Forum (BRI 19) held in March 2019, the number of partakers increased considerably with China "signing 173 cooperation documents with 125 countries and 29 international organizations"[8]. Italy became the first member of the Group of Seven to sign a memorandum of understanding on the initiative with China in March 2019. Third-party market cooperation which was first put forward with France in 2015 was also concluded with Japan in October 2018 during the first forum on China-Japan third-party market cooperation, with a combined value of $18 billion. Various forms of the "China plus" model were initiated in October 2018 when China and 17 other countries announced the building of the Belt and Road energy partnership. As of March 2019, China has signed 17 FTAs with 25 countries and regions, while nine more are under negotiations, involving more than 30 countries. Since the first BRI forum, the Mombasa-Nairobi railway and the Addis Ababa-Djibouti railway lines have started commercial operations; the China-Laos railway, the Hungary-Serbia railway, the China-Thailand railway and the Jakarta-Bandung railway lines in Indonesia are in trial stage; and the Moscow-Kazan high-speed railway is in the planning stage. The China-Europe freight train, since its inception till the end of February 2019 has totalled 14,000 trips, reached 50 cities across 15 European countries. In 2018, trips made by freight trains between China and Europe totalled 6,363 a year-on-year increase of 73 per cent. The number of return trips from Europe to China was 2,690—an increase of 111 per cent over 2017. The Air Silk Road between Luxembourg and Zhengzhou, capital of central China's Henan Province has reached 500,000 tons 789 flights in 2017. What appears to be a win-win for both is in reality, China's way to get unfettered access to the markets of these countries and thereby forge deeper connections and bonds where the countries do not have the option of 'backing out'. Furthermore, the Chinese see BRI as a way to reclaim their civilisational and political authority which was once lost to the West. The BRI was designed at the two levels—apparent and underlying. Without studying the underlying motivations behind the BRI, it is unfair to term it as a politico-economic measure. For the Chinese, the BRI is also a way to lessen China's exposure to the scourge of fundamentalism and socio-religious unrest. It is imperative for a country which is on the path of being touted as the next superpower to keep such influences and issues at bay. Moreover, it is also seen as 'the road' for resolving the energy issues which the Dragon might have to confront in the future. Growing energy needs is the hallmark of every nation which has its head and heart in the right place and with energy supply routes being revisited, Jintao's 'Malacca Dilemma' shall no longer be seen as a drag for the littoral will not be the nerve centre for serving China's energy needs. The BRI will serve more purposes and the Chinese are in no mood to let any aspect, real or fictional, remain unexploited. From being seen as the entrance to untapped markets to being the instrument for gaining control over critical infrastructure assets, the BRI is shouldering much of the burden of the Chinese ambition.

The connectivity on ground is buttressed by the technological and e-commerce links such as the digital road of fibre optic cables, international trunk passageways, mobile structures, etc. The 'Digital Silk Road' project—one of 12 subthemes discussed at BRI 19–could prove to be a game changer for the Chinese motive of staying connected. Less visible than ports and railways, China's expanding control over the world's digital communications networks would give Beijing unparalleled influence. Its growing clout in surveillance technology and lead in developing 5G, promises to make China a global tech challenger to the US. Ever since the Digital Silk Road was launched in 2017, China had begun building up an 'information expressway' of fibre optic cable links to Myanmar, Nepal and Kyrgyzstan. An 820-kilometres-long fibre optic cable is operational since July 2018 between Rawalpindi, Pakistan and Khunjerab Pass, China. By 2020 this optic cable is likely to be further extended from Rawalpindi to Djibouti creating an information expressway between Asia and Africa by a six thousand three hundred kilometres of underwater cable. China has offered help to countries as far away as Cuba, Egypt, Saudi Arabia and Turkey to embrace the convergence of three mutually exclusive cloud-based system for technologies—Internet of Things (IOT), Big Data, and Artificial Intelligence (AI). Most nations see this as a velvet glove but China is aware of the iron hand which adorns it. The US is aware of the Chinese motives and therefore has tried to exclude Chinese 5G equipment makers from their networks but China is insistent upon offering services of its indigenous suppliers to the 60 BRI countries.

In spite of the grand plans, 'all is not well' with BRI as it has been greatly impacted by certain barricades during its first five years of unfolding. The judiciousness of the decision is being frowned upon and so is the cloudiness surrounding its cost benefit analysis. The problem of secretly vilifying the

BRI, however, does not end here. The ongoing trade tussle with the US and economic slowdown and ambivalence of the nations who once stood rock solid behind the BRI, have all resulted in people asking questions, albeit not in a raised voice. "As domestic credit tightens and troubled overseas projects proliferate, China's four biggest infrastructure lenders reportedly made no loans to the Asian region in the first three months of 2019."[9] It may appear that the misty BRI is gradually digging its own grave, leading melting funds and boiling tempers. With time, the fund allocation will become abstemious and while China will do its best to generate sufficient foreign exchange surplus to fuel its dream, the enthusiasm around it would definitely be dented. But the BRI is here to stay. In the second Belt and Road forum, the rebranded BRI 19 aims to build a 'Clean Silk Route' by firstly overhauling its initial laissez-faire approach of project financing and implementation to a 'high standard' and 'high quality' endeavour. Secondly, Beijing is adjusting its policies with an emphasis to administer the activities of State Owned Enterprises (SOE) in overseas project contracting and investment. "In August 2017, the National Development and Reform Commission issued a circular on overseas investment, do's and don'ts and subsequently a code of conduct was promulgated in January 2018."[10] Under the new policies, all overseas enterprises would have to undertake constant and earnest diligence on societal impacts, sustainable development, and financial viability to ensure legal compliance, not only to Chinese law, but also to the legal acquiescing of the host countries and international laws. China gestured that it would recalibrate projects to address the concerns of debt burden by 'sustainable financing', especially for smaller countries and try and achieve boarder political sumptuary consensus for infrastructural megaprojects.

China's eagerness to adjust can be noticed in the renegotiated East Coast Rail Link (ECRL) with Malaysia at reduced cost. The countries which are likely to adopt the re-negotiating tactics in the near future are Maldives, Pakistan and Indonesia. Moreover, "elected governments have found Chinese counterparts relatively flexible on rescheduling loans, revisiting project costs or shifting the focus of the two sides' economic cooperation."[11] In order to entrench its presence in economic sectors, where it really matters, the new paylist of China has adopted the approach of mitigating its risks and being more responsive to local demands. Speaking at the BRI 19 forum, Xi vowed to ensure transparency and the "fiscal sustainability" of all projects.[12] China here is expected to play the role of a pacifier and whether the Chinese will be able to rise up to this occasion is something which can only be answered in retrospect.

On the home front, China is battling against skyrocketing cost for pension,[13] shrinking tax revenues and diminishing economic growth—all of which are a result of its own making. For instance, a rapidly ageing population is the ghost of the haphazard 'one-child' policy which had led to a severe shortfall in pension spending. While the optimists look at the BRI as the number one ambition, the realists believe that the ambition might have to be curtailed on the account of making pragmatic choices. It is this pragmatism which gets reflected in the Chinese Vision 2030—China's Thirteenth Five Year Plan (13-5).[14] With its ultimate objective to emerge as a "modern, harmonious, creative, and high income society"[15] by 2030, China insists on a thematic growth with focus on urbanisation, identification of policy priorities for inclusive growth and eco-friendly development. These themes, however, were given a Chinese interpretation and therefore, went beyond the confines of their literal meaning. As per the vision document, urbanisation meant a reduction in the urban-rural divide by upgrading the infrastructure in the rural areas[16] and ecological development meant development while being cognizant of ecological concerns. Given that China is battling against an ageing population, yet another priority for the Chinese was the reversal of the 'one-child policy' and replacing it with a 'two-child policy' with increased resource allocation towards poverty reduction programmes, skill development, robust social insurance system, etc.

TECHNOLOGY

Technology is a game changer, shapes relations among nations and determines hierarchy in international relations. Few economists could predict the rise of China as an economic powerhouse as they could not possibly foresee the impact of Internet in 1990. In recent times, the rapid diffusion of emerging disruptive technologies such as AI, 5G, and quantum computing may turn out to be facilitators of the rapidly raising stature of China in global affairs.

Industry 4.0[17]/MIC2025[18]

The world is standing on the brink of Fourth Industrial Revolution. Unlike the previous three times, this one challenges our concept of being human.

The notion of artificial intelligence and robotics taking over the world has been romanticised and demonised in an equal measure. The UK may have first embraced the steam engine and the US may have leveraged the Digital Revolution to emerge as a world leader but in case of fourth Industrial Revolution, the Chinese are not far behind.

In the earlier centuries, great power competitions, the focus was military puissance or territorial enlargement. However, with the return of great power competitions the struggle is over the new influencing tool kit—trade, technology, standards, setting the global rules and institutions. The capability to innovate new disruptive technologies particularly digital technologies has become a key factor in gaining international power. "Emerging technologies primarily shape the balance of power through military and economic means."[19] To establish the equilibrium of influence by military means, technology is used as the foremost force-multiplier in warfighting and success. The economic power of country also indirectly affects the balance of power as "countries cannot maintain military superiority over the medium to long term without an underlying economic basis for that power."[20] The Chinese communist leadership grasped early on that technology is one of the essential prerequisites to realign the power structure. An early project launched to display that China was an equal in strategic technology to the great powers of those days and did not require their support was the "two bombs and one satellite."[21] However, today it is no more a question of equivalence but a race to attain technological superiority.

Artificial Intelligence

China as a country suffers from Stockholm syndrome and it is because of this disorder that it has learnt to live under paranoia. A 'paranoid China' is an accepted reality. However when this 'paranoid China' becomes 'pressurised China', it ends up being hasty. It was this haste, caused by a lost match in 2016 and 2017[22] which made it design, develop and draft its Next Generation Artificial Intelligence Development Plan by July 2017. With its eyes set on being the global leader by 2030, China has put in motion a plan that would transform it into an advanced industrial economy which would revolutionise it into a leading technological economy. Artificial intelligence was brought in limelight in international politics by Russian President Vladimir Putin, "Artificial intelligence is the future, not only for Russia, but for all humankind," he said. "It comes with colossal opportunities, but also threats that are difficult to predict. Whoever becomes the leader in this sphere will become the ruler of the world."[23] To sum up the applicability of AI, it can be said that, "AI is actually the ultimate enabler, analogous to the internal combustion engine as well as electricity."[24]

On 18 October 2017, in his report to the Congress, Xi named artificial intelligence to be among the fundamental technologies that would metamorphose China in becoming a leading industrialised country. An AI powered economy will grow faster, will seize control of manufacturing and production, will provide universal healthcare to its people and will boast of a world class infrastructure. Furthermore, "its military will project more power, as autonomous weapons replace soldiers on the battlefield and pilots in the skies and as cyber troops wage digital warfare."[25]

China has fundamental advantages in building a robust AI ecosystem. Firstly, what matters most is not the innovation itself but its implementation in the form of a supportive government,[26] setting up of ambitious goals, willingness to take risks and quickly building the complementary infrastructure. Secondly, the considerable reach and extent of the data generated by Chinese technology giants is significantly importance. Thirdly, China's hypercompetitive and entrepreneurial economy provides greater chance for success. Fourthly, Chinese public at present is far more relaxed about data privacy. In November 2018, China announced an "AI national team" which comprised five companies tasked with distinct programmes. These companies were Baidu (autonomous driving), Alibaba (cloud computing), Tencent (medical imaging), iFlytek (speech language intelligence) and Sense Time (computer vision: face, image, object, and text). China is already well-placed to reach its AI goals. "Chinese companies accounted for 48% of the world's total AI start-up funding in 2017, and China's AI industry attracted 60% of global funding for AI between 2013 and 2018."[27] Furthermore, Chinese technology giants such as Baidu, Alibaba and Tencent (BAT) already use AI in a wide range of services. Moreover, the considerable reach and extent of the data available to Chinese technological companies will facilitate quicker learning by using algorithms and harmonising the predictive analysis process.

The Dragon will not stop before it assumes the top position in this race and is therefore pumping in more resources than are necessary. All the developmental plans are now AI powered and the tax regime is AI friendly.

The manner in which it has sought funding for its AI projects is daunting, and equally bedazzling is the amount of funding it has extended for similar projects. Following a heavily organised, top-down process, China has been able to mobilise government, industry and society to pursue this goal, something that has proven difficult to do anywhere else in the world.

AI is critical not only for economic resilience and national development, but because it has the capability to be a powerful catalyst which can develop into the main 'game changing and game levelling' military capability. This will result in the development of new types of platforms and systems which are capable of cognitively responding to and seamlessly adapting to fluid operational environments as well as carrying out missions without human intervention. It will also enhance the capacity of the decision maker to understand the strategic and operational environment, discern patterns and imminent threats and identify and track adversaries in complex and fast-moving environments. However, the implications of the development of these weapons go well beyond the operational realm. Success of China's advanced weapons systems programmes will also undermine the already sliding confidence in the capacity of the US to maintain an unquestioned military and technological advantage over China. This will result in degraded alliances wherein regional partners and potential partners are less likely to rely on the US and are more likely to hedge by deepening bilateral relations with China. More regional actors are turning to China for military sales, especially in South and Southeast Asia, which is likely to deepen the overall strategic relationship between China and these countries.

Quantum 2.0

In 2013, Edward Snowden's revelation[28] made the Chinese government sit up to his claims that the US intelligence was hacking into computer networks in Hong Kong and mainland China for at least four years and gave new urgency for an indigenous, secure cybersecurity system in the form of 'Quantum Communication and Quantum Computing'. In August 2016, the world's first quantum satellite, 'Micius' was launched by China. The 13th Five-Year Plan (2016–2020) enhanced the priority given to 'Quantum Mechanics' by including 'Quantum Control' in the category of "basic research related to national strategic requirements."[29]

Modern Physics has two major planks—Quantum Mechanics and

relativity. While relativity helps us to visualise and draw account of sizable things (gravity and space time), Quantum mechanics provides an insight into the microscopic aspects (atomics and subatomic levels). The first quantum revolution relied on the effect of microscopic realms which led to transistors, laser and semiconductors being developed. The second quantum revolution, which the world is presently experiencing, is about creating and manipulating individual quantum properties by superposition and entanglement.

The capstone of over two decades of research under Pan Jianwei was the Micius Satellite which has the capability of free space teleportation with cryptographic keys. The satellite has established a network with numerous ground stations. China is further building on this by establishing the world's largest ground based quantum optical fibre system (1240 miles) from Beijing to Shanghai. In the future China plans to extend this quantum network up to Europe by 2020 and establish a global network by 2030.[30]

While Chinese advances in quantum communication have outdone similar global achievements, quantum computing endeavours under Guo Guangcan is picking up. A semi-conductor quantum chip has been developed and mensuration of six hundreds of ensnared quantum particles has been performed. Chinese Academy of Sciences (CAS) and Alibaba Quantum Computing Laboratory are attempting to accomplish the consistent and comprehensible handling of 30 qubits[31] by 2020, by 2025 aims to develop computing speed equal to today's supercomputer, and subsequently by 2030 realise an archetype with computing function of 50 to 100 qubits.

5G

5G as the linchpin of the contemporary digital milieu is the centrepiece for emerging competition. The upgrade of global computer connectivity networks to 5G from 4G represents a leap from a soda straw to a firehose in digital power, which will actuate the online economy and render the fortitude and tenacity in evolving technologies to become mainstream. The rapid rollout and commercialisation of 5G mobile infrastructure and services is not only about having a profound effect on economy, but also about a bigger contest for influence and political manoeuvring. China is the first mover in 5G Technology with Chinese telecommunication giants such as Huawei and ZTE dominating the 5G network globally as manufactures of both core 5G equipment and essential 5G technologies. The US, on the other hand, is not manufacturing core 5G equipment although it is the leader in essential 5G technology. The US has attempted to exclude and stop the proliferation of Chinese 5G equipment. There is anxiety in the US due to the uncertainty in China's ability to embed 'backdoor' access in core 5G equipment manufactured by its telecommunication companies on the bidding of CCP.

The US campaign against Chinese 5G ambitions started in August 2018 when President Donald Trump signed US Defence Authorization Act, banning the US government from using Huawei and ZTE equipment. Huawei has repeatedly denied the allegations which have been exacerbated by its founder's, Ren Zhengfei, a former PLA officer with close links to the Chinese military. On 1 December 2018 in Vancouver, at the request of the US authorities Canada arrested Huawei Finance Chief Meng Wanzhou.[32] On 11 January 2019, Poland arrested Huawei sales official Wang Weijing and on 13 January 2019, Poland's Internal Affairs Minister Joachim Brudzinski called for a European Union and NATO joint policy to exclude Huawei from their markets.

US feels that China's 5G capabilities are posing a risk to 'Five Eye Network' (a seventy-year-old intelligence sharing network between US, Canada, Australia, UK and New Zealand), intelligence sharing and military mobilisation. UK's decision to allow Huawei to supply technology for Britain's new 5G networks could risk the continuation of the intelligence grouping. "If the US is unwilling to run military logistics networks through countries with any Chinese technology in their 5G systems, much less to expose sensitive military interoperability or intelligence-sharing operations to Chinese eyes and ears, it could substantially weaken the US ability to sustain robust defence partnerships abroad. This would open opportunities for China to fill the void and extend its own military influence in places with the technology infrastructure needed for next generation military applications. Countries like the Philippines, Vietnam, Thailand, South Korea and India are the battlegrounds to watch here. But as it stands now, Beijing is poised to export its 5G tech more quickly, more cheaply, with faster rollout and more diplomatic support particularly to strategically important but less wealthy states (BRI countries) where the potential for Chinese malfeasance does not carry as much weight against local development needs. This could have profound geopolitical implications."[33]

CYBER SUPERPOWER

From an Economic Powerhouse to a Cyber Giant: The Saga of an Emboldening China Continues

The definition of power has always been dynamic. It has changed from time to time to include the wheels and gears of control. In the age of cyber wars, cybercrime, cyber-attacks, cybersecurity, power has come to be associated with the controlling the information resources and flow in the cyber domain.

China's stupendous rise to an economic and political giant requires it go beyond watching its economic and geopolitical interests. It also has to look at carving and then preserving its position as a cyber-power should it want to maintain its position. The benefits of modernisation need to be milked further with the help of digital know-how. In its 'Internet Plus Initiatives'[34] document, the Dragon has unequivocally stated its desire to emerge as the default option for the supply of technology to the companies on its soil and gradually replace the 'United States' tag with that of the 'People's Republic of China'. Further, it will help combat the demographic irritant in the Chinese growth story.

The Dragon treaded the path of technological advancement at the pace of a rabbit which metamorphosed a nation obsessed with economic development into one which is obsessed with technology, digital world and start-ups. China houses world's largest internet users, owners of more than fifty percent of the world's online wallets and as a consequence, the hopes of almost all the technology giants in the world. While the government machinery of the PRC is encouraging its home grown technology companies such as Alibaba, Baidu and Tencent (BAT) to adopt indigenous technologies, the same have aggressively used foreign technologies to emerge as the 'Three Kingdoms' valued at USD 1 trillion. These 'Three Kingdoms' have over the years bought start-ups more aggressively than the titans of Silicon Valley. They are slowly spreading their tentacles into sectors such as robotics, artificial intelligence, deep machine learning, self-driven cars, healthcare, etc. The intention behind this expansion surfaces very clearly and that is to control the nerve centre of the world economy. The growth till now has been organic and therefore seems natural for a nation which is driven by the dynamics of power.

The ability to adapt and the capability to spend has made Chinese companies attractive to technology corporates which are waiting to be taken over and having their original identity to be subsumed. WeChat has given a stiff competition to WhatsApp and Tencent has acquired Supercell. The pace at which China-born and China-bred technology is making inroads into economies like South Korea and Japan indicates that China is in no mood to lag behind in this competition despite being a late entrant.

For an economy which is trying its best to not break under the pressure of trade wars, the lofty BRI, an ageing population, increasing pension costs, plummeting GDP and waning tax revenues—technological innovation and subsequent domination will act like an elixir. Given that China is fully cognisant of this fact, it has been pumping resources on gathering technology, setting up research centres and hiring the right fit. One can witness this from the increase in the Chinese partake in the venture deals which jumped by almost 100 per cent in about half a decade.

Additionally, the anti-immigrant sentiment in the US has given a fillip to the recruitment of the right people with the necessary expertise by the Chinese firms. It will not be surprising if Shanghai becomes the new Silicon Valley. In the event that China fails to accomplish that, it is simultaneously investing in the Silicon Valley and its investment had topped USD 6 billion by mid-2018.

"China's digital economy is expected to reach $16 trillion by 2035, with a penetration rate throughout the overall economy of 48%."[35] The Chinese digital adaptability is transformational and can be judged by the fact that on 11 November 2018 (Single's Day, in China), Alibaba Cloud was able to process up to 175,000 orders every second. Alibaba's payment platform processed US$ 17.8 billion in 24 hours. The delivery software that Alibaba relies on managed to successfully process over 650 million orders in one single day.

Controlling Information

Internet is empowering and the Chinese forgot the power of the Internet before encouraging technological advancement. With over 700 million people using the Internet, China was exposed to attacks on two fronts—first, it had the potential to question the omnipotence and omnipresence of the Party and second, it made them dependent upon foreign technology and software thereby making the otherwise insulated country vulnerable to a cyber-siege. The filtering and the funnelling of the online content with the help of firewall has kept a check on 'what gets posted' on social media websites. However, the Internet savvy users have managed to circumvent tough censorship by relying on their lexical ingenuity to produce content which is often interpreted as 'dissent' by the authorities and hence has been appropriately snubbed in form of banning and arresting the bloggers on the charges of defamation, abetment and incitement. For China, cybersecurity and cyber control is synonymous and one cannot be compromised for another.

Countering the anti-Party narrative has in fact given rise to a pro-Party narrative with the help of an active information technology cells which have been entrusted with the responsibility of spreading and building a pro-government discourse via Internet. The people engaged in this task are like modern-day spin doctors with the aim of strengthening the stability of the government and maintaining its legitimacy. Through their content, the online commentators[36] urge (in some cases) and brainwash people (in others) to think in the way the government wants them to. The comments by these supporters contain a pro-government undercurrent and bolster state's preferred positions. However, some on these 'independent' online commentators have been unmasked and thus state apparatus has therefore not yielded the results it was expected to.

The Chinese leaders have proceeded to use the tech entrepreneurs to cleanse Internet and erase the vilifying content along with digging into the details of the citizens thereby emerging as an online policemen. By keeping a control on 'what goes on' in the online space, China can decide whom to reward and whom to punish.

Leave No Access Point Unexploited

Historically, espionage has played a central role in Chinese strategy with Sun Zu devoting an entire chapter[37] in his book 'Art of War' to Espionage. The subject also featured in Romance of Three Kingdoms as Zhuge Liang's empty-city strategy.[38] In the Republican Period (1913–1949), the communists under Mao Zedong achieved comprehensive intelligence success by demoralising the Kuomintang. Novels *Decoded* and *In the Dark* by Mai Jai (Jiang Benhu), China's most famous spy thriller author, are set in the republican period and are annually making the national bestseller list. Just like spy-craft of old, cyber espionage allows rivals to steal information and alter the balance of information. Cyber espionage is evolutionary in nature, low in expense and exposure and impacts international relations fundamentally.

Hacking into the systems of Taiwan[39] and the defence contractors of the US, the Chinese military has become a repository of sensitive information.

With time, an attack on the network of NASA titled as Titan Rain Attacks,[40] gave Chinese intelligence the capability to launch both an offensive and defend its own cyber-space with much fervour.

Remote Access Trojans (RATs) in the form of email attachments, images, hyperlinks, or as access to infected websites were used to gain control of defence contractors of the US. The Chinese information operation has both military and civilian domains. Subsequent to the 2015 PLA reforms, all strategic assess of space, cyber and electronic warfare from all the PLA services and former General Departments were combined to form the Strategic Support Force (SSF). The aim of creating the SSF was to plug the inter domain gaps creating a discipline—a central, non-kinetic force for the future war. Two new departments which were created as part of the SSF were Network System Department and Space System Department. The Network System Department integrated the earlier GSD Third and Fourth department. The main assets under the Network System Department are twelve operational bureaus, Unit 61539 (also called the Beijing North Computing Centre or 418 Research Institute) and three engineering bases at Shanghai, Beijing and Tianjin. The Engineering bases manages different programs—Shanghai engineering base looks after the program 863-917 (Great Firewall of China) and two standardisation committers (WG-3 and WG-7), and the bases at Beijing and Tianjin specialise in cryptography and network attacks.

The military assets are also been supplemented by a cyber-militia which today has a membership of over ten million patriotic hackers driven by nationalism. The factoring in of the, amalgamation of civilian individuals and organizations into a formal structure can also be identified in the establishment of the cybersecurity innovation centre by '360 enterprise security group' in December 2017.

Cyber Strategy

Released in December 2016, the strategy governing the cybersecurity of China aims to elevate China to the status of a 'cyber-superpower'. The international dimension of the Chinese cyber strategy is based on the 'Four Principles' of global Internet governance and the 'Five Propositions' of building a cyberspace community of shared destiny (4+5)' formula. These formulas were first proposed in the Second World Internet conference in Wuzhen by Xi Jinping. "The 'Four Principles' of reforming the existing internet governance system are: respecting cyber sovereignty (core and foundation), maintaining peace and security in cyberspace (purpose and objective), promoting open cooperation (route) and building good order (premise and guarantee). The 'Five Propositions' of building a cyberspace community of shared destiny were concerning the digital gap, cultural diversity in cyberspace, digital economy, cyber security, and Internet governance."[41] On 19 April 2016 at the National Meeting on Cyber Security and Information Technology, Xi Jinping laid out the domestic aspects of cyber strategy which are based on four broad objectives—"embracing the Internet, the Internet as a positive channel for the expression of public opinions, breakthroughs in core Internet technologies, and construction of a cyber-security assurance system."[42]

The main issues which can be derived from the Chinese cyber strategy are—firstly, the web and its manifestation are beneficial forces which need to be embraced to provide new vitality and vigour to the economy; secondly, there is a need to create and sustain a positive energy online by control. Thirdly, there is a need to establish an indigenous technological ecosystem so as to ensure general cybersecurity and protection of critical information infrastructure. Fourthly, the constituted cybersecurity system needs to shield the national interest. Xi while articulating the importance of informatisation said, "Without cybersecurity there is no national security, and without informatisation there is no modernization."[43] Moreover, while emphasising on the need to manage the content of the internet, Xi said, "If our Party cannot traverse the hurdle represented by the Internet, it cannot traverse the hurdle of remaining in power for the long term."[44]

Cyber Security Law[45]

While the Chinese are ready to embrace the Internet, they have not done so without regulating the cyberspace. Laws governing the cyber space have been enacted to protect the cyberspace from both domestic onslaught and outside threats. When Xi issued a statement to the effect that, "cyber-security and informatization are a single body with two wings, the two wheels of a single drive and require unified planning, unified deployment, unified promotion, and unified implementation,"[46] he was not being indirect about placing cybersecurity right at the top of the priority list in order to promote and perpetuate order, stability and control. Cyber security is paramount for any country but for a country like China which needs to maintain that 'things are under control' at all times, it becomes indispensable to its image. The regulatory regime targets three aspects—indigenization, data privacy and data localisation. All these three aspects focus on legally governing the cyber space, breach of which invites severe penalty. From encouraging people to use domestically cultivated hardware and software to giving rise to a multi-level protection scheme to contain potential threats—all aim at protecting the cyberspace. The cybersecurity laws regulate and enforce this indigenous process. Article 19 of the cybersecurity refers "to the development of national internet information department in China as a nodal centre for preparation of a catalogue on the likely list of equipment and products to be sold in China".[47] The Security law also firmly communicates that overseas organisations operating in key information infrastructure like energy, transportation and finance will have to undergo security assessment test of their data and equipment by public security agencies that have power to freeze assets of the individuals or organisations based overseas. A step further in this direction is data localisation which does the funnelling of the so-called damaging Western influences. The data localisation prohibits the data which originates in China from being stored or analysed outside China. Additionally, all foreign firms are required to provide the government with source codes. This exerts a two-fold impact—first, it adds to the repository of data that China holds close to its chest thereby augmenting its AI development programme, and second, the intelligence agencies gain access to individual and company data in accordance with its National Intelligence Law and Counter-Espionage Law. The third issue is data privacy that is the manner in which data is collected. Collection of data in China at all times needs to conform to the laws, prohibits third party disclosures and maintains the principle of 'prior notice and consent' of the users.

Cyber Governance

Internet at its inception in 1970s was not regulated. And there was no governmental control or censorship. Subsequently, its widespread reach and acceptance in the 1990s led to the introduction of copyright, firewalls and private appropriation of Internet. Today with data gaining a strategic importance and digitisation becoming embedded in every activity of our life, some degree of automatic movement of data is integral to a digital landscape. However, if a few companies or countries have a monopoly on the data, they can unleash a new form of data imperialism by colonising the data. It was this fear—that no one should be allowed to practise this cyber hegemony as it could be used in anti-national activities—which is the starting point of Chinese cyber sovereignty. The Chinese cyber sovereignty concept refers to this subordination of cyberspace to the values and interests of the nation and talks about three main principles—firstly, no country should interfere in other countries' internal affairs or abet unwanted influence in the other country which undermines its national security; secondly, countries should honour each other's sovereign right to choose their own model of regulation and polices, and the model so chosen must be based on equality; and thirdly the present system of governance of Internet from the current organisation needs to be moved to international forums like the United Nations, leading to the move of governance from 'multi-stakeholders' to a 'multi-party'.[48]

Cyber sovereignty as a concept is distinct from cybersecurity. "While cybersecurity pertains to protecting infrastructure and process connected to the Internet, cyber sovereignty is concerned with the information and content the Internet provides."[49] China's main role in promoting cyber sovereignty is to control the narrative about nation and the party. Today, controlling the content on Internet is done by the 'The Great Firewall of China' which filters and monitors all data at the six data entry points to restrict perceived harmful information for the nations.

It is in interest of China that cyber sovereignty as a tenet is always upheld. Given that Xi Jinping's intention of staying in power has been made amply clear, it is important that any form of dissent is nipped in the bud. The strong commitment of Xi Jinping to the Cyber domain can be seen from the fact that he has formed and chaired two "leading small groups on Central Internet Security and the Information Leading Group."[50] The main worry of the Chinese government today is internal stability and the control of information to manage unrest. With dimensions of airing information shifting from stationary sources to mobile and fluid sources in today's world, this concern has been heightened with the ever increasing user base. The main position taken by China is the primacy of the nation in the cyberspace and a concern of possible interference by foreign actors on whom the technology is dependent.

"The Chinese position in international diplomacy has changed from a more passive and reactive approach in the past to the current which is largely proactive and seeks to use its influence to shape the global agenda. The Chinese tactics for furthering their aims can be summarized as leveraging their large user community to gain concessions, build and support domestic companies, advocate the concept of cyber sovereignty in international fora and construct information networks in the developing world."[51]

Xi Jinping, while reaffirming the relevance of cyber sovereignty said, "We should respect the right of individual countries to independently choose their own path of cyber development, model of cyber regulation and Internet public policies, and participate in international cyberspace governance on an equal footing."[52] It is felt by a few that the anxiety created by this competing vision of Internet governance may lead to fragmentation of Internet and may lead to a splintered Internet controlled by nations or regions. However, at present, it this does not seem to be true as efforts by China are intended primarily as security measures aimed at protecting the political stability of the Chinese Communist Party and not in any way having any economic motive. However, there is a possibility that this could with time be reframed and resurface as cyber protectionism. Given how crucial this matter is for the Chinese, with time, one will witness a deeper and a more extensive dialogue surrounding cyber sovereignty which will be spearheaded by China.

HUMAN RESOURCE

Knowledge Capital

China has never underestimated the power of knowledge. In fact, the Chinese have taken pride in investing in expanding their knowledge base from time and time and it is this power which has brought them to the forefront in many arenas. Even in colonial China, knowledge was placed at par with material riches. The ferocious protection given to the Chinese philosophies and literature and the fact that China continues to draw from it is indicative of the superior status which 'knowledge' has occupied. However, Beijing is not oblivious to the reality that controlling the world would require more than just dollars. It would require acquiring the intellectual capital, dominating the lingua franca of business and establishing the centres of learning which can impart a heady mix of ideology and intellect. All this would be needed to fulfil the Chinese ambition of Pax Sinica.

In terms of resource allocation, China has done whatever it takes to upgrade its universities to match the international standards. From designing the curricula to suit the modern needs to putting in millions for research—China has done it all. It is this sheer need to be the 'knowledge capital' of the world which has led to four of its universities featuring in the top 100 universities in the world. This obsession with quality of education is not new. From the days of Deng, the Dragon has been working towards a system which has today put it on the world map when it comes to the quality of education imparted by its schools and universities.

The spread of xenophobia and the rising corruption in the education sector in the US has made China popular among the students of South and Southeast Asia, and China has not been oblivious to the massive opportunity this presents for it to include education in developing its international relation strategy around it. Over the years, one witnesses the once-upon-a-time snooty American universities melting towards the Chinese system of education. For instance, the acceptance of the Chinese university entrance exam Gaokao Scores for admission by University of New Hampshire and University of San Francisco are attempts to attract more Chinese students.

Pregnant with ideology and intellect, China has made education its mission and the aggressiveness with which it is pursuing the same can be seen from the fact China outpaced US in the count of scientific articles published. There has also been a drastic increase in citations to Chinese authors in academic circles. In terms of obtaining patents for its inventions, China has "issued about 1.36 million patents on inventions by the end of last year, working out to about 9.8 patents per 10,000 people",[53] thereby underlining the importance of scientific research and innovation.

In the field of language learning, China understands the importance of learning English. While it has tried its best to spread love for the Chinese through the Confucius Centres, the fact that English has been irreplaceable as a medium of exchange has been accepted by the Chinese, albeit grudgingly. It is for this reason that Beijing intends to produce maximum English speakers in the next decade. A step in this regard was taken when in December 2016 the National Education Examinations Authority (NEEA), Ministry of Education, China, and the British Council (BC) signed a Memorandum of Understanding (MOU) to link the British English tests—International English Language Testing System (IELTS) and Aptis[54]—to China's Standard of English Language (CSE) Ability. The linking of IELTS and Aptis to China's CSE was announced on 15 January 2019 which marks the official mapping of the CSE to the international examination systems. Linking IELTS and Aptis with CSE will ensure that the Chinese curriculum is designed to foster English proficiency among its students. Furthermore, the methodology of teaching English in order to get the desired results shall too become a part of the existing pedagogy so that the Chinese learners do not lag behind when it comes being fluent in English.

Innovation Imperative

From time immemorial, China has been a leader in innovation having invented compass and gunpowder to name a few. However, China fell short of capitalising on its innovations; rather the West manoeuvred to gain from them. Now, the tables have turned. China has been trying to become a world leader in technology and idea-driven innovation.

China needs to pursue an 'innovation imperative' in order to continue its international ascent and overcome the middle-income trap. The way in which China seeks this imperative, in turn, will shape its economic strength, military power, and give it an intangible benefit of perceived leadership. The innovative imperative entails that China has to meet both short- and long-term objectives. The short-term objective would be affected through technological 'catching up' while the long-term objective would involve innovating new products and processes. China's strategy, in order to achieve the innovation imperative and move up the value chain, has been to unify its state machinery, military, and society at large. "China has dramatically increased its budget for innovation and increased its participation in international bilateral research partnerships."[55]

"China's spending on research and development (R&D) was up 11.6 per cent in 2017, reaching USD 280 billion. It has a target for gross expenditures on R&D to GDP of 2.5 per cent by 2020 and is now sitting at 2.12 per cent."[56] One of the most significant policies which gives new dynamic to Chinese market is PRC's Indigenous Innovation Policy, which has as its target to reduce foreign technology in the Chinese market to less than 30 per cent by 2025. The three-pronged strategy calls for the development of indigenous Chinese innovation, the integration of foreign companies' technology into Chinese firms through Joint Ventures (JVs), Mergers and Acquisitions (M&As) as well as "re-innovation" by modifying western technology to make it Chinese.[57]

Beijing's comprehensive plans are clearly mapping out a future for China to move into the vanguard of world innovation. The broad targets set by its strategy for innovation-driven development are—to be an innovative country with a full national innovation system by 2020, to be a leading global innovative country by 2030, and to be a major global hub for science, with innovation the key factor in policy-making and institutional planning by 2050.

In addition to its aggressive targets and massive spending, the PRC has implemented major reform of all aspects of China's innovation system. In the past three years, the programmes of all Chinese ministries and agencies that fund industry R&D have been wound up and replaced with five programmes and seven arm's length professional agencies managing the new peer-review process.[58]

"Reforms are also occurring in universities and national laboratories. The salaries of scientists have been increased, plagiarism is being dealt with more aggressively, and talent programs have been upgraded to attract the best and brightest researchers from around the world with promises of sparkling new facilities and lots of bright postdoctoral staff."[59]

ACTIVISM IN ITS PERIPHERY

One cannot choose to have a Dragon as their neighbour, one just has it. 'Ask about your neighbours, then buy the house' is not possible in the context of the territorial arrangement and earmarking. Therefore, once a country with the size and magnitude of China decides to redraw and renegotiate boundaries, the countries of a 'lesser world' have no choice but to relent. As China's activism grows, its strategic interests will stand out against its neighbours. Historical experience makes us believe that rising powers suffer from a dogmatic dilemma of suspicion that other are out to get them and obstruct their march to greatness. They flex their muscles and test the resolve of any one who protests and benefits from their seeming weakness in resolve.

"Territory provides the identity autonomy and coherence to a state."[60] Since the modern state came into being, disagreements over territories have become a prime matter of difference between them, often leading to conflict. The Government of China, on assuming power in 1949, proclaimed that it would reconsider and review treaties by its predecessors with foreign powers, and either "reorganise, abrogate, revise or renegotiate them."[61] The Chinese explain most of their claims of sovereignty by saying that the territory has been illegally taken away from them through "unequal treaties"[62] by foreign powers during the 'century of humiliation' and now they are reclaiming it in order to reunify it with the Chinese motherland.

China has a land border of approximately 20,000 km and a coastline of about 18,000 km. It shares land borders with 14 countries and its maritime boundary with 9 countries. Domestic challenges have compelled China to opt for cooperation in many of its boundary disputes and thus, barring India and Bhutan, China has resolved all its land border disputes and is yet to settle it's maritime. Put simply, Beijing makes concessions on border issues to stabilise its domestic base. On 10 October 1960, Myanmar became the first country to have a defined boundary with China. The main reason to resolve the boundary dispute was the recognition of Tibet as a part of China by its neighbours. Following Myanmar, Nepal signed a boundary agreement with China in 1960 and here too the political upheavals in Tibet of 1959 played a crucial role as they were a tacit indication to Nepal to prevent Tibetans from using Nepal for anti-Chinese protests. This also restricted the movement of Tibetans at the Nepalese border. North Korea and Mongolia signed boundary treaties with China in 1962 to present the dispute resolution model to the USSR so that it could also opt for a settled border with China. China signed boundary treaties in 1963 with Pakistan taking advantage of the ambiguity vis-à-vis the status of Kashmir. Moreover, "When the contestant state is weak China has moved quickly to resolve the dispute—only when the USSR disintegrated that Beijing moved quickly to achieve resolution with the Central Asian Republics."[63] China settled its border with Kazakhstan, Kyrgyzstan and Tajikistan, which coincided with the ethnic unrest in the XUAR in April 1990 so that it would get these countries' assistance in curbing the challenges emanating from separatist groups in XUAR and across the border. It is noteworthy that China usually does not favour multilateralism for resolving its territorial issues. However, to get support from CAR countries to eliminate threat to the XUAR, it got into a multilateral mechanism to stabilise the border.

Bhutan Border Issues (Unresolved)

The boundary dispute between China and Bhutan came to the forefront in 1950s when Mao cited his 'Right Palm Five Fingers Strategy' by which he claimed that "Tibet is China's palm. Nepal, Bhutan, Sikkim, Ladakh and NEFA are the five fingers. Now that palm has been restored to China the five fingers should go with it."[64] Moreover in 1954, China published *A Brief History of China* where in a portion of Bhutan was included as a prehistorical realm of China. In July 1958, another map published in 'China Pictorial Magazine' claimed more Bhutanese land and later on, China occupied 495 sq km of

Central Bhutan. China's control over Tibet in 1959 furthered China's claims on Bhutan which were totally dependent upon justifying its claims on Tibet. However, an examination of the historical linkage between Bhutan and Tibet from the eighth century to the middle of twentieth century proves that although Bhutan had a close and conflicting relationship with Tibet, it was mainly cultural and religious in nature and did have any political linkages.

Today Bhutan, apart from India, is the only country in China's neighbourhood that is yet to have its border with China delineated and demarcated. It is also the only country in China's neighbourhood which does not yet have diplomatic relations with China. China-Bhutan border is 477 km long, out of which nearly a quarter is disputed. The first trilateral talk between China, Bhutan and India began in 1972 but it was only in 1984 that the bilateral negotiations without India began. The first major agreement on 'Maintenance of Peace and Tranquillity in the Bhutan-China Border Areas'[65] was signed in 1998. It was then that China, for the first time ever, recognised Bhutan as a sovereign country. This was a complete reversal from its 'Right Palm Five Fingers Strategy' policy. In 1999, the thirteenth round was held when the Chinese side put forth a 'package deal' for Bhutan. Till date, 24 rounds of 'Border Talks and Expert Group Meeting' and a Joint Technical Field Survey (to harmonise the reference points and name of the disputed areas) have been held with the last round being held in August 2016 in Beijing. In the autumn of 2017, there was a standoff for 73 days (18 June–28 August 2017) in the Doklam area of the disputed boundary between Bhutan and China which resulted in no talks being held in 2018.

China claims approximately 269 sq km and 459 sq km of territory in Western and Central Bhutan respectively. China has made the establishment of diplomatic and trade relations a precondition for resolution of the boundary dispute; whereas, Bhutan wants it to be the other way round. In the 2018 National Assembly election in Bhutan, left-leaning Lotay Tshering led Druk Nyamrup Tshogpa (DNT) party won 30 of the 47 National Assembly seats, which indicates that Bhutanese voters appear to be increasingly favouring opening up trade links with China. A favourable dispute resolution could play a critical role for China: "firstly in furthering its strategic depth against India's north-eastern periphery; secondly in restraining its Tibetan dilemma from spilling over into Bhutan; and lastly, in stopping Bhutan from being guided by Indian concerns alone."[66]

India Border Issue (Unresolved)

Nearly six decades have passed since the Indo-China war of 1962 but the border issue remains unresolved. It has turned into one of the most protracted border disputes in the world. Since 1960, when the first round of border talks was held, officials from India and China have sought to negotiate a solution to the border issue many times.[67] The India-China 3,488 km border is divided into three sectors—western, middle and eastern. India, following its Independence, believed that it had inherited settled borders from the British. However, China felt that the British had left behind unsettled boundary between the two. On the Eastern side, the dispute pertains to the Johnson Line proposed by the British in the 1860s that extended up to the Kunlun Mountains and put Aksai Chin in the then princely state of Jammu and Kashmir. Independent India used the Johnson Line and claimed Aksai Chin as its own. China initially did not demur when India said so in the early 1950s; however, in the years that followed it reversed its position and stated that it had never acceded to the Johnson Line and therefore did not see why it should cede Aksai Chin to India.[68] In the Middle sector, the dispute is a minor one. It is the only one where India and China have exchanged maps on which they broadly agree. The disputed boundary in the Eastern sector of the India-China border is over the McMahon Line. Representatives of China, India and Tibet in 1913–14 met in Shimla where an agreement was proposed to settle the boundary between Tibet and India, and Tibet and China. Though the Chinese representatives at the meeting initialled the agreement, they subsequently refused to accept it. The Tawang tract claimed by China was taken over by India in 1951.[69] India and China continue to cope with the undesignated boundary, resultant perceptual differences, and the trust-deficit in the relationship. The Sino-Indian boundary haggle has persisted since negotiations commenced during the 1980s to arrive at a mutually acceptable arrangement,[70] which would embody and reflect principles of accommodation, sensitivity and sovereign-respect in amicable and beneficent compromise. Nevertheless, the border has stayed tranquil and peaceful in spite of China's militarised incursions in Depsang (April 2013), Chumar (September 2014) and Doklam (2017) sectors.

By the beginning of the 21st century, the two sides had agreed not to let the border dispute affect bilateral engagements. This was inked into the 'Agreement on Political Parameters and Guiding Principles for the Settlement of the India-China Boundary Question signed in 2005'.[71] Today Sino-Indian bilateral interface and multilateral interchange is reposing elements of confrontation, competition and cooperation in alternating and concurrent hue. In 2017, the bilateral ties were stained by brackishness over the China-Pakistan Economic Corridor (CPEC), followed by the Doklam standoff. However, 2018 was a remarkable turnaround with the first informal summit of the top leaders at Wuhan and resumption of joint military drill of the two countries, thus abating some tension. Moreover, China's open aversion to India's attempts to become member of the Nuclear Suppliers Group and continuous stalling of New Delhi's bid to declare Masood Azhar[72] (2009, 2016, and 2017) as a global terrorist has opened wide the crevice between the two countries. China also continues to overtly exert economic embrace in South Asia, in Nepal, Maldives and Sri Lanka, where India has traditionally sought to maintain a sphere of influence.

Economic consonance has often been pointed to as a strong case in the relationship, suggesting that the rising trend of trade has helped to muzzle tensions. The growing trade has been accompanied by a widening trade deficit operating against India at 200 per cent over the past couple of years. Moreover, India's demand for a greater market access in China has repeatedly been turned down.

Near Seas

The Near Seas of China are the South China Sea, East China Sea and Yellow Sea (Bohai Sea and Korea Bay). The South China Sea (SCS), a strategic maritime space of East Asia, has emerged as one of the hotspots in the Indo-Pacific region with growing potential to erupt into unplanned encounters, a limited military conflict, or even a major war that would involve more actors. The South China Sea stretches roughly from Singapore and the Strait of Malacca in the southwest to the Taiwan Strait in the northeast covering about 3.5 million sq km. The maritime features and maritime zones in South China Sea have been a source of conflict between China and South East Asian Countries for decades. The maritime features consists of more than 200 tiny islands and several uninhabited rocky outcrops, atolls, sandbanks and reefs; the contested islands are in the north—Paracel Islands; in the south—Spratly Island; and in the east—Scarborough Shoal. Paracel islands are claimed by Taiwan and Vietnam and have been occupied by China since 1974. The Spratly Islands are completely claimed by Vietnam, Taiwan and China and in parts by Philippines, Malaysia and Brunei. Scarborough Shoal is claimed by both China and Philippines. China, since a standoff with Philippines in 2012, has uninterrupted Coast Guard presence in at Scarborough Shoal. The issue of sovereignty over the maritime features has been a bone of contention for a long time; however, tension intensified in early 2008 when conflicting claims were submitted for Extended Continental Shelves by China after Malaysia and Vietnam had submitted their claims. Chinese sovereignty claims over the maritime feature is based on historic rights and eleven dash line claim submitted after the World War II.[73] Although China ratified the United Nations convention on 7 June 1996, it has filed a reservation statement to not accept the binding decisions of Article 298 of the Convention. Although the UN Convention on the Laws of the Seas (UNCLOS) defines the maritime zone along a country's coast, it does not have any jurisprudence to address contesting claims of sovereignty over maritime features. It will be unfair to call only China's claims as exaggerated when other South East Asian countries haves similarity interpreted 'baseline'[74] provisions in a flexible manner.

In January 2013, Philippines instituted arbitral proceeding against China under Article 287 and Annexure VII of the UNCLOS. In July 2016, the award of the Arbitral Tribunal asserted that China's historical rights based on the nine dash line[75] was contrary to the UNCLOS. China refused right from the outset to accept the arbitration award and the Chinese Ministry of Foreign Affairs declared that it was "null and void and has no binding force, China neither accepts nor recognizes it."[76] After a rather low-profile year in 2017, when both China and the international community contemplated the impact of the Permanent Court of Arbitration Ruling, 2018 witnessed much more active efforts. In 2018, China expanded construction activities on 30 features, in the Subi, Mischief and Fiery Cross reefs in the Sparlty islands and Woody in the Paracel Islands. More importantly, it 'weaponised' features in the South China Sea by landing nuclear strike-capable bombers, deploying anti-ship cruise missile-carrying bombers and deploying Electronic Warfare equipment. On these islands, in May 2018, China, for the first time, landed long-range strategic bomber H-6K bombers on Woody Island. "If the H-6K were to appear on similar runways on Mischief or Fiery Cross in the Spratlys to the south, Australia or US territory of Guam could come within their range. If China was to base more advanced surface-to-air or anti-ship missiles on the Spratlys, it could strike anything moving in or out of the South China Sea."[77]

As a response to this 'weaponisation of South China Sea', the US government decided to withdraw an invite that had been given to China for the Rim of the Pacific exercises in May 2018. The weaponisation of the artificial islands has spiked tensions and further lowered the chances of settling the dispute peacefully.

Apart from sovereignty issues, which are centred on ownership, another issue which has led to a number of deadlocks is about how the sea would be governed and utilised. China is emphatic that foreign War Ships need prior permission to transit their territorial sea. According to the UNCLOS, "innocent passage is a right that foreign War Ships have to sail within another country's Territorial Sea as long as they traverse the zone in a swift and direct manner without conducting any prohibited activities such as military exercises and surveillance."

The China-US showdowns in the South China Sea have at times also become dangerous. For instance, on 30 September 2018, a Chinese Lu Yang destroyer came within 45 yards of a US Navy Ship USS Decatur. "From a legal perspective China's interpretation of UNCLOS demonstrating that the Convention does not grant the coastal state expansive powers to regulate foreign military activity in the EEZ."[78] That is why China has increasingly downplayed UNCLOS in defending its position, arguing that its domestic laws supersede UNCLOS on these matters.

Operations in the South China Sea have developed into 'grey zone' warfare, employing a mixture of military coercion, economic inducement, information warfare, and even historical narratives—pushing where the 'red line' is and expanding the range of the grey zone, still under the threshold for war. Communist China used to employ the maritime militia earlier so as to supplement PLAN which had fewer capabilities then. Today, the use of maritime militia is an instrument of choice as actions by militia can be framed as private actions. "This plausible deniability makes the militia force ideal instruments for pursuing national aims in the 'grey zone' between war and peace. Militia forces tend to operate smaller and more manoeuvrable vessels, which are better equipped for plying in shallow waters and engaging small foreign vessels. Moreover, because they are far more numerous than China's naval and coast guard assets, militia forces can cover much broader swathes of ocean, enhancing presence and bolstering maritime domain awareness. The maritime militia is now standing on the front line of disputes, as during the

2009 USNS Impeccable incident (involving two maritime militia fishing vessels from Sanya city), the 2014 Hai Yang Shi You 981 confrontation (escort operation to protect the drilling platform as Vietnamese maritime law enforcement vessels challenged Chinese presence), and the 2017 attempt to intimidate the Philippines near Thitu Island."[79]

More importantly, Beijing's South China Sea strategy is targeted not only at competing claimants, but also non-claimant stakeholders with vital interest in the region. Involvement of these third parties provides Beijing with a pretext to continue its militarisation; for instance, Beijing continuously calls-out US-conducted FONOPs as military escalations. Some members of Association of Southeast Asian Nations' (ASEAN) also tend to quietly accommodate China's assertiveness. An example of this is deliberate reticence on China's militarisation of the artificial features is that no ASEAN collective action was registered after China began using its militarised features in the South China Sea. Only Vietnam has officially asked Beijing to remove them but it received no backing from its group of fellow ASEAN members. Moreover, Malaysia's Prime Minister, Mahathir Mohamad, told US Vice President Mike Pence at the ASEAN–US Summit in November 2018 that sending the Seventh Fleet ships to the region would not be welcomed. Philippines seem to be unconcerned about pressing the arbitration award on China, while on the contrary President Rodrigo Duterte is playing ponderous 'Political footsie' with China. In his maiden visit in October 2016, Duterte signed 27 deals for 75 infrastructure projects worth $24 billion while Xi, in his first visit to Philippines, signed 29 deals for $5 billion, including a joint energy exploration in the contested waters.

Over the past two decades, the East China Sea maritime and territorial disputes have been a key flashpoint in East Asia. China and Japan lay claim to islands (known as Senkaku in Japan and Diaoyu in China) that cover around 81,000 square miles. The Senkaku/Daioyu islands were claimed by Japan in 1895 and until 2012[80] were owned by three Japanese citizens, subsequent to which they were purchased by the Japanese government.

China began claiming the Islands in the 1970s, citing historical rights. The maritime claims are disputed, with Japan claiming Exclusive Economic Zone (EEZ) from Ryukyu Island to the median line between Chinese and Japanese continental shelves. China and Taiwan, however, claim that their EEZ could include all of East China Sea given their continental shelf claims.

Although discussion on aiming to develop a crisis management mechanism began in 2012, it was only in June 2018, after nine rounds of high-level discussion, that a mechanism for maritime and aerial communication was put in place.

As China's navy capabilities improve and the margin of supremacy of Japan and US alliance reduces, the likelihood of potential incidents is growing. The rising nationalist sentiments and historical mistrust could manifest into a clash between Chinese fishing and coast guard vessels, deployment of Chinese oil drillings rigs across the median line, China declaring an Air Defence Identification Zone (ADIZ) covering East China Sea and even the deployment of unmanned systems in air as well as undersea.

Far Seas Strategy

The rise of China power has made it increasingly outward-looking in economic and military affairs. China's 80 per cent of oil imports is through International Sea Lanes (ISLs) in the Pacific and Indian Ocean. The strategic vulnerability of the Strait of Malacca has led to China expanding its influence and presence in the maritime space, which in turn is influencing diplomacy, partnership building and naval modernisation, thereby raising consciousness of the two ocean strategy. From the maritime perspective, the development of naval capabilities—significant expansion in marine corps, construction of second aircraft carrier, development of Type-55 destroyers and enhancement of submarine launched ballistics (JL-3) missile with range up to 9000 km—suggests that Beijing's maritime priorities (graduate from) 'near seas' off China's eastern seaboard to 'far seas'.

The "Two Ocean" Strategy came into prominence in 2006. However, since the pursuit of the BRI, the Two Ocean Strategy has been revived.[81] The foundation of the two ocean strategy is the development of ports in the Indian Ocean. "The major ports of interest in the Indian Ocean are: Gwadar/Jiwani in Pakistan, Colombo Port City and Hambantota in Sri Lanka, Payra in Bangladesh, Kyaukpyu in Myanmar, Melaka Gateway and Kuantan in Malaysia, Khalifa in UAE, Aden and Mokha in Yemen, Dolareh in Djibouti, Mombasa and Lamu in Kenya, Dar-es-Salaam and Bagamoyo in Tanzania, Beira, Narinda and Techobanine in Mozambique. China is also in negotiations for Chittagong Port in Bangladesh, Gadhoo in Maldives and Kra Isthmus Canal in Thailand."[82] These projects would be developed initially by private players as commercial facilities and in all likelihood be subsequently modified for military purpose. The two, BRI and two ocean strategy working in synchronisation with each has led to the modernisation of the PLAN, construction of more maritime bases aboard and presence of more military to protect its supply line aboard the necessary promptitude. The outlook of military has also transformed from regional to global with increased contribution in UN Peacekeeping and increased demonstrated commitment to Shanghai Cooperation Organization (SCO) tasks. "Moreover, as its hard and soft economic presence expands, it will require both Chinese civil servants and business elites. Finally, in terms of geopolitical strategy, it is likely that—as the BRI progresses closer to the Middle East—China will play an increasingly greater role in arbitration in the conflict zones of the Middle East. Essentially, Beijing has a vested interest in ensuring peace in this region, so as to allow the construction of the Belt portion of the BRI to pass through. Moreover, insofar as peace and economic development can occur in the region, China would gain valuable sources of oil and gas imports. As such, it is expected that Chinese presence in the Middle East will increase in the coming years."[83]

China's anticipated predominance in the Indo-Pacific region is transforming US relations with its allies and partners in the region. Washington, with its allies and partners, is actively building embryonic balancing coalitions (Quadrilateral Security Dialogue) in light of uncertainties about future Chinese power. "At the same time, none of these nations wants to choose between the United States and China; none wants the United States to leave the region; none wants China to dominate the region; and none wants to be drawn into an effort to contain China."[84] As China continues to dominate the economic development and regional security planning in Asia, a sense of appurtenance and desperation has arisen. China's neighbours are not likely to dispute China's influence and prosperity but will not welcome their loss of strategic independence. China's ascendance in the Indo-Pacific region could manifest itself as China will try its best to constrain the US and its allies by limiting their freedom of action but may not seek to confront the US owing to the high 'face' saving cost in case of failure.

China's strategy is to weaken the US' trustworthiness as regional security guarantor and relegate its allies to the sidelines. "From Beijing's perspective, the main issue is how to manage, and profit from, America's decline. The challenge, from Washington's perspective, is how to manage China's rise within the US-led order without diluting American role and presence."[85]

For the world today, the biggest question is how to manage China's rise and mould its diplomatic behaviour, even as China has done its best to underplay its emboldening initiatives by calling them either issues of sovereignty or labelling them as rightful historical claim. One cannot deny that these garbs are only meant for misleading the rest of the countries. The truth is China's burning desire of achieving invincibility through these measures. An emboldened China will negotiate from a position of strength and will ensure that its message and one-sided dialogue will not get lost in translation.

NOTES

1 Katrin Bennhold, "As China Rises, Conflict With West Rises Too," *The New York Times*, January 26, 2010, https://www.nytimes.com/2010/01/27/business/global/27yuan.html.

2 John Lee, "Lonely Power, Staying Power: The Rise of China and the Resilience of US Preeminence", *Strategic Snapshot*, No. 10 (September 2011), p. 1.

3 Hamid Soltani, A Civilised Beginning: The Human Social Journey (Pennsauken: BookBaby, 2016)

4 When the economic reforms commenced in 1978, China ranked ninth in world Gross Domestic Product (GDP) ranking with USD 214 billion; while today it is it at the second position with a GDP of over USD 10 trillion.

5 In 1978, China accounted for just ½% (half percentage) of world trade and now, it has outperformed USA to become the global leader in trade.

6 Focus Economics, "China Economy - GDP, Inflation, CPI and Interest Rate," *FocusEconomics*, Economic Forecasts from the World's Leading Economists, April 16, 2019, https://www.focus-economics.com/countries/china.

7 The Belt and Road Initiative (BRI) is the cornerstone of what Xi Jinping has hailed as the "project of the century". Since the 19th Party Congress, along with 'Xi Jinping Thought on Socialism with Chinese Characteristics for a New Era', the charter of CCP has received two amendments: firstly, the enshrining "Xi Jinping Thought on Socialism with Chinese Characteristics for a New Era" and secondly, "following the principle of achieving shared growth discussion and road imitative". The reference of BRI in the charter signifies that it is a long-term project. Resolution of the 19th National Congress of the Communist Party of China on the Revised Constitution of the Communist Party of China, October 24, 2017, http://news.xinhuanet.com/english/2017-10/24/c_136702726.htm

8 China Daily, "The BRI Progress, Contributions and Prospects," *China Daily Website*, April 23, 2019, http://chinadaily.com.cn/a/201904/23/WS5cbe5761a3104842260b7a41_2.html.

9 Jamie Horsley, "Can China Deliver a Better Belt and Road?", *Foreign Policy*, April 22, 2019, https://foreignpolicy.com/2019/04/22/965685-china-beltandroad-governance/.

10 Li Ziguo, "For the Public Good: The Belt and Road Initiative delivers shared benefits as vision turns into reality," *Beijing Review*, April 18, 2019, http://www.bjreview.com/Special_Reports/2019/Second_Belt_and_Road_Forum_for_International_Cooperation/From_the_Magazine/NO_16_2019/201904/t20190417_800165108.html.

11 Andrew Small, "A Shorter Belt and Road by China Will Be Even More Dangerous," *ThePrint*,

April 25, 2019, https://theprint.in/opinion/a-shorter-belt-road-by-china-will-be-even-more-dangerous/226849/.

12 BBC, "Xi Vows Transparency over Belt and Road," *BBC News*, April 26, 2019, https://www.bbc.com/news/business-48061951.

13 According to the Ministry of Finance, the government had to contribute 1.2 trillion yuan in 2017 to fund the shortfalls in pension spending.

14 Dr. Wendy Hong, Denise Cheung, David Sit, China's 13th Five-Year Plan (2016–2020): Redefining China's Development Paradigm under the New Normal, China's Policy Think Piece Series Issue No. 3, Nov 2015, Fung Business Intelligence Centre.

15 China 2030: World Bank Report, A "modern society shall be industrialized and urbanized that enjoys a quality of life that is on par with the Western world." As a "harmonious society, the aim is to have inclusive growth and at building a society in which everyone has a common stake in the country's economic, social, legal and political institutions while maintaining ecological balance." As a "creative society, China sees itself building its future prosperity on innovation. Creativity will manifest itself not just in product and process technology but also in cultural and artistic pursuits." As a "high-income society, China's aspiration is to enjoy a per capita income on par with advanced economies and to have a large middle class that acts as a force for stability, good governance and economic progress; eliminating poverty as it is known today."

16 Improving the rural infrastructure; by developing new "Small to Medium sized Cities (SMC)", implement steps to increase rural per capita income, and reform of 'hukou ' system.

17 Fourth Industrial Revolution, coined by Klaus Schwab, is also the title of his 2016 book.

18 In May 2015 the China's State Council released 'Made In China 2025' (MIC 2025). MIC 2025 is a ten years action plan to transform China into a global leader in manufacturing and innovation. It is believed to be China's response to Industry 4.0. A English translation of MIC 2025 is available at http://www.cittadellascienz.it/cina/wp-content/uploads/2017/02/IoT-ONE-Made-in-China-2025.pdf.

19 William H. McNeill, The Pursuit of Power: Technology, Armed Force, and Society Since A.D. 1000 (Chicago: University of Chicago Press, 1982).

20 David A. Baldwin, "Power Analysis and World Politics: New Trends versus Old Tendencies," *World Politics* 31, no. 2 (January 1979), pp. 161-194, https://www.jstor.org/stable/2009941.

21 Minnie Chan, "The Day China Entered the Nuclear Age", *South China Morning Post*, Oct 17, 2014, https://www.scmp.com/news/china/article/1617933/day-china-entered-nuclear-age

22 In 2016, an artificial intelligence (AI) system called Alpha Go based on machine learning defeated in match in Seoul a Weichi world champion. Again in May 2017, Alpha Go defeated a Chinese Weichi world champion. In China, millions watched the matches and were astonished by the fact that a machine made by a country which did not play the game could beat an expert from a country where the game had been played for over 2500 years.

23 James Vincent, "Putin Says the Nation That Leads in AI 'Will Be the Ruler of the World'," Verge, September 4, 2017, https://www.theverge.com/2017/9/4/16251226/russia-ai-putin-rule-the-world

24 Walter Frick, "Why AI Can't Write This Article (Yet)," *Harvard Business Review*, July 24, 2017, https://hbr.org/cover-story/2017/07/the-business-of-artificial-intelligence#/2017/07/why-ai-cant-write-this-article-yet.

25 Wired Staff, "The AI Cold War That Threatens us All," Wired, October 23, 2018, https://www.wired.com/story/ai-cold-war-china-could-doom-us-all/.

26 In July 2017, the China's state council released the New Generation Artificial Intelligence Development Plan (AIDP). The opening paragraphs of AIDP demonstrate Chinese views regarding AI: "AI has become a new focus of international competition. AI is a strategic technology that will lead in the future; the world's major developed countries are taking the development of AI as a major strategy to enhance national competitiveness and protect national security." An English translation of AIDP 2017 is available at https://www.newamerica.org/cybersecurity-initiative/digichina/blog/full-translation-chinas-new-generation-artifical-intelligence-development-plan-2017/. In September 2018 the China Academy of Information and Communication Technology released the "Artificial Intelligence Security White Paper".

27 Hannah Illing, "Helena Legarda: The EU Should Invest in Dual-use Technologies," *The New Federalist*, April 22, 2019, https://www.thenewfederalist.eu/helena-legarda-the-eu-should-invest-in-dual-use-technologies.

28 Lana Lam, "Exclusive: Whistle-blower Edward Snowden Talks to South China Morning Post," *South China Morning Post*, June 12, 2013, https://www.scmp.com/news/hong-kong/article/1259335/exclusive-whistle-blower-edward-snowden-talks-south-china-morning.

29 Xinhua News Agency, "Outline of the 13th Five-Year Plan: Double the income of Residents in 2020," *China.com*, March 18, 2016, https://economy.china.com/news/11173316/20160318/22110334_all.html.

30 Xinhua News Agency, "China to build global quantum communication network in 2030," *Xinhuanet*, November 2, 2014, http://news.xinhuanet.com/english/china/2014-11/02/c_127169705.html.

31 Qubits is the unit of quantum mechanics and can be visualised as an equivalent of the present bit (binary digit) which is used in communication and computing.

32 Meng Wanzhou, the Huawei Finance Chief, is the daughter of the Founder of Company Ren Zhengfei.

33 Phillip Orchard, "5G, China and the Race to Dominate High-Tech," *Geopolitical Futures*, January 30, 2019, https://geopoliticalfutures.com/5g-china-race-dominate-high-tech/.

34 Xinhua News Agency, "'Internet Plus' Action Plan Unveiled," *China.org.cn*, July 4, 2015, http://www.china.org.cn/business/2015-07/04/content_35980397.htm.

35 Sara Hsu, "China's Digital Economy's Growth Will Soon See It Outpace The Traditional Economy," *Forbes*, November 24, 2017, https://www.forbes.com/sites/sarahsu/2017/11/24/chinas-digital-economy-will-become-the-economy/#6b583d15430d.

36 The online commentators are used for incognito buildup of a favourable image of the state and augment trustworthiness of state message by 'astroturfing'.

37 In the book 'Art of War', Sun Tzu describes in Chapter XIII (Use of Spies) that, "Fore knowledge cannot be elicited from spirits; it cannot be obtained inductively from experience or by any deductive calculation... but can only be obtained from other men." Sun Tzu describes five types of spies whom he calls the "divine manipulation of the threads ... and the sovereign's most precious faculty."

38 During the course of fighting in the Three Kingdom period, Zhuge Liang and his small army in a city called Xichang had to face a big army of Sima Yi. Zhuge Liang opened the doors of the city and ordered his men in civilian dress to sweep the streets. Sima Yi on approaching the city assumed this an ambush and walked away in place of attacking the city. Today quoted as 32nd stratagems among the Thirty Six stratagems.

39 The hacker war between China and Taiwan began in 1999 when Chinese hackers defaced a

large number of government websites of Taiwan in retaliation to Taiwan's suggestion of state to state relations with China. Subsequently in 2003 and 2004, a large number of governmental computer networks were hacked again.

40 Titan Rain was a series of coordinated cyber-attacks detected in 2005 on NASA, FBI and Department of Defense (DOD) of US, suspected to have been conducted by PLA unit 61398 since 2003. This was the first instance of state-sponsored espionage from China that was made public and gave rise to distrust and suspicion against China.

41 Elsa Kania et al., "China's Strategic Thinking on Building Power in Cyberspace," *New America*, September 25, 2017, https://www.newamerica.org/cybersecurity-initiative/blog/chinas-strategic-thinking-building-power-cyberspace/.

42 Lu Chuanying, "China's Emerging Cyberspace Strategy," *The Diplomat*, May 24, 2016, https://thediplomat.com/2016/05/chinas-emerging-cyberspace-strategy/.

43 Xinhuawang, "Xi Jinping: Building China from a network power to a network power," *Xinhuanet*, February 27, 2014, http://www.xinhuanet.com//politics/2014-02/27/c_119538788.htm.

44 Kania, "China's Strategic Thinking on Building Power in Cyberspace".

45 China's first Cyber security law was passed on November 7, 2016, and came into effect from June 2017.

46 Kania, "China's Strategic Thinking on Building Power in Cyberspace".

47 Abhishek P. Singh, "China's First Cyber Security Law," Institute for Defence Studies and Analyses, October 14, 2016, https://idsa.in/backgrounder/china-first-cyber-security-law_apsingh_231216.

48 The 'Multi-stakeholder' governance is advocated by U.S, Germany and India is a model where governments, industry, civil society and technical community are consulted while taking any policy decision and in this way concerns of various stakeholders are adequately addressed. The 'Multi-party' governance as advocated by China means a state-led system in which civil society and business are present but regulated to consultative roles, thus government's authority cannot be challenged.

49 Niels N. Schia and Lars Gjesvik, "The Chinese Cyber Sovereignty Concept (Part 1)," *Asia Dialogue*, September 2, 2018, https://theasiadialogue.com/2018/09/07/the-chinese-cyber-sovereignty-concept-part-1/.

50 Shannon Tiezzi, "Xi Jinping Leads China's New Internet Security Group," *The Diplomat*, February 28, 2014, https://thediplomat.com/2014/02/xi-jinping-leads-chinas-new-internet-security-group/.

51 Niels N. Schia and Lars Gjesvik, "The Chinese Cyber Sovereignty Concept (Part 2)," *Asia Dialogue*, September 2, 2018, https://theasiadialogue.com/2018/09/07/the-chinese-cyber-sovereignty-concept-part-2/.

52 Chuanying, "China's Emerging Cyberspace Strategy".

53 China Daily, "R&D Input '2nd-highest in the World'," *China.org.cn*, February 20, 2018, http://www.china.org.cn/business/2018-02/20/content_50569194.htm.

54 Aptis is a general English test to assess language skills: speaking listening, reading and writing. It is used to assess foundational English skills.

55 Canadian Security Intelligence Service (CSIS) Report, Re-Thinking Security: China and Age of Strategic Rivalry, (Canada: CSIS, 2018), p. 105, https://www.canada.ca/content/dam/csis-scrs/documents/publications/CSIS-Academic-Outreach-China-report-M

56 Canadian Security Intelligence Service, "Re-Thinking Security", p. 106.

57 Ibid. p. 108.
58 Ibid. p. 106.
59 Ibid. p. 107.
60 Alexander B. Murphy, "Historical Justifications for Territorial Claims", *Annals of the Association of American Geographers*, Vol. 80, no. 4, 1990, p. 535.
61 Francis Watson, The Frontiers of China (New York: Preager, 1966), p. 9.
62 The Chinese called the following as unequal treaties: "1842 Nanking Treaty, the 1858 Aigun Treaty, the 1858 Tientsin Treaty, the 1860 Peking Convention, the 1881 Yili Treaty, the 1887 China-Portuguese Treaty, the 1895 Shimonoseki Treaty, the 1898 Convention for the Extension of Hong Kong Territory, the 1901 Boxer Protocol, etc."
63 Sudha Ramachandran, "China Plays Long Game on Border Disputes", *Uyghur American Association*, January 28, 2011, https://uyghuramerican.org/article/china-plays-long-game-border-disputes.html.
64 Barnett Doak A, "Mao's Strategy," p. 110.
65 Medha Bisht, "Bhutan: Internal Development and External Engagements," *Country Brief*, January 2010, p. 31, http://www.idsa.in/sites/default/files/countrybrief_Bhutan.pdf.
66 Tilak Jha, "China and Its Peripheries: Limited Objectives in Bhutan," *Institute of Peace & Conflict Studies*, August 1, 2013, http://www.ipcs.org/issue_select.php?recNo=529.
67 Till date, 21 rounds of border talks have been held between India and China. The last meeting between Special Representatives on the Border was held on 24 November 2018 in Chengdu China.
68 Shivshankar Menon, Choices: Inside the Making of India's Foreign Policy (India: Penguin Random House, 2016).
69 Mohan Guruswamy and Zorawar D. Singh, India China Relations: The Border Issue and Beyond (New Delhi: Viva Books, 2009), p. 31.
70 China and Indian have engaged in Confidence Building Measures (CBMs) on the border with bilateral agreements signed in 1993, 1996, 2005, 2012 and 2013.
71 "Agreement between the Government of the Republic of India and the Government of the People's Republic of China on the Political Parameters and Guiding Principles for the Settlement of the India-China Boundary Question," Ministry of External Affairs, Government of India, April 11, 2005, https://www.mea.gov.in/bilateral-documents.htm?dtl/6534/Agreement+between+the+Government+of+the+Republic+of+India+and+the+Government+of+the+Peoples+Republic+of+ China+on+the+Political+Parameters+and+Guiding+ Principles+ for+the+Settlement+of+the+IndiaChina+Bou.
72 Pakistan-based terror outfit Jaiṣh-e-Muhammad chief. He has been designated as a global terrorist by the United Nations in May 2019.
73 The eleven dash line map was first used by the Nationalist Government of the Republic of China in 1947. The eleven dashes laid out the extent of claim of China in the SCS. It was prepared for the Republic of China's Navy to take control of islands in SCS that had been occupied by Japan in the Second World War. After the People's Republic of China was found in 1949 and the Kuomintang forces fled to Taiwan. The executive Yuan of the (Pre-1949) Republic of China ... released a map titled "Position of the South China Sea Islands" with eleven dash. In 1953 two dashes around the Gulf of Tonkin were removed to allow to come to an agreement with Vietnam. Leading to 9 dashes on the map.
74 Baseline is the line that divides the territorial sea and internal waters. Its role in UNCLOS is

central as all claims for maritime zones are based on Baseline. They are two types of Baselines: Straight Baselines and Normal Bassline. Large number of East Asian countries use a straight base line claims as strategic positioning of their claims to keep margins for political bargaining.

75 The Tribunal concluded "...that to the extent China had historic rights to resources in the waters of the South China Sea, such rights are extinguished to the extent they are incompatible with the exclusive economic zones provided in the convention", Re-Arbitration Between the Republic of the Philippines and the People's Republic of China PCA Case No. 2013-19, Award, Supra note 2, p. 2061.

76 Statement of the Ministry of Foreign Affairs of the People's Republic of China on the Award of 12 July 2016 of the Arbitral Tribunal in the South China Sea Arbitration established at the request of the Republic of the Philippines, 12 July 2016.

77 CNN, "Troubled Waters: How Beijing Won't Back Down over the South China Sea," *Att.net*, December 19, 2018, https://start.att.net/news/read/category/news/article/cnn-troubled_waters_how_beijing_wont_back_down_over_th-cnn2.

78 R. Pedrozo, "Preserving Navigational Rights and Freedoms: The Right to Conduct Military Activities in China's Exclusive Economic Zone," *Chinese Journal of International Law* 9, no. 1 (2010): pp. 9-29, doi:10.1093/chinesejil/jmq007.

79 Conor Kennedy, "The Struggle for Blue Territory: Chinese Maritime Militia Grey-Zone Operations," *The RUSI Journal* 163, no. 5 (2018): pp. 8-9, doi:10.1080/03071847.2018.1552450

80 In September 2012 Japan government purchased three disputed islands from the private owners.

81 Alex Payette and Thom (Guorui) Sun, "China's Two Ocean Strategy: Controlling waterways and the new silk road", (Institute of International and Strategic Relations, May 18, 2017), p. 2, https://www.iris-france.org/wp-content/uploads/2017/05/Asia-Focus-31.pdf.

82 BK Sharma, "Net Assessment of China's Strategic Forays in India's Neighbourhood," *Bharat Shakti*, May 3, 2019, https://bharatshakti.in/net-assessment-of-chinas-strategic-forays-in-indias-neighbourhood/.

83 Ibid., p. 9.

84 Evan S. Medeiros, *China's International Behavior: Activism, Opportunism, and Diversification,* (Santa Monica: Rand Corporation, 2009), p. xxiii, https://books.google.co.in/books/about/China_s_International_Behavior.html?id=aW4icdPZcK8C&printsec=frontcover&source=kp_read_button&redir_esc=y#v=onepage&q&f=false.

85 Mohan Malik, "China and Strategic Imbalance", *The Diplomat*, July 14, 2014, https://thediplomat.com/2014/07/china-and-strategic-imbalance/.

5

Influential China

The world may have changed in its appearance but the desire to rule the world has not changed its flavour. Power was and continues to remain one of the deadliest desires of humankind and owing to its very nature, what has merely changed is the manner of its pursuit. From being concentrated in the hands of a few western countries to being broader in its fulcrum—the centre and the manifestation of power has changed but its core has not, and the political climate, both nationally and internationally, has suffered because of this shift. However, what remains to be seen is the manner in which the dynamics of the relationship between power and people has evolved. While for the US, the power now lies in the hands of the fourth estate which is responsible for making and breaking the leaders and leviathans, for a country like China it has merely changed hands within the Party.

In the context of China, it is imperative to acquire correct understanding of how and why this shift was prompted and more importantly, who prompted this shift. Was the shift in the global power centre engineered by China or is China simply bearing the fruit of a natural shift? Has China been able to gain a genuine respect from the international community or are the countries merely scared of standing up to a country as large and as powerful as China? What does it mean to 'influence China'? What has China done to emerge as a major influencer in the post-modern times? The answers to these questions are not simple. In fact in the quest for searching for these answers, one may end up facing tougher questions. However, in order to dissect and understand the Dragon, it is important to go beyond the obvious and see how China has tried to influence the rest of the world and to what extent it has been successful in its endeavours.

A WAVERING AND UNCERTAIN WORLD

Hans J Morgenthau in his book *Politics Among Nations* considers "nine elements including geography, natural resources, industrial capacity, military preparedness, population, national character, national morale, the quality of diplomacy and the quality of government as the components of national power".[1] However, the reality is that "those best endowed with power do not always get the outcomes they want"[2]. The truth of this statement is illustrated by the example of the US, which despite its power and prowess could not hold a candle to Vietnam. A nation which had tasted freedom after much strife had only passion on its side. Another example of desperation taking power head-on was the failing grip of communism over countries like Hungary and former Czechoslovakia which later emerged as independent nations after the disintegration of the erstwhile Soviet Union. History, therefore, does not always belong to the powerful and the definition of victory is no longer as straitjacketed as it used to be. Conflicts are not always known for their outlays and outcomes but also for their obsession. A fledgling trying to protect its sovereignty often wins in the eyes of the world, result notwithstanding. These days the war often belongs to the underdog, and in this constantly shrinking world it has become imperative to be 'seen' as a 'soft power' if you are a giant and to be seen as an 'underdog' if you are in the process of becoming a giant. Each nation has its story to tell and the manner in which it chooses to do determines whether the same is slated to be a bestseller.

When Joseph Nye coined the term "soft power",[3] he knew he was giving rise to an alternative which most countries would jump at for their image-building exercise. Soft power for Nye is a political verb and not a political adjective. In other words, the term soft power encompasses all the non-aggressive, non-confrontational and unobtrusive methods of weaving a favourable narrative which ensures the projection of a positive image before the international community in a manner that other countries would wish to tread the same path. For a very long time, the US was seen as a personification and a metaphor for the term. However, with a change in its approach, China took the matters in its own hands and tampered with the very definition of the term soft power.

With Hu Jintao's assuming the leadership, discourse surrounding soft power took a new leap. President Jintao was of the opinion that China must emerge as a soft power and expressed his desire in the Report to the 17th Party Congress of 2007. For Hu it was essential that China be viewed as a soft power and not as an aggressive, pugnacious nation. It was his efforts which communicated to the world that the Dragon does not always spew fire. One such attempt in this regard were the 2008 Olympics which gave the impression that China is a strong country with deep roots.

While China's commitment to being a soft power cannot be questioned, what needs to be understood at this stage is the manner in which it is measured. In international relations, power has always been a political construct but the manner in which it is expressed may not always be political. Cultural engagement, linguistic influence, extolling common historical past, etc. are ways in which a nation garners respect in the eyes of the world. For China it was about being active on global media platforms, setting up of Confucius Centres, opening its universities to the international student community, use of giant pandas as diplomatic gifts to other countries[4], etc. However, where China flounders is the manner in which it tries to weave the narrative of its softness. Its attempts are essentially exclusionary. 'The Chinese Dream' is a slogan which is anti-rest of the world. Whereas the American Dream was all about America being the greatest nation in the world because it tries to come to the rescue of the weakest, the Chinese Dream was only about China. Yet another folly in the Chinese understanding of "soft power" was the manner in which it used the terms 'civilisation' and 'civilised'. Nations across the world take pride in their histories and therefore, to label the ancient Chinese civilisation as the pinnacle of human civilisation will automatically imply that the Western world and its history was barbaric. The Chinese have always turned to their past for drawing inspiration; however, in the 21st century, when the narrative is all about creating a harmonious world order, cherry picking historical influences to spread the message of world peace is a convoluted approach and not the one which supports the notion of soft power.

The Chinese have given their interpretation to the notion of soft power, which necessarily is not a derivative of the original meaning. The words might be the same but the import is very different. Along with cultural engagement, China is rampantly using economic tools to drive across the point that in order to be a soft power one may not necessarily embrace the concepts of democracy, free speech and universal human rights. One can be a soft power without aping the West and adopting their ideology. Emerging as the largest trading partner for some countries, undertaking massive infrastructure development for others and building the ambitious Belt and Road project are all expressions of soft power.

A major deviation from Nye's definition of soft power can be seen in the manner China uses the term. It does not project itself as a role model worthy of imitation; however, it manages to capture the attention of the foreign audience because of what it offers to them, both tangible and intangible. Another factor which contributed to growing popularity of the Chinese version of 'soft power' was the talk of a "smart mix"[5] advocated by Hillary Clinton during the Obama administration in order to arrive at a nuclear deal with Iran in November 2014.

Power Changing Forms and Shades

The US no longer occupies the numero uno position in the world order and therefore, one finds that with rising China and Russia, the world is witnessing an ideological conundrum. The soft power of Uncle Sam is losing its appeal to heat of the "sharp power"[6] of the Dragon coupled with its notion of soft power. The Chinese unapologetically and unabashedly uses sharp power to yield influence in every form possible—from using academia as a pawn to outright open coercion. It is this constant use and expression of sharp power which has made the Western world apprehensive of the motives of China despite its best efforts to not create ripples in the present day world order. Sharp power makes democracy look jaded and less attractive because somewhere it glorifies authoritarianism owing to its tendency of 'getting the job done'.

The Chinese concept of power is not novel. In fact, the definition, the expression and the manifestation of power in China owes its existence to the ancient doctrines and writings of its religious scholars. Additionally, it derives legitimacy for its actions on the basis of historical evidence which both in terms of occurrence and interpretation has never been doubted. Using *Guanxi* to foster unity in an otherwise fragmented situation and *Yizhan* to justify its aggression against India, erstwhile Soviet Union and Vietnam is indicative of the manner in which China packages and then markets its actions to its own people and to the world at large. The Party leaders have always been aware of the sway history, culture and tradition have on the Chinese masses and therefore, have never shied away from squeezing every ounce from them (both conceptually and ideologically). It was Deng Xiaoping who felt the need for conducting a power audit before entering into strategic alliances and in doing so introduced *zonghe gouli*, which literally means 'Comprehensive National Power'. The purpose of *zonghe gouli* was to go beyond power assessment formulas developed by the western scholars and look at Comprehensive National Power (CNP) as an aggregate of multiple factors. While the factors covered within its ambit are being debated upon till today, the underlying objective of devising an indigenous power assessment formula was to annihilate the opponent not just politically and diplomatically but also psychologically. In fact, Chinese scholars have given rise to some sort of a CNP Index to throw clarity on what actually constitutes it and given the impressive growth China has clocked for over three decades, one cannot undermine the importance and contribution of CNP in it. However, China of today is beyond power assessment formulas and the growth which comes with accurate decision-making.

From the foregoing, it is necessary to see China's growth in a multi-dimensional manner. In the 21st century, Chinese growth is more about its "Core National Interests"[7] and an uncompromising attitude towards its pursuit. The phrase 'Core National Interests' was first introduced in 2011 thereby clubbing governance, sovereignty, and development together[8]. These core national interests became the crux of the Chinese concept of growth. In 2015, yet another term was added to this group, that is, security. In order to expand the umbrella of the core national interests, China passed the National Security Law[9].

It is interesting to observe the manner in which the Chinese have defined the elements of their core national interests. While the West invested its faith in Westphalian Sovereignty of absolute non-interference which gave the conflict ridden Europe its peace, the Chinese looked at Zhu Quan (Sovereignty) as a 'Mandate of Heaven (Tian Ming)'. What was 'power sharing' for the West was 'power concentration' for the Chinese—a tool for survival. China firmly held on to its concept with absolutely no readiness to relook, rethink or revise. It is this blind faith in its own interpretation of the term which led to its fierce defence of its territoriality. China has often used the "Treaty of San Francisco"[10] to justify its stand on Paracel, Spratlay, and Taiwan, etc. The passion with which China today safeguards its core interests gets reflected in its stance on South China Sea. Realising the sensitivity of that area, China has virtually altered its position on sovereignty in order to justify its construction of 'Air-Defence Identification Zone'. The shift in the definition of 'sovereignty' has led to China being protective towards its cyber space, and at the same time work towards developing deep-rooted, strong and great power relations.

Extrapolation of 'sovereignty' is neither unheard of nor unfamiliar for the Chinese. The notion of non-interference exceeds to include 'National Reunification' as its natural corollary. Since the Chinese believe that the two are inseparable, it sought to 'get back' Hong Kong from the British and Macau from the Portuguese. In the same vein it stated in no clear terms that recognition of Taiwan as a separate and an independent political entity would result in a military takeover.

Even though President Xi is completely in tune with the details and nuances of the National Reunification Project, the manner in which he will choose to execute the same will bear the hallmarks of his essentially Chinese understanding and conditioning. His idea of 'bringing together China' is not to reassemble China for the sake of the world but for the sake of China. It is a way of eradicating the horrific memories of the 'Century of Humiliation' and help China and the Chinese regain their lost glory. It is this firm resolve which makes China propel harder in the arena of geo-politics and geo-economics amidst the prevailing bedlam.

Yet another dimension of power is the 'power of knife' also known as 'hard power' and while over the years China has tried its best to not appear as a supporter of the power of knife, it has time and again hinted that should the need arise, it will resort to its use. There is a popular Chinese saying, "To fight for peace, peace will prevail; to compromise for peace, peace will disappear."[11] The Dragon, therefore, shall not contain its fire should the need arise. China has seamlessly worked towards becoming an economic and military might to reckon with. These tireless efforts to become a possessor of power in all its forms has made the rest of the world take notice of China with respect and apprehension in equal measure.

SHARPENING THE KNIFE

The Chinese Communist Party (CCP), known for its amoebic tendencies, could replicate its genetic material and give birth to its extensions in order to ensure that it grows in all directions. The People's Liberation Army, an Ideological offspring to the state, also known as the 'Red Army', is one such mitotic extension of the CCP which began in 1927. The outfit was started by

Mao in order to have armed conflicts with the opponents and adversaries. However, the giant military body has evolved since then.

A clear change in its structure, messaging, size, technology and response to external stimuli can be seen. These changes can be attributed to the leaders which China has had. With its initial conditioning being limited to engaging in a protracted battle after pulling the enemy within the Chinese borders to modernising it from within and without—China's People's Liberation Army (PLA) has grown from strength to strength without compromising on a harsh criticism of itself on occasions. Its keen observation coupled with introspection has undoubtedly worked miraculously in its favour. Reforms were initiated by Deng when the lacunae in the PLA were split open during the Vietnamese conflict. These reforms were brought about when the PLA began the exercise of learning through observation. As a keen observer, China studied a series of armed conflicts including but not limited to the Falklands War of 1982, the Libyan bombings of 1986, etc. in order to upgrade itself. From manipulating the enemy into its borders and making its territory as ground zero to focussing on armed brawls and regional conflicts, Deng undertook a large-scale and an all-encompassing modernisation of the PLA. When the baton was passed on to Jiang Zemin, he built on the reforms and legacy of Deng. However, it was during Zemin's tenure that the technological obsolescence of the Chinese army was revealed. He realised that the defence forces were technologically incapable to fight in the modern times and therefore, it was Zemin who announced the 'Military Strategic Guidelines for the New Period' with the objective of bringing about a metamorphosis in the defence forces in terms of improving the quality of the forces and prepare them for local wars under modern technology conditions.

Hu Jintao envisioned a bigger and a meatier role of the Chinese forces at a global level. The clarity in his objective gets reflected when he married the internal and external military concerns of the Chinese with world peace. For him, the two were not mutually exclusive and therefore one witnesses an active participation by the Chinese forces in the peacekeeping missions of the United Nations[12] as well as counter-piracy operations. For Hu Jintao, Chinese sovereignty, security and intactness were non-negotiable and had to be protected at all costs and in an equal measure was the PLA's engagement in international conflict situations. It was at this juncture that the importance of a strong naval presence was felt. While the Chinese could tackle a military tussle on the land, they were still far behind when it came to gaining control of the waters. It was during Hu's stint that the PLA began emphasising on space and cyber operations, strategising for offensive engagements, establishing military bases in other parts of the world and securing overseas interests.

The journey of giving rise to a formidable defence forces began with Deng Xiaoping and was steadily taken to another level by Jintao. However, what accelerated the pace of the journey was the spate of reforms introduced by Xi Jinping whose concentration was as much on the internal organizational restructuring as on the outward appearance strength. In his report at the 19th congress Xi said, "The party will strive to basically complete national defence and 'military modernization' by 2035 and fully build the people's army into a 'world class military' by middle of the century." The measure taken by President Xi aims at rightsizing the military and follow a force development plan with a set of benchmarks to achieve the objective of a "world class military". The force development plan has three noteworthy features—first, restructure the forces to conduct joint operations in a modern high-tech battlefield by replacing the seven 'Military Regions' (MR) by five 'Joint Theatre Commands' (JTC). Unlike the MR whose jurisdiction was confined to China's frontier, the JTC are responsible to operate far beyond their frontiers; second, are the clear domain specific five services—Army, Air Force, Navy, Rocket Force and Strategic Support Force; third, centralisation and strengthening of Xi's control over the CMC and reaffirmation of the belief that the central task of military is to preserve the party. In this process, Xi has taken urgent steps to change the spotlight of the Chinese forces from land to sea; from a regional to a global force; and from being an information based force to an intelligence based force. These efforts unmask the reality of the PLA and give the observers a glimpse into his game plan, that is, to be able to fight a 360 degree war, to be able to launch an offensive should the need arise and to not be taken by a surprise attack under any circumstances.

The emerging locus of the PLA Navy (PLAN)—from 'offshore waters defence' to a mix of 'offshore waters defence' and 'open-seas protection'—echoes China's ambition for a far reaching operational capability. In July 2013, Xi Jinping in a meeting of the CCP Politburo to discuss Maritime Power stated that China needed to "do more to take interest in the sea, understand the sea, and strategically manage the sea, and continually do more to promote China's efforts to become a maritime power."[13]

The attempts made by China towards making it appear powerful beyond its territorial borders have manifested in the form of the ambitious BRI, establishing its military bases outside of its territory, and emerging as a voice in international conflicts. The growing ambition of the PLA and its presence abroad has positioned it as a reliable player in the global arena as well as an exacting and a fierce force which is capable of playing a dual role of protecting the China's interests.[14] This image gets further enhanced when the world watches the size of the budgetary allocation towards military advancement and upgradation of the existing arsenals. A solid air force with a world class apparatus and weaponry, expanding naval bases and the size of the Marine Corps[15], stockpiling of assault ships and fleet-support ships, etc. leaves no ambiguity in understanding the ambition of the Chinese.

The latest defence white paper "China's National Defence in New Era" released on 24 July 2019 brings out six main issues; Firstly, "Socialism with Chinese characteristics has entered a new era" where peace is an irreversible trend but a "world is not yet a tranquil place." The white paper justifies Chinese force restructuring and modernisation requirements, which it feels is guided by rising strategic competition due to shift in US strategy from counter terrorism and extremism to competition and possible conflict with US unleashed by the 2017 National Security Strategy and 2018 National Defence Strategy. Secondly, unlike the earlier nine white papers, where China had not named any country while discussing, "Anti-China forces". The present 2019 white paper clearly brings up the US as practicing "hegemonism, power politics and unilateralism" and undermining the global security by increasing its defence expenditure and pushing "additional capacity in nuclear, outer space, cyber and missile defence." Thirdly, the strategic direction for China continues to be Taiwan and it considers reunification as an unfinished agenda and there is no ambiguity in its assertion that "China, must be and will be reunited" even if it means use of force. Fourthly, the white paper recognizes nuclear, outer space and cyberspace as the major security domains, with nuclear as the "strategic cornerstone to safeguard national sovereignty," outer space as the critical domain for capability development for unhindered space utilization and cyberspace as a sovereign requirement that has been tied to national security. Fifthly, the white paper clearly lays down the service-wise priorities for military modernization in the future; PLAN, PLAAF, PLARF and newly created PLASSF have been given due impetus. Capability wise in the near term, the emphasis would be to complete its mechanization and to bridge the technology gap with US in new domains and in the middle term, create capabilities to prevent US military superiority. Sixthly, the paper highlights, the Chinese emphasis on combat readiness, "Military training in real combat conditions across the armed forces is in full swing. Since 2012, China's armed forces have carried out extensive mission-oriented training tailored to the specific needs of different strategic directions and exercises of all services and arms, including 80 joint exercises at and above brigade/division level. The PLA Army (PLAA) has organized training competitions and conducted live exercises codenamed Stride and Firepower. The PLA Navy (PLAN) has extended training to the far seas and deployed the aircraft carrier task group for its first far seas combat exercise in the West Pacific. It has organized naval parades in the South China Sea...and conducted a series of live force-on-force exercises.... The PLA Air Force (PLAAF) has...conducted combat patrols in the South China Sea and security patrols in the East China seas and operated in the West Pacific.... The PLA Rocket Force (PLARF) has organized force-on-force evaluation-oriented training and training based on operational plans at brigade and regiment levels, strengthened training for joint strikes, and completed regular exercises such as Heavenly Sword."

Whether China is ready for coping with the conflicts of 21st century can be answered in affirmative but will China dominate militarily given its preparation, procurement and progression can best be answered in retrospect. Understanding the nature of future challenges is the key to their approach and resolution, but how soon China will be able to decode them remains to be seen.

INSIDE THE NUCLEUS OF THE NUCLEAR CHINA

During the Mao regime, China was overtly critical of the merit in acquiring nuclear weapons by labelling them as 'paper tigers'. However, there is always a massive discrepancy between what China says and what China does. Covertly, China began the process of working towards a nuclear arsenal after the fall out with Russia. Hiding behind the tagline, 'People's War', China initiated the process of becoming a nuclear state without deviating from the doctrine of 'no first use'. It has been extremely particular when it comes to projecting an image of a responsible nuclear power. While its nuclear doctrine seems well structured today, Beijing initially had a very rudimentary nuclear policy. There was a consensus among the Chinese elite vis-à-vis the need to upgrade the armed forces; however, its pace and budget were the topic of debate. Over the years, Beijing managed to arrive at a balanced nuclear policy which was based on a 'credible survivable nuclear deterrent' and a counter-strike capability. The Defence White Paper of 2010 does not explicitly mention the words 'no first use' but clearly outlined China's "unequivocal commitment that under no circumstances will it use or threaten to use nuclear weapons against non-nuclear weapon states or nuclear-weapon-free zones."[16] That said, while assessing the nobility of the Chinese intention one needs to be fully cognizant of the fact that China has developed strong underground storage facilities in the regions of Gobi Desert and Tibetan Highlands in order to safeguard its borders and launch a counter-attack against Russia and India should the need arise.

The Chinese nuclear doctrine is designed on the principles of *youxiaoxing* (effectiveness), *zugou* (sufficiency), and *fanweishe* (counter deterrence.) One can clearly identify the three stages in the China's journey towards becoming a nuclear power—first, when it possessed nuclear weapons but did not possess the bandwidth to effectively use them; second, when it became confident of inflicting damage to its adversaries; and third, when it gained the capability of hoodwinking the adversary about the location of its missiles.

Since 1964 (when China conducted its first nuclear test) China has till date conducted 45 nuclear tests. China has undertaken major restructuring and modernisation of its nuclear arsenal under the Rocket Force. China's maintains a triad of nuclear capable delivery system with the arsenal size of 220-310 nuclear weapons. The land-based platforms (75–100) consist of silo-based DF-5A and DF-5B; the solid-fuelled road-mobile DF-31 and DF-31A; and the more-limited-range DF-4. This force is complemented by road-mobile, solid-fuelled DF-21 MRBM for regional deterrence missions. The sea-based platforms consist of JL-2 SLBM on JIN-class nuclear powered submarines. The air-based platforms consist of stealth strike aircrafts—the J-20, J-31 and strategic bombers.[17] In order to counter ballistic missile defence system, China is working on Multiple Independently-targeted Re-entry Vehicles (MIR), Manoeuvrable Re-entry Vehicles (MaRV) and Hypersonic Glide Vehicles in order to enhance its responsiveness. Moreover, in the last few years, the nuclear research and design organisation in China—China Academy of Engineering Physics, and the uranium enrichment facility—China National Nuclear

Cooperation, have been given enhanced funding and support by the Chinese Government.

Space

While China was not a significant space power throughout the first four decades of the space age, its space capabilities have significantly improved over the past 20 years. In the late 1990s, the US-adopted policies designed to thwart China's ability to access space-related technologies. China responded by accelerating the pace of its space programs. China today has quickly become a major player in the space domain with the ability to influence significantly both the informatisation of the military and astro-nationalism events in the coming centuries.

The informatisation of the PLA has been a key component of China's military modernisation since the times of Jiang Zemin. Space today is one of the key components driving the PLA informatisation. Signifying this importance of space driving China's informatisation, the 2015 Defence White paper asserts, "Outer space has become a commanding height in international strategic competition. Countries concerned are developing their space forces and instruments and the first sight of weaponisation of Outer Space have appeared."[18] Furthermore, China created its space force as a part of Strategic Support Force (SSF) in 2015. The Chinese military is developing two major space launch capabilities—space-based C4ISR[19] and counter space capabilities. C4ISR capabilities are function of detecting, monitoring, communication (data, image and voice) and geo-spatial positioning. Satellites are indispensable for gaining the C4ISR dominance in battle space. China has, in March 2019, 299 satellites—198 remote sensing (Yao Gan), 66 communication and 35 navigation satellites.[20] The remote sensing capabilities consist of both Electro-Optical (EO) and Synthetic Aperture Radar (SAR) sensors with resolutions up to sub meters with capability to evaluate geophysical specifications of the earth such as disaster monitoring, crop yield assessment, land survey and scientific experiments. However, it is believed that a number of the remote sensing satellites are equipped with Electronic Intelligence (ELINT) payload for military purposes.[21] In the coming future, commercial launches are planned:

- "Super view"[22] (Gaojing), a 24 satellite constellation, by 2022
- "Jilin"[23] (Chang Guang Satellite), 60 satellites by 2020 and 138 satellites by 2030

These will make it possible to make a ten-minute revisit to each and every location on the Earth.

China is attempting to enhance its broadband access and services especially to underserved regions by exponentially increasing its communication satellites. Today China has 66 communications satellites out of which four are for military purposes and plans two major Low Earth Orbit (LEO) constellation—'Hongyan'[24], a 320 satellite constellation developed by China Aerospace Science and Technology Corporation (CASTC) by 2025 and "Hongyon",[25] 156 satellite constellation developed by China Aerospace Science and Industry Corporation (CASIC) by 2020.

In navigation satellites or geo-spatial positioning, Chain has launched 49 satellites out which 35, which are a part of the Beidou Programme are operational; 15 second and 20 third generation. The Beidou navigation system has been providing global coverage since 27 December 2018 with an accuracy of 5 meters in the Indo-Pacific region (including 50 nations of BRI) and 10 meters accuracy to the rest of world. All smartphones as well as over two million cars in China are already Beidou navigation system compatible.

In order to gain information, dominance is important to secure space and network superiority by 'Counter Space Operations'. Chinese counter space strategy involves creating a D3SOE (Deny, Degrade, Disable, Space Operations Environment) by the use of anti-satellite weapons to "blind and deafen the enemy". [26] Since China conducted Kinetic Kill Anti Satellite (ASAT) test by direct-ascent missile on 11 January 2007 to destroy the weather satellite FY 1L, it has continued to develop, test and operationally deploy more sophisticated soft kill application such as Rendezvous and Proximity Operations (RPO) as precursors to co-orbital technology.[27] China first exhibited its robotic Rendezvous and Proximity Operation (RPO) in June–August 2010 and involved Shi Jian 12 and SJ-06F satellite. Subsequently, three satellites—Shiyan 7, Chuangxin 3 and Shijan 15 (2013), SJ-17 (November 2016–February 2018) and TJS-3 (January 2019) have ventured into activities cohering with RPO. The RPO activities have gained significance as they are of dual use—engaging in peaceful work (they remove harmful orbital debris) as well as repairing or disabling others satellites. On 26 September 2006, China used ground-based lasing system to illuminate a US satellite as it passed over Chinese territory. There are reports that China has developed the capability to modify and control the ionosphere by high-energy microwaves over a target area by creating a barrier to signals passing through it thereby disrupting GPS systems and jamming radio waves used in voice communication and radars.[28]

Astro-Nationalism/Astro-Politics: The New Space Race

Although the traditional struggle over terrestrial supremacy is far from over, the arena of space offers a new field for the realisation of influence strategies of 'great power'. In the coming two decades or so, China wants to dominate the outer space, especially the Moon and other celestial bodies. China's aspirations can be understood from the comments of Ye Peijian, the Head of Chinese Lunar Exploration Program (CLEP), who when asked by a reporter, "Why China is going to moon?" at the CCP's annual plenary session in 2017, Ye Peijian replied, "The Universe is an Ocean, the Moon is the Diaoyu Islands, Mars is Huangyan Island. If we don't go there now even though we're capable of doing so, then we will be blamed by our descendants. If others go there, then they will take over, and you won't be able to go even if you want to. This is reason enough."[29] This reply suggests that China sees Moon and Mars as places of astro-political importance. The present geocentric approaches to outer space are mainly concerned about how space influences affairs on the Earth and downplays the astro-strategic terrain in 'cislunar'.[30] The idea of astro-politics[31] is a significant development and if it was to be compared to any 20th century geopolitical idea, it would be of Halfords Mackinder's Heartland Theory[32] as both aim to develop technologies to control strategic resources and gain advantage over other nations. The importance of the astro-strategic terrain is highlighted by Everett C Dolman in his book *Astropolitik*, "What appears at first as a featureless void is in fact a rich vista of gravitational mountains and valleys, oceans and rivers of resources and energy, alternately dispersed and concentrated, broadly strewn danger zones of deadly radiation and precisely placed peculiarities of astrodynamics."[33] A pertinent question here could be—What is the strategic value of the Moon? Paul Spudis in his book, *Value of Moon* brings out the significance of the Moon in astro-politics, "The moon's greatest value is its capacity to create new spacefaring capabilities through the exploitation of its material and resources."[34] The Chinese White Paper of 2015 emphasises the relevance of astro-politics by mentioning that "whoever controls space will control the earth"[35]. The White Paper of 2016 lays down a vision "to build China into a space power in all respects: acquire key technologies and conduct experiments on such technologies to raise our manned space flight capacity, laying a foundation for exploring and developing

Cislunar Space."[36] Moreover, Xi believes that the "Spirit of aerospace is akin to the spirit of long march"[37] and will play a leading role in rejuvenation of the Chinese nation.

China's first human spaceflight—Shenzhou 5—atop Long March 2F rocket, carried China's first Taikonaut Lieutenant Colonel Yang Liwei on 15 October 2003. Subsequently, China's space station programme—Tiangong (Heavenly Palace)—has been able to launch two space laboratories—Tiangong-1 on 29 September 2011 and Tiangong-2 on 15 September 2016—which have given China hands-on understanding and adequate facilities and systems to take its next surge—the deployment of the Chinese Space Station (CSS)—Tianhe (harmony of the heaven)— weighing sixty tons. Two experimental modules 'Wentain' and 'Mengtain' will constitute the CSS. The first module is likely to be launched in the latter half of 2019. The CSS is likely to be fully functional in 2022 for a period of 10 years with three taikonauts, with each staying for 3–6 months. Bai Mingsheng, the chief designer of China's first cargo spacecraft Tianzhou-1, in an interview to China Central Television, stated that, "China might be the only country that will run a space station in the foreseeable future. We could invite other nations to carry out experiments on our space station, making it an international scientific platform for all humankind."[38] On 28 May 2018, China invited all UN members via United Nations for Outer Space Affairs (UNOOSA) to participate in the CSS. If China is able to entice foreign partners it will be able to corrode the domination of US in space and this kind of grand standing offers China influence and power, especially the ability to influence others to do what they want them to do. After the stationing of the CSS, China could intensify efforts on launch vehicles such as Long March 9 to lift 140 tonnes for its manned China's Lunar Exploration Program (CLEP) in 2030s. With such technically sophisticated outer space accomplishments, China will show up the influence to manufacture alternate structures and norms for outer space.

In outer space governance, China has been an active participant in both the United Nations Committee on the Peaceful Use of Outer Space (COPUOS) and Conference on Disarmament (CD). In COPUOS, China has advocated equitable access and utilisation of space resources to all countries, while in CD, along with Russia, it has continued to push for a Treaty on Prevention of the Placement of Weapons in Outer Space (PPWT). Overall, China has identified outer space governance as an area which is still evolving and where it can configure the normative schema as per its interests.

Advanced Weapon System

China believes that technological development is critical for maintaining deterrence in an environment in which "...the emergence of new deterrence forces, based on new technology such as information, cyberspace, space, and new-material technologies, is revolutionarily changing the mechanism, method, and area of operation. It heralds a completely new method of deterrence, symbolized by constructing asymmetrical method of deterrence."[39] Asymmetric capabilities such as autonomous unmanned systems, manoeuvrable re-entry vehicles, directed energy, electromagnetic railguns and emphasises on development of artificial intelligence applications remain PLA's priority.

Over the past five years, China has become a global leader in commercial and military autonomous Unmanned Aerial Vehicles (UAV). It has also successfully tested the ability to use artificial intelligence (AI) to link over 100 UAVs as part of resilient and networked 'swarm'. Moreover, the Chinese research community has been involved in the development of autonomous Unmanned Underwater Vehicles (UUV), the proliferation of which will offer China an opportunity to address critical vulnerabilities in its undersea domain. Presently, the operationalisation of autonomous unmanned systems infused with AI is the most critical future battlefield game changer for the PLA.

China is attempting to develop multiple weapons that are launched by ballistic missiles but could vary from predictable ballistic trajectories upon re-entry. These manoeuvrable weapons would pose a particularly daunting challenge for existing missile defences and could upset delicate balances in the missile versus missile defence competition in the Western Pacific. China's Hypersonic Glide Vehicle (HGV) programme is also advancing, having completed seven tests since 2014. The programme is largely catalysed by concerns that US advanced missile defence systems, particularly and most recently the Terminal High Altitude Area Defence (THAAD), are severely undermining, if not abrogating. China's strategic and conventional nuclear deterrent.

China's industry has successfully developed several directed energy weapons, predominantly lasers and microwave weapons. These weapons are designed to carry out several missions including the close-in defence, jamming of platforms, and possibly missile defence. Continued development of both satellite-carried and ground-based laser dazzlers that can blind, jam or destroy satellites constitutes a particularly worrying threat to space-based architecture.

Progress in the development of EM railguns and hypervelocity weapons has lagged behind the development of other systems. China's interest in EM railguns and weapons should be seen as part of the broader cascading implications of the missile versus missile defence competition that the introduction of Hypersonic Glide Vehicles (HGVs) and other Manoeuvrable Re-entry Vehicles (MaRV) weapons are generating.

STRATEGIC STORY TELLING

Giving rise to false narratives is not a new weapon in the arena of international politics. In fact, there have been occasions when facts have been buried deep inside the stories which the nations have told their electorates and international supporters. The war between the US and erstwhile Soviet Union might have been cold but the story telling was certainly not. For instance, in 1980s, the Kremlin took it upon itself to paint AIDS as an American biological weapon, thereby making it an outcome of the American brand of politics instead of a disease.

With time, the weapon of spreading stories woven in the chambers of the political leadership found favour with many new age media platforms. It became much easier to accomplish political goals through the instrumentality of print and electronic media and paid trolls. However, China in the new age has made it its mission to use its sharp power to its advantage. Influencing the electoral process, manipulation of election results, navigating policy making to suit its own needs, posing as a stakeholder in the decisions of the companies and moulding the public opinion are components of China's bigger agenda some time now. Furthermore, the Chinese government has ensured that it uses all the resources at its disposal to colour the public perception and impress upon the Chinese diaspora an image which is neither tyrannical nor authoritarian.

The manner in which the Chinese have used different methods of power has created much confusion in differentiating between the contours of soft power and sharp power. The line separating the two has been deliberately blurred to such an extent that one cannot discern when and where one ends and the other begins. A consequence of this hazy display is the uncertainty on the part of other countries to strategise in relation to China. In some cases, the nomenclature used for this version of China is 'China Threat 3.0'[40]. China uses every possible mode as paraphernalia for the sharp power to be injected into the system. Culture, language, religion, media, customs, academia, diaspora—all have been reduced to playthings in the hands of the Chinese political leadership to employ sharp power.

Apolitical Appearance, Political Purpose

An amateurish China had maintained a policy of 'non-interference' vis-à-vis the political process in other nations. However, an expert China knew better. When the reality of the 21st century dawned upon the Chinese, they realised the merit in influencing the political processes in other countries, especially with those with which it engages for trade and business. It was the fear of being left out in controlling the share of the world economy that made China take the centre stage in gaining the trust of those countries through sizeable investment in their economies, bribing their politicians, control of the Chinese diaspora present in those countries as well as bailing them out in the hour of need. An aggressive and an active China amassing support from the world outside of its own has become a force to reckon with. China's ambition of emerging as a dominant player in the world affairs is unambiguous. President Xi, in his report to the Chinese Communist Party's in October 2017, stated that "...by 2050 China will have become a global leader in terms of composite national strength and international influence." [41] With its eyes firmly on the future, China knows what it needs.

The Chinese used its economic enthusiasm to first gain Africa on its side and then to meddle in its political affairs. For Chinese, Africa is important for more reasons than one. With only 9 per cent of farmland, China needs food grains, and Africa, with 60 per cent arable land, is the granary of the world. Additionally, the continent is well endowed in terms of natural resources and oil. Thus, the economic aid and political meddling comes with a strong motivation. For instance, in South Sudan, China has been alleged of political doublespeak. On one hand it has been taking the forefront as a peacekeeper and on the other has been clandestinely extending military support to the incumbent regime in order to safeguard oil investment. One can make similar observations when one looks at the policy China had adopted towards the Democratic Republic of Congo and Nigeria where the Chinese story began with doing business and making progress in it to a full-time security presence. China is acutely aware of the nature of interests it is looking to protect. With its eyes firmly set on the future, it has supplied arms to the political regimes in South Sudan, Congo, Liberia and Zimbabwe to prevail over the political opposition in those countries and gain political allegiance. Beijing's presence in Djibouti marks the role China wishes to play in the Second Continent (Africa) and how serious it is about the same.

With the Aussies, China did not start on a positive note. In fact, the relations between Australia and China were strained for a considerable part of the 20th century. However, with the passage of time, China emerged as one of the most crucial trading partners of Australia and the proof of the same was the inking of the bilateral Free Trade Agreement (FTA) between the two on 17 June 2015. But before their FTA, it was China that helped Australia in avoiding the global recession of 2008. The tie-building exercise has not only been at a macro level but also at a micro level and this can been seen in the heavy influx of the Chinese students in the Australian universities. Studies show that out of every 10 students in Australian University, one comes from China and the Chinese constitute approximately 900,000 of the total population of Australia. However, the Chinese students are under a strict diktat not to participate in any anti-China demonstrations. Thus, the surveillance by the Orwellian Big Brother is a part and parcel of the lives of the Chinese students even when they are offshore. Yet another manner in which China has made itself crucial to Australia is through campaign donations. Given that Australian rules permit acceptance of donations from foreigners to fund the political campaigns, China has exploited that channel and emerged as a platinum donor of the largest political party of Australia in the 2017 elections. It was this loophole in its electoral process that made Canberra pass the anti-foreign intervention legislation in 2018 and strengthen the penal provisions for the foreign espionage offences which included declaration of activities by the people working for foreign donors in Australian politics.

With the Kiwis, China shares what is popularly known as the five firsts—first nation to concur to China's accession to World Trade Organisation (1997); first nation to acknowledge China as a market economy (2004); first nation to negotiate and sign a FTA with China (2008); first western nation to became a member of Asian Infrastructure Investment bank (2015); and first western nation to sign MOU on BRI (2017). Chinese students have also emerged as the largest group of international students studying in New Zealand's education institutions. However, China's underlying intentions of forging deep ties with New Zealand include influencing the political decision-making, keeping a track of the overseas Chinese communities and maintaining a strong ally in the Pacific. This was further corroborated when a Canada spy agency released a report in 2018. The report claimed that "New Zealand provides a vivid case study of China's willingness to use economic ties to interfere with the political life of a partner country."[42]

China had made no attempts to hide its intention of emerging as a supporter of conservative regimes across Asia and Africa. However, it now has a number of European countries on its radar. The Chinese have visibly entered into countries such as Poland, Portugal, Macedonia, etc. and through investments and trade partnerships; they have been indeed been welcomed as trading partners. For instance, over 25 per cent of Portugal's largest energy utility is now owned and controlled by China.

China came to the rescue of Portugal through massive investments when the latter was severely impacted by the economic meltdown of 2008. Since then, China has emerged as Portugal's eleventh largest trading partner. This relationship was further cemented when the Chinese FDI jumped from 0 to USD 6.6 billion in less than a decade. In 2011, China once again bailed Lisbon out when it was under the siege by the triptych European financial institutions.

Similar moves were made by China in relation to Greece where concessions were made for the Chinese-owned shipping group as well as for the acquisition of a majority stake in the power grid operator.[43] The overt economic aid came with a covert understanding to not indulge in 'China bashing' and a paid 'political interest' to China on two occasions. First, in July 2016, along with Hungary and Croatia, it blocked a strong statement by the European council to support the arbitrational award of the International Arbitration Court ruling on South China Sea. Second, in June 2017, Greece blocked EU statement denouncing China's human rights record ruling it as "unconstructive criticism of China".

In a paper titled 'Central Europe for Sale: The Politics of China's Influence', it is mentioned that "for the first time, Chinese assertiveness in international relations is met with open arms by leading Central European politicians who no longer regard it as a potentially troubling, undemocratic regime but as a full-fledged partner and even in Zeman's and Orbán's case, political inspiration."[44] Czech Republic's foray in the sphere of international relations and diplomacy began only in 1989 when it had emerged as a strong voice against the totalitarian regimes. While it never openly vilified China for its political system, Czech Republic displayed its loyalties when it openly supported the Dalai Lama. Upon it accession to the European Union, Czech Republic vociferously critiqued the relationship the regional trading bloc shared with the Dragon. However, with the global meltdown, Czech Republic's rigidity towards China too melted with the kind of business opportunities which China offered and by 2014, the narrative of Czech-China relations had completely changed. What began as a cold and distant relationship, dense with condescension of the Chinese political fabric and values had metamorphosed to a warm, affable, bilateral friendship spearheaded mainly by the Czech President Miloš Zeman whose pro-Chinese attitude is an outcome of the expansion in foreign trade and investment. In 2016, Xi Jinping became the first Chinese head of state to visit Prague, which resulted in a strategic partnership and was hailed in Prague as a sovereign autonomy from European restraint in action and thoughts. The ties have been cemented to such an extent that President Zeman has labelled Prague as the 'entry gate' for China into European Union. Czech Republic's strategic location made China position it as a key member of its ambitious BRI.

China is what China does and what China does is further its interest, making them 'appear' mutual with other countries. Economic investment and political engagement are mere tools to influence the regimes in other countries, their nature notwithstanding. Through its political agency known as the United Front Work Department, China has put to use the three magic weapons of Mao in order to tell the Party's version of "China's story: by encouraging overseas Chinese of all sorts to become active promoters of the Party-state's views in their own domiciles. This promotion includes using material from China in publications, forming associations to highlight positions on issues like Taiwan or more recently, the One Belt, One Road policy (BRI), meeting local politicians and winning them over, and using the status of voters in democracies to influence domestic policies in ways to promote CCP interests".[45] United Front Work Department is thus relevant to a number of foreign governments where a sizeable Chinese elite are present. The overwhelming role played by the organisation has made Xi add 40,000 cadres to its ranks, thus outranking the Party and the Propaganda Department.

Overseas Chinese

When one talks about the influence China yields, it is not just political or economic influence one refers to. Influence here has a much broader meaning which encompasses Chinese living outside China. Internal influence would imply indoctrination and control of the Chinese living within China. External influence implies relations which China has with other countries. But what about the Chinese diaspora? The answer to this question lies in the number of Chinese living outside China. There are about 15 million Chinese [46] who left the shores of the People's Republic of China since reforms. However, this diaspora has not been able to leave China completely because the Party sees it as a resource and a tool to build a positive image of China.

Chinese living outside China may not share any connection to China more than China being their country of origin, yet the Party promotes unity among them and tries to instil in them the love for their motherland. Organising community meetings, literary festivals and cultural activities to promote Chinese language and extol its rich historical past fosters unity among an otherwise fragmented Chinese diaspora and makes them a politically active and a cohesive group.

In order to positively influence the Chinese diaspora, the government has set up 'Overseas Chinese Affairs Office' which aim at incentivising repatriation of the Chinese citizens by offering them support, preferential treatment, business opportunities, etc. These incentives are coupled with 'birth right tours' to establish an emotional connect with their home country. The persistent efforts of the Chinese government have led to a massive increase in the repatriation rate. For instance, over 80 per cent of Chinese students who went abroad for higher education eventually returned to China. The entire purpose is to make China look attractive to the youth and keep them intoxicated on nationalistic sentiment and fervour. However, dissent even among the Chinese diaspora is frowned upon. Loyalty towards the Party cannot be compromised and if a Chinese student is found opposing any of the political moves and/or manoeuvres of the Party, he/she is intimidated by fellow Chinese.

Furthermore, if the university organises an event which is against Chinese sensibilities, the same is vehemently opposed. For the Chinese government, the student community[47] studying in universities aboard is an effective tool to communicate its interests. The Party does not lose the sight of the Chinese living and/or studying abroad and monitors their movements and activities to ensure that they do not participate in any anti-China activities or harbour or spread opinions which are not conducive to the image which China is trying to build. The Chinese Students and Scholars Associations[48] plays the dual role of being a cementing force along with being a spy. Their specific agenda is to observe public opinion and intervene in the event any anti-Party or anti-Beijing opinion develops.

The Party regards the Chinese diaspora as a major source of capital as well as a major technological and political influence. It has made attempts to tap into this resource to serve China's political interests and help in the country's development given that they understand the modalities of running a business in the country of their residence.

Even though China does not openly accept the role it plays in influencing and controlling the Chinese diaspora, its intentions are clear from the paraphernalia and the apparatus it has placed in other countries. Being a megalomaniac, it believes that by keeping a constant eye on the Chinese living abroad, it will be able to take over the process of image building and the construction of pro-China narrative.

MONEY CAN NOT BUY LOVE BUT INFLUENCE

The Open Door Policy of Deng Xiaoping laid the foundation of China's emergence as the growth engine of the world. Given the pace at which China has jumped on to the bandwagon of 'global economy', it is not surprising that there are very few countries in the world with which China does not have an economic relationship. For China, economic diplomacy has paved the way for a smoother political interaction and export of political influence. Therefore, China's strategy of using economics to settle political scores is not new. In fact, Beijing is known for behaving in an underhand manner when it comes to fulfilling its political and foreign policy objectives. It has been accused of imposing restrictions, manipulating regulations and erecting technical trade barriers in order to prevail its will. While it is not easy to pierce the veil of normalcy to unearth the reality behind trade relations and trade volumes between two countries, it is fairly easy to connect the dots when a heavy economic embargo usually follows a political standoff.

Japan was at the receiving end (September 2010) when China blocked its shipments of rare earth minerals owing to the increasing pollution levels. However, the timing of such a blockade was dangerously close to the detention of a Chinese fishing trawler by Japan. It is also not a coincidence that China continued to supply rare earth minerals to Hong Kong and Singapore. The experts saw this Chinese obstinacy as a retaliatory measure and not as a concern for the environment. China was not above using economic leverage to settle scores on the political front and that was the precise message the world received.

Norway was yet another nation which had to withstand the Chinese wrath thereby negatively impacting the export of salmon to China. The announcement of a Chinese dissident for the Nobel Peace Prize in 2010 was met with severe opposition. China not only boycotted the event but also sent warning signals to the diplomats of other nations as well. This led to at least 18 countries 'missing' the ceremony and threatened the Free Trade Agreement which China had with Norway.

Under the garb of health concerns and quality control, China rejected bananas from Philippines at the same time (2012) when the latter refused to withdraw from Scarborough Shoal. Philippines was made to suffer even more severely when China slowed down the inspection of perishable fruits exported by Philippines and imposed restrictions on tourism.

At an individual level, China penalises the corporations which do not submissively accept its stance and foreign policy positions. It never shies away from making countries, consumers and corporations[49] suffer due to the perceived or actual deviance. Beijing resorts to coercive measures, and given the size of the Chinese economy and share in the world trade, the coercive measures are usually economic in nature.

In the decade gone by, China has broadened its well-set economic toolkit in order to have a carrot and stick approach. Countries which have threatened its national interests such as foreign policy objectives on territorial issues have been cracked down in some measure by restricting trade or by slashing tourist quotas. In the coming decade, China will leverage its growing economic power as a strategic asset to influence and further reduce its appetite for dissent.

World's Favourite Moneylender

China understands the challenges which a country faces when it is grappling with political instability and/or economic crunch. Not too long ago, China was also a trying to find its ground after its 'Century of Humiliation' came to an end. Thus, China knows the trick of winning over a strife-laden, developing/ under-developed country through the instrumentality of debt.

Chinese has mastered the art of predatory lending and it is this facet of their foreign policy which has made China the world's favourite moneylender. Countries like Sri Lanka have taken loans to the tune of USD 15 billion in order to begin economic reconstruction after decades of political turmoil. China is not only a stakeholder in the Sri Lankan economy as a debtor but also as a facilitator of the development of the Sri Lankan infrastructure.[50] Sri Lanka, on the other hand, was forced to accept the presence of Chinese conglomerates on their soil and also permit the use of Hambantota port for strategic purposes. The terms of the loan agreements obliterate renegotiations and external checks and balances which have majorly hit the economic sovereignty of Sri Lanka.

In case of regional trading blocs like ASEAN, China has used its influence over Indo-China to ensure that the countries in that bloc do not put up a united front against any ASEAN resolution which opposes the Chinese claims in and over South China Sea. In order to buy proxy veto in ASEAN, China provide billions of dollars to Cambodia in aid.[51]

The strategy behind lending to a country is not always a political advantage in the present. On occasions, debt has been specifically offered keeping in mind an agreement or a future event. Lending to Papua New Guinea is one such instance where the Chinese are patiently waiting for the expiry of Compact of Free Association to gain inroads into the Pacific, thereby using it for a greater political gain in the future.

Most countries which are unable to repay Chinese debts are selling its stakes in the Chinese-financed projects and trying to exit the existing arrangements. However, these countries are in a debt trap and find themselves at a major disadvantage because a rescheduling in the existing contracts[52] will force them to award the construction and infrastructure contracts to Chinese companies thereby worsening their economic condition and allowing the Chinese to seek control of the assets.

While one may be tempted to assume that this exploitative form of lending by China is restricted to its Asian neighbours, the reality is that even the European Union is feeling the heat of this form of lending mechanism. China has been steadily increasing its economic[53] and the consequent political[54] presence in Europe by investing into the individual economies of the regional trading bloc. The investments are not restricted to infrastructure companies or technology giants, but also in sports teams. Powerful countries within EU are calling for measures which require China to be more open about its investments; economies which are neck deep in debt such as Greece and Portugal are trying their level best to prevent the same as they too have borrowed heavily from China and any strong measure from the EU would prove to be counter-productive for them.

China, through its systematic investments and economic aid, is trying to emerge as a global economic and political powerhouse with the definite objective of being one of the paramount voices in international affairs.

EDUCATION AND MASS MEDIA

Educating the World the Chinese Way

In its mission to control every form of storytelling and information sharing, the Chinese have left no stone unturned. From seizing control of the academia to establishing centres of Chinese language and culture, China has made its intention crystal clear—to install filters in every outlet and to use every bit of information and intelligence which comes its way. The expulsion of prominent Chinese-born American academic Professor Huang Jing[55] in August 2017 for being an 'agent' of China on the grounds that China was interfering with the domestic politics of Singapore is an unprecedented move which has brought to the fore the role of academia as a tool for furthering China's state objectives.

The Wilson Centre, in its report titled 'A Preliminary Study of PRC Political Influence and Interference Activities in American Higher Education, unravels the intent behind a 2016 Ministry of Education directive. It states that overseas students are seen as a population to be mobilised in support of their country and connected through organisations like the Chinese Students and Scholars Association (CSSA), party cells and consulates. Together with diplomats based at the embassy and consulates, overseas students are expected to superimpose their narrative over those of Tibetans, Taiwanese, Mongolians, etc.[56]

Yet another manifestation of the Party's intention is establishing Confucius centres of learning which overtly aim at spreading the Chinese language and culture thereby building a favourable image of China but covertly trying to further Chinese thought and ideological fabric. State-sponsored centres had a definite aim of promoting the propaganda of the Party with a strong support for censorship practices. The establishment of these institutes was a strategy to make the presence of China felt amongst the student community along with keeping an eye on the campus activities.

The rate at which Confucius centres have mushroomed is unbelievable. In over a decade and a half, the centres have outnumbered the aggregate of the total number of students serviced by Spain's Instituto Cervantes, France's Alliance Francaise and UK's British Council. "The enthusiasm for the Confucius phenomenon can be gauged from the fact that there are 525 Confucius Institutes and 1,113 Confucius Classrooms in 147 countries and regions, offering 410,000 language courses to two million people."[57] Additionally, the Confucius Network became popular because of its generous funding, free course materials and even trained teachers and instructors provided by the Chinese government.

The Confucius centres were projected as a tool to facilitate learning and exchange between people belonging to different cultures, races, regions, etc. However, the reality of these centres was unmasked when they began to interfere and influence the academic environment of the host countries. Values of freedom of speech, freedom of expression, freedom of thought, critical thinking and freedom of questioning the answers were targeted in a subtle manner so as to discourage dialogue and codes of democratic behaviour. They were allegedly the eyes and ears of the Chinese government to monitor the activities of the Chinese students. At the same time, these centres indulged in active image building sans the taint of Tiananmen Square, Dalai Lama, Taiwan independence, etc. and garnered support for the Chinese model of economic control and development and its emergence as a growth engine. The idea behind these centres was to reduce them to a mouthpiece for the Party to reach out to the student community at large. When the true nature of these centres was unravelled, the Chinese were at the receiving end of a huge backlash for manipulating the thought process of the future leaders and for spying on the host countries. However, this has not stopped China from rising as an international hub for the pursuit of higher education. With courses and scholarships being offered to students of specific countries, it is clear that

China wants to appear as one-stop solution for the international student community.

Speak No Evil

Back in 2006, Freedom House released a report titled 'Speak No Evil: Mass Media Control in Contemporary China' in which it had stated, "The CCP exerts near complete control over the country's 358 television stations and 2,119 newspapers—the primary media available to more than one billion Chinese citizens."

Touted as the 'fourth pillar' of a free and democratic world, mass media has grown in both strength and impact and China is acutely aware of what might transpire if this fourth pillar is unleashed. Therefore, to keep a check on the content and the manner in which the same needs to be conveyed, China has ensured that it holds media with a firm gauntlet. Manipulating mass media in all its forms to give rise to a partisan, favourable public opinion is an open secret in China. Media platforms serve Chinese propaganda on a platter and the laws allow themselves to be interpreted in the most whimsical manner. Furthermore, the Party has been using multiple tools to generate and conflagrate an opinion which places it in a positive light. The extent of influencing the public opinion is not limited to the borders of China. In doing so, it uses multiple channels and vehicles to not only engage in right messaging and a positive image building, but also erasing negative opinions which can have a damning impact on the Party.

In order to fulfil its stated objectives, the Party uses state-owned and state-operated media houses such as the Xinhua News Agency, China Central Television Network, and China Radio International. These media houses do not have the liberty to spread news in a manner they deem fit. The information that is passed through them, the text and the context of that information and the news which is covered is first filtered by the Party. The news is spread in multiple languages such that no one is deprived of it and that it reaches the nooks and corners of the country. The vocabulary used is simple yet powerful to ensure that the message of the Party reaches the foreign audience without diluting its impact.

The media companies and houses also partners with the local outlets to tap into foreign media and funnel Chinese content through them. These partnerships are entered into for specific purposes and therefore are meant only to spread the messages of the Party to further enhance its image.

The Party also gives a verisimilitude of encouraging journalists who are not familiar with China to write about China. These journalists, who are told about China by the Party in training programmes organised by the Party, are hoodwinked into believing what is being projected. Scholars have often written about China keeping in mind its strict censorships laws and have therefore, compromised on their intellectual honesty. If they are found criticising China or writing anything which is even remotely hurtful to the Chinese interests, China can deny them their visas..

On 31 December 2016, CCTV (China Central Television) was launched in a new avatar as China Global Television Network (CGTN). CGTN is a group of six international television channels, a video contact provider and array of facilities of social media which operates on a multi-language (English, Spanish, French, Arabic, Russian) platform. China Radio International (CRI), which is a part of China Media, has a global presence with 80 radio stations in forty countries and broadcasts in 65 languages. In order to 'sell' the Chinese perspective of international news, CGTN, China Daily, China Media Group and Xinhua News have also entered into partnerships with foreign media houses via stake holding or financial support.

The global clout of China over print media can be judged from the last-minute cancellation in November 2017 of the book *Silent Invasion* authored by Clive Hamilton about the burgeoning influence of CCP in Australian politics by the publisher Allen and Unwin. The publishers cancelled the publication "after legal advice that they could be sued for defamation by the Chinese government".[58] Similarly in October 2017, one of the world's leading academic publishers, Germany-based Springer Nature had to block access to over one thousand articles containing sensitive keywords like 'Taiwan', 'Tibet' and 'Cultural Revolution' from its website.[59]

As China grows in power, its attempts at curbing free speech are rapidly increasing. It does not believe in creating a democratic atmosphere for the news agencies and therefore, it refused Al Jazeera English (2012) to work in China and did not grant permission to a CNN crew to interview Tibetans in rural Nepal (2012). When a Hong Kong-based investment group became a majority shareholder in Forbes Media (2014), it was certain that the days of free reporting by Forbes are over.

China controls what goes in print and what is uttered in speech. By doing so, it believes that it is able to protect its image and since the control of the purse and the narrative is in its hands, it can use media the way it fancies.

A PANDA ON MY VERANDA[60]

"There's a panda on my veranda, it's been there most of the night, I don't think I would have believed it, but it's there in black and white." China is behaving "just as other rising powers have behaved in history: it is laying down new markers, drawing new lines in the land, air, water, sand and snow all around its periphery, seeking to expand its territorial and maritime frontiers, forming and reforming institutions, and coercing others to fall in line."[61] The panda paw marks are everywhere—be it the Arctic, Small Island Developing States (SIDS) or Eurasian land mass.

Arctic Policy of China: In Uncharted Maritime Space

The water encircling the North Pole has for thousands of years remained ice-bound, but fuelled by climate change, the northern ice cap is rapidly shrinking, ushering in an arena of growing competition along the Northern Sea Route (NSR).[62] The unchartered maritime space along the NSR is now navigable for two–four months in a year and is likely to become navigable year around by 2030. The warming of Arctic could not only unravel the colossal hydrocarbon reserves that lie beneath the Arctic but also change global shipping lanes and the resultant trade flow. Although over a dozen countries stake claim to the Arctic and the NSR, it is Russia which is spending billions since 2013 in a bid for dominating[63] the NSR and the regions. China, despite its geographic distance, has hastened activities in the Arctic and is promoting itself as a "Near Arctic State". Historically, Chinese interests in the Arctic are indicated by the following: a research station on the Norwegian archipelago of Svalbard since the 1990s; Observers status on the Arctic council since 2013; biggest foreign investor in Russia's Arctic liquefied natural gas projects (Yamal LNG[64]: 16.5 million tons of natural gas by 2019); and a white paper published by China on 26 January 2018 on Arctic Policy that linked the NSR to the BRI calling it the "Polar Silk Road".[65] The Polar Silk Road white paper proposes China's resolve to accelerate activities in the Arctic by seizing the 'historic opportunity' but remains obscure about its security interests in the region.

The paper advocates transforming the Arctic's governance from regional to global[66] which, if formalised, would diminish the influence of the Arctic states and bestow non-Arctic states a louder voice. Finally, the paper attempts to elicit distinction between the sovereign rights of Arctic states and rights of non-Arctic states under UNCLOS regarding resource extraction and fishing in the Arctic by emphasising that the UNCLOS has jurisprudence to high seas and international seabed while the Arctic is a common heritage of humankind.

China's economic footprints in the Russian Arctic involve rejuvenation of sea ports. The Russian Ports for which the Chinese investors have expressed interest are—Murmansk, as a transhipment hub for NSR and Arkhangelsk, on the Northern Dvina River, as a greenhorn project.

In the Nordic Arctic, "Finland and Norway have also proposed the Arctic Corridor[67] that will connect the city of Rovaniemi in North Finland with the Norwegian port of Kirkenes, to further strengthen the international utilization of the Northern Sea Route (NSR). The program includes the rebuilding of the Kirkenes deep-water port and the construction of a railway, a logistic hub in Rovaniemi and an air logistic Hub in Helsinki that is linked to the Baltic Tunnel. Once completed, ships can dock at Kirkenes, where cargoes are loaded to the railway and sent southward through rail connections in Helsinki, and then through the proposed Helsinki-Tallinn tunnel to central Europe. To China, the Arctic Corridor presents an extraordinary opportunity for cooperation under the Polar Silk Route (PSR) framework. Chinese companies have received invitation to discuss the possibility of getting involved in these projects, and a brochure in Chinese has been prepared for the same."[68] Moreover, in the Nordic Arctic, China is collaborating with Finland, Norway and Russia to construct a 10,500 km fibre-optic cable link across the Arctic Circle.

In the upcoming competition to gain control of the future independent state—Greenland—China intends to hold the first place. The Greenland government in search of investors to finance the development met Export-Import Bank of China (EXIM), China Communications Construction Co (CCCC), and Construction Engineering Group (BCEG) in 2017[69]. In March 2018, the Greenlandic public enterprise Kalaallit Airports, responsible for the construction and operation of three new airports, announced that it had selected the CCCC as one of six preselected companies and consortiums[70] despite the official disapproval of Denmark who had said that it would readily provide cash in an attempt to avoid this potential Chinese influence on Greenland[71].

To recover after the severe economic crisis of 2008, Iceland could only welcome the advances of a commercial actor like China, especially in the uncertain context of its economic relations with the EU. The economic rapprochement was concretised by the signing of a Free Trade Agreement (FTA) in 2013, a first between a European State and China, which involved a three-year currency swap agreement between Chinese and Icelandic central banks, worth ¥3.5 billion ($507 million)[72]. Cooperation in renewable energy (geothermal) and polar sciences was also undertaken. Today, Icelandic geothermal know-how is being used in 40 cities in China[73]. Planned port projects in the Northeast of Iceland, both in Finnafjordur and Dysnes, have been attracting potential Chinese investors. This economic rapprochement of China and Iceland has been reflected in terms of regional geopolitics. In 2013, at the Arctic Circle conference, former President of Iceland, Olafur Ragnar Grímsson, played a major role in China's admission to the Arctic Council as an observer member in spite of the European Union opposing it.

Overall, the influence of China in the Arctic is characterised by a gradual and calculated transition from the scientific to the political, ultimately leading to the construction of legitimacy within polar States.

Small Nations and Small Islands Developing States (SIDS)

China, in its rapid push to economic and political influence across the globe, has targeted Small Nations, and Small Islands Developing States (SIDS). Small Nations and SIDS, being the weaker partners in an asymmetric relationship with China, are offered concessional loans to fund their much needed infrastructure projects. If these countries are unable to repay the loan, China could demand concessions in return for debt relief.

Nepal

Nepal is a nascent democracy with its associated weaknesses and insecurities. With the Nepali populace now aspiring for rapid development, China, with its economic might and its strategic geopolitical aspirations has stepped in to woo and lure Nepal. Over the last few years, through developmental interventions as well as diplomatic engagements, China has assumed importance in Nepal's foreign policy. China's engagements with Nepal are multifaceted and spread in all domains, including economics, people-to-people relations, defence, and security.

"The recent flurry of infrastructure building in Nepal signifies the amalgamation of two ambitious plans—Nepal's state building through technological advancement and China's massive 'Belt and Road Initiative' (BRI). Highways to facilitate physical connectivity across the China-Nepal border have resulted in re-routing of earlier trade passages. Following the 2015 Nepal earthquake, building, re-building, re-opening border points and re-routing of trans-Himalaya trade routes have become the main points of convergence for the two countries."[74] Major road projects wherein Chinese enterprises are involved are—reconstruction of the Friendship (Araniko) Highway[75], construction of the Kimathanka–Khandbari–Dhankuta[76] road, repair of Syafrubensi–Rasuwagadi[77] road, construction of the bridge connecting Yari (Nepal)–Pulan (TAR),[78] and the construction of the Kathmandu Ring Road (KRR)[79] project.

As a landlocked country, Nepal seeks to diversify its strategic economic dependencies. Nepal had been looking for third country transit trade options via China. On 28 April 2019, China and Nepal have signed a protocol to operationalise their 2016 Transit and Transport Agreement (TTA) which will enable the landlocked Himalayan country to access "Chinese Sea Ports of Tianjin, Shenzhen, Lianyungang and Zhanjiang; three land ports in Lanzhou, Lhasa and Shigatse"[80] and allow Nepal to carry out exports through six dedicated transit points for its foreign trade, ending Nepal's dependence on India for goods and trade. China and Nepal have agreed to extend the Qinghai Tibet Railway (QTR) in China from Keyrong (TAR) to Nepal. In the BRF 19 held in Beijing from 25–27 April 2019, "The Nepal-China Trans-Himalayan Multi-Dimensional Connectivity Network, including Nepal-China cross-border railway"[81] has been listed as one of the 35 corridors to be laid by China under the BRI format.

China is also supporting the capacity building of the aviation sector in Nepal. China has supplied six aircrafts to Nepal Airlines Corporation (NAC).[82] China is involved in the construction two major airports in Nepal. China's CAMC Engineering is constructing the Pokhara Regional International Airport (PRIA).[83] The construction of the Gautam Buddha International Airport[84] at Bhairawaha (Lumbini Zone) is also be done by Chinese Company. Nepal and China have also agreed to construct dry ports at six border points.[85]

In the energy sector, China is actively assisting Nepal in the construction of a number of hydropower projects. Some of the major hydropower projects in Nepal wherein Chinese enterprises are involved in construction are—Upper Trishuli 3A, Chameliya A, Kulekani-3, Upper Tamakoshi, 750 MW West Seti, Upper Marshyandi and Kabeli-A. China was also given the contract for construction of the 1200 MW Budhigandaki hydropower project which was subsequently scrapped. Nepal is now connected by Internet through China after the operationalisation of an OFC line via Rasuwagadhi in 2017.[86] Moreover, a large number of China Study Centers (CSC) have sprouted in Nepal to promote the Chinese culture.

China has been offering various military training courses to Nepal Army, Nepal Police and Nepal Armed Police Force of Nepal.[87] China has pledged a sum of ¥200 million (approximately $ 29 million) towards the capacity building of Nepal Army in March 2017.[88] China is likely to "provide heavy equipment and other logistics for the Nepal Army on United Nations peacekeeping missions as well as for disaster management".[89] China has constructed the Nepal Armed Police Force Training School which was handed over in 2017.[90] China's PLA Army and Nepal Army conducted their first Joint Counter Terrorism Military Exercise 'Sagarmatha Friendship 2017'[91] in April 2017.

Panama

In June 2017, Panama abruptly ended its ties with Taiwan and established full diplomatic relations with China. The decision not only caught the US flat-footed, but has been a massive coup for China as the few countries that recognise Taiwan are in the Latin America and the Caribbean (LAC). This strategic action of Panama has had major impact in the region as a few months later, Dominican Republic also established diplomatic ties with China.

China is not new to the region and is already the second-largest user of the Panama Canal having a share of nearly 20 per cent of total cargo flow, and in the free port of Panama, 'Colon trade zone', China accounted for 35 per cent of imports ($3 billion) in 2017. Panama may be a small country with an area 75,417 sq km and population of four million people but it has a strategic importance due to its canal linking the Atlantic and Pacific oceans making it one of the world's busiest International Sea Lanes (ISL). Panama's developing economy and political soundness make it fit to be a transshipment and logistic nerve centre to broaden China's trade in LAC.

The diplomatic shift in June 2017 was preceded by 41 agreements being signed in September–November 2017, and the state visit of President Juan Caicos Varela in November 2017 to China. "Through these agreements, Panama obtained most favored nation trade status and 'approved destination' status. In addition, China committed to finance a feasibility study on a high speed railroad between Panama City and Costa Rica."[92]

Xi's visit in early December 2018 lead to another 19 new agreements being signed although the announcement of bilateral FTA was delayed. China already has three FTAs in place in the LAC—with Chile, Peru, and Costa Rica—all singed during the period of Hu Jinto. The pace of activities over the past two years points toward the single-minded purpose of Panama to close an FTA with China at the earliest.

Although on the face of it, China's clout in Latin America and Caribbean is economic and it is growing by the day, China is on the heels of catching up with US as the leading trading partner of nearly all leading economics in LAC. The Latin America exports mainly commodities (69 per cent) to China which includes such as soybeans, iron ore, copper and crude oil.[93] The increased importance given to a relationship with LAC has become readily apparent in the era of Xi Jinping who has visited 12 LAC countries in his first five years (2013–2017).[94]

Small Islands Developing States (SIDS)

The creation of several overseas bases of strategic influence is closely tied to China's growing maritime capabilities which are significant for the expansion of its strategic space. The mechanism of entrenchment in the maritime domain has been far more calibrated. Targeting leaderships and economic vulnerabilities of island states, China has effectively deployed its economic levers of loans, grants, creation of logistics infrastructure such as roads, ports, transshipment hubs, airfields, etc. to buy acquiescence of countries and shape their policies in advancement of its strategic objectives.

Djibouti

"In 2008, China began naval-escort missions in the Gulf of Aden, following a series of UN Security Council resolutions authorizing countries to conduct counter-piracy operations in the area. In the ten-year period from 2008, China dispatched 30 naval-escort taskforces to the region, at a steady rate of three a year."[95] The naval escort mission was a good enough reason for China to call for the need of a logistic base to replenish its forces operating in the area. Djibouti, on the northeast coast of the Horn of Africa and along the Bab-el-Mandeb Strait, provides a gateway to Suez Canal. This strategic chokepoint is also in demand with other foreign forces operating from Djibouti. "Camp Lemonnier is the forward operating base of US Africa Command, and America's only full-fledged naval base on the African continent."[96] The North Atlantic Treaty Organization, the European Union, the Japanese, and the Italians have also leased land around Camp Lemonnier.

Initially when China began its base construction at Djibouti, the base was called 'an overseas logistical supply facility' which was subsequently changed to 'supply base'. Beijing has never called the base a 'military base' because of its state ideology of non-interference into sovereign matters of other states. As peace keeping missions mandate come with consent of the host country and licitness of the Security Council, they provide the *locus sigilli* for the overseas base.

Following the opening of the base, China has strengthened its hold by providing generous financing for the Doraleh Multipurpose Port project and Hassan Gouled Aptidon International airport. The Chinese base and the extensive financing for infrastructure projects have drawn the Djibouti government into the sphere of China's influence.

Why should China be singled out if it has developed an overseas military base and judged at variance from other powers with overseas bases not only in Djibouti but also all over the world? The issue is not about construction of overseas bases but the hidden agenda approach adopted by China to achieve the same, that is, the use of the UN mandates and debt, which invites suspicion.

São Tomé and Príncipe

São Tomé and Príncipe is a small island nation located in Central Africa (Gulf of Guinea). China's diplomatic relationship with the island nation was established in April 2017. Subsequently in January 2018, China "... pledged to provide the archipelago with $146 million for the modernization of its international airport and construction of a deep sea contained port, which could serve as a logistic hub for Chinese exports to Central Africa."[97]

If China were to develop the deep sea part at São Tomé and Príncipe into a naval base, China would have presence both in the east (Djibouti) and west of the African continent, as a result of which it would be "able to deploy its fleet and troop to safeguard trade route."[98]

Maldives

Maldives was identified in 2015 as one of the 18 locations where China would build ports within a decade.[99] Maldives is of great strategic significance for China. Firstly, the southernmost atoll of Maldives (Addu Atoll) lies 619 km directly North of Diego Garcia which is central to US power projection in the Indian Ocean and houses one-third of US Afloat Prepositioning Force. A base in Maldives will provide China the capability to closely and directly monitor US and Indian military activities and also increase its reach and readiness to respond to contingencies. Secondly, all east-bound shipping from the Red Sea and the oil cargo from the Persian Gulf, whether transiting through the Malacca, Sunda, Lombok or Ombai Wetar Straits, converges in a funnel between the Eight and Nine Degree and Equatorial Channels straddled by India's Lakshadweep and Maldives' island chains giving them strategic control over the International Shipping Lanes (ISL). A base in Maldives would also provide China the ability to monitor ships that are eastward bound from Cape of Good Hope to Australia, South China Sea and Pacific Oceans. Thirdly, nearly all shipping routes from China pass within close proximity of Maldives which could provide China a valuable pit stop as also a transhipment hub in furtherance of its mercantile commerce, and other strategic objectives.

China expanded its engagement rapidly from almost nil in 2004 to covering a large canvas today, ranging from defence, infrastructure, tourism, education, health, and culture. Xi Jinping visited Maldives[100] during 14–16 September 2014 which led to signing of nine agreements in infrastructure development maritime and health sectors. Later in 2017, during President Yameen's visit to China,[101] another set of 12 agreements[102] were finalised including a Free Trade Agreement (FTA). China has invested heavily in infrastructure development in Maldives.[103] Some of the prominent ones are China-Maldives Friendship Bridge connecting Male to Hulhule, a 14.2 km road project in Laamu Atoll, the Hulhumale Airport development, housing projects on number of islands as well as the development of a number of tourist resort. In April 2015, both countries signed a five-year defence agreement[104] under which China will provide military assistance worth $4.2 million on gratis basis to Maldives. As of 2017, China is Maldives biggest trading partner with the total trade growing from $16.6 million in 2005 to $172.6 million in 2015. Tourism is the main industry of Maldives and China is the biggest contributor in this industry.[105] Since 2011, China accounted for over 29.1 per cent of the total 1.2 million tourists. China's investments in Maldives are estimated at around $2.77 billion which is equal to around 77.15 per cent of the GDP ($3.59 billion, 2018) of Maldives.

On 23 September 2018, President Yameen was defeated by Ibrahim Solih in the presidential elections. In the Majlis (legislative body with 87 seats) election held on 06 April 2019, the Maldivian Democratic Party (MDP) led by Mohamed Nasheed and President Ibrahim Solih secured 65 seats as compared to the coalition[106] which was able to secure only 13 seats. The change of government followed by President Ibrahim Solih's party winning the Majlis elections could bring a paradigm shift in China-Maldives relations. The new government has already repealed the controversial foreign free hold amendment and the Free Trade Agreement signed with China has also been put on hold. However, given the huge economic dependency of Maldives, and the fear of alienating China, it is unlikely that a complete reversal of engagement would take place. Most of the projects initiated under the previous regime are likely to continue.

Pacific Islands Countries

The Pacific Ocean (63.6 million sq miles) is the world biggest ocean occupying nearly one third of the Earth's surface. The Pacific Ocean is dotted with 14 independent, freely associated, and dependent states which constitute the Pacific Island countries. The Pacific Island countries can be divided into three ethno-geographic sub regions—Micronesia, Melanesia and Polynesia. The Pacific Island countries occupy a total landmass of 1.85 million square miles but their Exclusive Economic Zone (EEZ) of 7.7 million sq miles is over four times their landmass. "The Pacific Island countries may be small island countries but are large ocean nations."[107]

The region's vast maritime expanses have long been controlled by the US Navy whose base in Guam is central to its ability to project power in the western Pacific. China's growing influence in the Pacific Islands is a consequence of its economic influence. Especially when implemented as an expression of

South–South cooperation, that influence is establishing a high level of bonding, awe and reverence for China in the region. Irrespective of cause and effect, China enjoys extensive influence across the region and that is affecting the relations that the Island countries have with their traditional friends. Although China is challenging the western power in other parts of the world, the calculations are different in the Pacific due to the special characteristics of the region—small size, remote, geographically dispersed, limited resources, and narrow economies. Here relatively small investments allow China to gain influence over a number of governments in the region. China could then access or even control vast waters of vital strategic importance.

Melanesia

Melanesia is an ethno-geographical sub-region of Pacific Island countries which are located in an arc north and east of Australia and south of the equator. The sub-region has four independent countries—Papua New Guinea, Fiji, The Republic of Vanuatu, and Solomon Islands, French holdings (New Caledonia) and Australian holdings. Historically, during World War II Melanesia was a ground of island hopping campaign between Allies and Japan. Today, the strategic relevance of Melanesia is that it overlaps with the 'Second Island Chain' which extends from the Ogasawara Islands and Volcano Islands of South Japan through US territory of Northern Mariana Islands in Micronesia up to Papua New Guinea.

Papua New Guinea (PNG): PNG is the sub-region's biggest country and its economy is dependent on the resource sector—petroleum, gas and mining. Its medium-term outlook is optimistic provided the large-scale resource projects take off. In the recent years, China has significantly expanded its political influence, economic footprint and military relations with PNG.

A few signs of growing political influence are:

- PNG, prior to Hague arbitral award over South China Sea with Philippines in July 2016, expressed its support to China's position.
- PNG Prime Minister Peter O'Neil has visited China 12 times since 2011, including his visit in July 2016 seeking influence to back PNG's desire to host the APEC in 2018.
- PNG became the first country in the Pacific Islands to sign the BRI as well as a member of Asia Infrastructure Investment Bank.

- In the APEC summit in 2018 held in PNG, no joint statement was issued as China objected to the clause—"we agree to fight protectionism including all unfair trade practices."

Following are the indicators of an expanding Chinese economic footprint in PNG:

- China is the top importer of PNG's mineral and hydrocarbon.
- In 2012–2018, China heavily invested in infrastructure projects worth $ 4.78 billion.
- China holds over a quarter of PNG's external debt.
- Huawei was chosen to lay the 3,390 miles underwater cable in spite of better offers from Australia.

In the military domain PNG, signed a military cooperation agreement in July 2018.

Fiji: After a military coup in Fiji in December 2006 when it was isolated by the West, China used the opportunity to not only maintain a position of political support, but it also enhanced its economic engagement. "Between 2011 and 2018, China committed $340 million in aid to Fiji and over delivered—doling out 340% of that amount across forty two projects. Today, Beijing holds $249.2 million of the country's external debt, about 37% of the total."[108]

Vanuatu: In 2017, China's Shanghai Construction Company renovated the Loganville Wharf (360m) in Espiritu Santo Island which was the largest military base in the Pacific during World War II. Although the renovation is intended to give a boost to the island's tourism industry and economy by permitting larger cruise ships and cargo ships to berth at the Wharf, reports from Fair Fax media in April 2018 reported that China had discussed a permanent military base on Espiritu Santo. However, the idea of making a military base was rejected by Vanuatu. China is undertaking a large number of infrastructural projects in Vanuatu—upgradation of International Airport, construction of Prime Minister's Office, government complexes and a stadium. The influence of China over Vanuatu can be judged from the fact that on 9 July 2019, Chinese police was allowed to enter Vanuatu and extract six Chinese nationals who were criminal suspects without facing a local court.

Micronesia

The Micronesia arc of islands is located north of the equator and east of Philippines. The arc is formed by US territories (Guam and Common Wealth of North Mariana Island [CNMI] in the west), and Compact of Free Agreement (COFA) states—Marshal Islands in the east and Palau and Federated States of Micronesia in the south. The Compacts of Free Association (COFA) agreements gives these microstates subsidies and visa-free US residence for their citizens in exchange for the right to base its troops on their territory and block other countries from doing so. The compact helps create a security zone that guards US interests in the Pacific. If compact were to slip into the Chinese influence it could put the US territories, especially Guam, in jeopardy.

In recent years there have been concerns that COFA as an agreement was likely to lapse or get abrogated by member nations due to perceived US inaction and the increasing influence of China. However, the same seems unlikely now with the US congress extending the necessary agreement for Palau till 2044. In all likelihood, it would extend the same for Marshall Islands and Federated States of Micronesia before it lapses in 2023.

Polynesia

In the eastern Pacific, Polynesia is bounded within an isosceles equilateral triangle with Tonga to south, French Polynesia to the east and Hawaiian islands to the north. The area bounded by Polynesia is huge due to the wide dispersion of the island. The other islands countries in the sub-region west to east are Tuvalu, Samoa, Tokelau, Kiribati, and Cook Island.

Over the last few years Chinese strategic activities in Polynesia have increased briskly to fill the void by the diminished US and French influence. Although the Polynesian leaders still maintain their special relationship with traditional partners, they are not hesitant in expanding their relations with China. It is accepted by most Polynesian leaders that China would be a leading power in the next few years.

"In Tonga, Chinese money has left the country dependent on Beijing. Under a scheme currently contested in Tongan courts, China Electronic Systems Engineering (CESEC), a company linked to the PLA, paid Tongasat, a company controlled by Pilolevu, Tonga's Princess Royal, US$ 50m in 2008 for parking a satellite in the Polynesian kingdom's skies. The bulk of the funds, half of which should have gone into the national budget, went to the company, according to Tongan court documents. Tonga borrowed $114m between 2008 and 2010 from Beijing. Its debt to China is now equivalent to 43 per cent of the country's gross domestic product. Beijing's engagement in Tonga is highly strategic due to China's Beidou system satellite slots for missile guidance and command and control."[109]

In French Polynesia, China has increased its investment. In Hao Island, a project to export live fish to China has resulted in a major investment by the Tianrui Group in Tahiti Nui Ocean Foods.

Eurasian Landmass: Pivot of Influence

Halford J Mackinder in 1904 in his article 'The Geographical Pivot of History' and later in 1919 in his book *Democratic Ideals and Reality: A Study in the Politics of Reconstruction* propounded the 'Heartland Theory' and the importance of Eurasian landmass. Mackinder, while explaining the influence which would have come from controlling or commanding the Heartland, used the maxim "who rules East Europe Commands the Heartland; who rules the Heartland Commands the World-Island; who rules the world Island Commands the world."[110] In the BRI too the land component is Mackinder's Heartland. This now Chinese 'Heartland', aims to forge a new blueprint of influence over the Eurasian continental landmass by containing the Russian influence in Central Asia and East Europe, providing alternative routes for trade and strategic supplies, and enabling development of China's western region.

Although China and Russia may be contesting for a sphere of influence and assets in the shared Eurasian landmass, they have metamorphosed their relationship from being competitors to partners to contain the West. On the economic front, Russia has enhanced its engagement with China which have enabled it to overcome the western sanctions over Ukraine. China has made major infrastructural investments in Russian Far East, and Chinese companies have in turn gained technological know-how by working in sectors such as exploration, extraction, refinery and transportation of petroleum, natural gas and petroleum products. China is also keen to gain access to Russian Arctic's huge economic largess and augment its technological ability by partnering with Russia. In Central Asia, China is coming forth as a dominant player and in BRI-19, President Vladimir Putin fully endorsed the BRI and suggested the merger of the Eurasian Economic Union with the BRI. In the domain of military activities, sale of the latest version of S-400 missile defence system, SU-34 Jet Fighter, and joint exercise in the form of Vostok-2018 are pointers towards their increased bilateral engagement. Today China due to its economic clout clearly holds the role of the dominant power in the relationship and it is this increasing power which it is using to gain influence over the Heartland.

EMBOLDENED INFLUENCE: 3Ws

In the history of humanity, wars have involved the use of military and kinetic energy weapons. In the cyber age, military and kinetic energy weapons are still powerful deterrents but are no longer enough and need to be supplemented by controlling the narrative, both during peace and wartime. The Chinese control the narrative by the application of Emboldened Influence (3Ws)—public opinion warfare, psychological warfare, and legal warfare. The aim of the three warfares is "intended to control the prevailing narrative and influence perceptions in a way that advances China's national interest, while compromising the capability of opponents to respond."[111]

In the overall context, the idea of 3Ws aims to expand conflict from military domain to political domain by "building a story to create conditions for a resolution of conflict on favourable terms to China without resorting to physical war."[112]

Public opinion warfare aims to "tell China's stories well" and spread its voice far and wide. China uses its state owned media to mould public opinion and promote the ideological aspiration of CCP both domestically and internationally. In 2009, the international media expansion campaign was launched by Hu Jintao with a commitments of over $9.3 billion which involved rebranding the international television channels to CGTN, opening of new bureaus in Washington, Nairobi and London, following the Chinese saying of 'borrowing the boat to get to the sea' by buying up broadcast space on foreign radios, commercial content sharing agreements with foreign local newspapers and manipulating social media by hired commentators who 'manufacture consent'.

Psychological warfare believes that the bona fide target in any conflict is the understanding or intellectual ability of the hostile decision-maker and its domestic audience. Psychological warfare is not something new and in all probability historical, soldiers banked on barbarity for terrifying their enemies by their intense looks or dreadful behaviour. Today with the complex intertwined nature of politics and economics, the agents of psychological warfare operations, such as technology and economic statecraft, ensure that their reach resonates globally resulting in rapid shifting of theme leading to 'dynamic narrative shaping' and blurring its application in peacetime and wartime, and between military and the civilians. The ancient Chinese psychological warfare is rooted in *Art of War* and the *Thirty Six Stratagems*. In today's context (that is, 1949 onwards), if we were take the a typology of Chinese psychological warfare tasks, five broad ones emerge—first, muster (physically and mentally) popular support to justify one's cause; second, project China's invincibility as a nation because of its military might, advances made in science and technology, and its economic capacity; third, weaken the opposition's determination for any confrontation; fourth, promote contention in the enemy's sentiments and opinions causing disunity, division and animosity; and finally, enforce psychological defence to annul or subdue enemy's counter psychological liveliness. The Chinese scope and sphere of psychological warfare has broadened and could involve different dimensions of narrative-shaping such as imposing of import tariffs on bananas with Philippines after the 2012 Scarborough Shoal standoff or threat to sell the US debt holdings.

China approaches the legal warfare (lawfare) as an offensive tool capable of controlling or constraining the opponent through law. Lawfare involves adopting domestic and international legal customs, conventions and agreements to seize the political initiative by projecting China as an aggrieved party. The target whose perceptions are the main focus in 3Ws are—first, China's domestic populace to fortify the party's licitness to rule; second, global public in order to promote the Chinese story; and finally, the rival claimants to continuously alter facts and figures in China's favour.

Beijing's response to the South China Sea arbitration outcome "sought to delegitimize the arbitration process and achieved some success in undermining the coalescence of consensus in support of the ruling, while engaging in coercive signaling and deniable attempts to punish the Philippines".[113] China's comeback has included cyberattacks against the Philippine government websites, formalising the "combat readiness patrol" in the South China Sea by H-6K bombers and promoting the narrative that the US is responsible for imbuing the militarism in the South China Sea.

In the case of Arunachal Pradesh, which is a part of India, China asserts on ascribing it as "South Tibet" in all its official articulation. "The Ministry of Civil Affairs of China issued a so-called 'notification' on its website on 13 April

2017 assigning names to six small towns in the state of Arunachal Pradesh."[114] Chinese Foreign Ministry spokesperson Lu Kang, pronounced that the names echoed, "China's territorial claim over South Tibet is supported by clear evidence in terms of history, culture and administration."[115] Moreover, China has always shown dissent for any diplomatic visit to Arunachal Pradesh. It lodged a protest when Dalai Lama visited Tawang Monastery and Indian Prime Minister Narendra Modi visited Arunachal Pradesh on 2 April 2019.

During the Doklam incident against India, the 3Ws were an indispensable constituent of China's strategic and operational approach. China's reaction and the rollout of the 3Ws began primarily focussed on three aspects—China is a just power; India is the hegemon who has violated China's sovereignty; Doklam is Chinese territory from times immemorial and China has a legally binding treaty (The Convention of 1890) to justify the fact. The aspects were immediately lapped on by the Chinese media along with Global Times[116] on 26 June 2017 and the People's Daily[117] on 27 June 2017 which publishing news on the same themes. The editorial page of Global Times on 27 July 2017 mentioned that the Indian External Affairs Minister, Mrs Sushma Swaraj lied to the Indian Parliament and said that in case India does not pull back its troops, they will face the same situation as they did in 1962. This was followed by a racist and derogatory video on Xinhua called "The Spark: 7 Sins of India" on 16 August 2017.[118]

As the conflict has evolved towards greater "informationisation", the 3Ws will be the game changer as "...a significant shift away from current understandings of conflict as defined primarily by the kinetic and tangible, towards one focused more on thought processes, mental impressions, and the will to act. The doctrine will remain an essential component of China's information war strategy for decades to come and will continue to evolve. China is playing the long game and seeking to further refine each element in the trilogy, operating with increasing sophistication and establishing positions now that can be exploited in the future with the goal of redefining norms beyond the periphery, into the Arctic and even in space".[119]

China has emerged as one of the top influencers of our times and while certain aspects of the Chinese way may not suit our palate, we cannot be oblivious of the aftertaste of 'Chinese food' and what an interaction with a Chinese leads to. From the poles to the polls (Nepal), China has touched and influenced every aspect of a nation's existence. It might not have been successful in creating Chinese satellites yet, but the day in not far when we will see many nations going the Chinese way. Over the years, China has emerged as a substitute to the US and has become a formidable entity which can no longer be overlooked.

NOTES

1 Hans J. Morgenthau, Politics Among Nations: The Struggle for Power and Peace (Peking University Press, 2006), pp. 148-188.

2 Joseph S. Nye, The Future of Power (New York: Public Affairs, 2011), p. 8.

3 'Soft Power' was initially advanced by Joseph S Nye in his seminal book *Bound to Lead: The Changing Nature of American Power* in 1990 and subsequently modified for a more general understanding of power in his book *The Future of Power* in 2011. Nye defines power "As an ability to affect others to achieve the outcome one wants." "Nye split power into two forms Hard and Soft. Hard power is a command power which is based on threats and inducement, and relates to tangible military or economic resources, while soft power is a co-optive power which is based on attraction and establishing preferences, and with the use of intangible culture, ideology and institutional resources."

4 In the 1970s, gifting of giant Pandas to American and Japanese Zoos marked the first cultural exchange of the PRC with the west which is called 'Panda Diplomacy'. However, subsequent to 1987 the Pandas were not gifted but offered on 10-years loan for a fee of US$ 1,000,000 per year and with a provisions that any cub born during the loan period belongs to China.

5 In order to achieve the desired aim effectively it was felt that elements of soft and hard power need to combine so that they complement and reinforce each other. The 'smart' mix was first professed by Hillary Clinton in January 2009 at her confirmation hearing before the Senate Foreign Relations Committee. This application of smart power, synchronising the effects and sustainable application of all the instruments of national power—"diplomatic, economic, military, political, legal, and cultural—picking the right tool, or combination of tools, for each situation...With smart power, diplomacy will be the vanguard of foreign policy." "Clinton: Use Smart Power In Diplomacy", *CBS News*, January 13, 2009, https://www.cbsnews.com/news/clinton-use-smartpower-in-diplomacy/

6 The term "sharp Power" has been coined by Christopher Walker and Jessica Ludwig of the National Endowment for Democracy. Sharp power attempts to manipulate and co-opt media, culture, academia, tourism and diaspora by weaving an intricate web of coercion, persuasion, political power and inducement by directly employing manipulation, influence peddling, bullying and intimidation to impose their will.

7 'Core National Interests' are largely associated with issues of sovereignty or territorial integrity however they could be defined across a large number of subjects such as national security, social development, stability and 'loss of face'. The ability to uphold these Core Interests depends on the power that a country wields and its global stature at that time. Countries which become powerful, enunciate core interests openly and go about upholding these, while others, who are not, don't enunciate them on the count that it is futile to enunciate core interests which cannot be upheld. Enunciation of core interests also enables a country to draw red lines which indicate the amount of concession that it would make on a critical issue of

interest. It states, "China is firm in upholding its core interests which include the following: state sovereignty, national security, territorial integrity and national reunification, China's political system established by the Constitution and overall social stability, and the basic safeguards for ensuring sustainable economic and social development." Available in English at http://www.gov.cn/english/official/2011- 09/06/content_1941354_2.htm

8 In September 2011, the Chinese Peaceful Development Policy paper formally enunciated Chinese Core National Interests. The paper went beyond the basic issues of "Sovereignty and Territorial Integrity" to include issues such as "national security, China's political system, social stability and ensuring of sustainable economic development". It states, "China is firm in upholding its core interests which include the following: state sovereignty, national security, territorial integrity and national reunification. China's political system established by the Constitution and overall social stability, and the basic safeguards for ensuring sustainable economic and social development." Available in English at http://www.gov.cn/english/official/2011-09/06/content_1941354_2.htm

9 National Security Law was passed on 01 July 2015 at the 15th meeting of the Standing Committee of the 12th National People's Congress. Article 2 of the National Security Law states, "National security refers to the relative absence of international or domestic threats to the state's power to govern, sovereignty, unity and territorial integrity, the welfare of the people, sustainable economic and social development, and other major national interests, and the ability to ensure a continued state of security." "National Security Law of the People's Republic of China," *China Law Translate*, July 1, 2015, https://www.chinalawtranslate.com/en/2015nsl/

10 United Nations Treaty Collection, "Treaty of Peace with Japan (with two declarations): Signed at San Francisco, on 8 September 1951," Treaties and international agreements registered or filed and recorded with the Secretariat of the United Nations 136 (1952), https://treaties.un.org/doc/Publication/UNTS/Volume%20136/v136.pdf.

11 Deng Yuwen, "Opinion: In New Era, Chinese Diplomacy Will Be a Display of Hard Power," *South China Morning Post*, July 20, 2018, https://www.scmp.com/comment/insight-opinion/article/2117726/xis-new-era-chinese-diplomacy-will-be-display-hard-power.

12 In 2018 more than 3,000 peacekeepers of China in 10 UN missions are deployed. Moreover, China has also committed to keep another 8,000 additional peacekeepers on stand by for any contingency.

13 Ryan D. Martinson, "Jinglue Haiyang: The Naval Implications of Xi Jinping's New Strategic Concept," *Jamestown*, January 09, 2015, https://jamestown.org/program/jinglue-haiyang-the-naval-implications-of-xi-jinpings-new-strategic-concept/.

14 The incremental improvement of PLA power projection capability can be found in its military exercises. The PLAAF in 2017 fly the H-6K medium-range bomber, past the first island chain into the western Pacific.

15 The PLAN has announced to expand its Marine Corps from 20,000 to 100,000 which will enable the Marine Corps "to protect the maritime lifelines and its growing interests overseas".

16 "China's National Defense in 2010", Information Office of the State Council the PRC, March 2011, Beijing, https://media.nti.org/pdfs/1_1a.pdf

17 Department of Defense Washington, DC, "Military and Security Developments Involving the People's Republic of China," 2018, https://media.defense.gov/2018/Aug/16/2001955282/-1/-1/1/2018-CHINA-MILITARY-POWER-REPORT.PDF.

18 "China's Military Strategy", Defense White Paper 2015, The State Council Information Office

of the People's Republic of China, May 2015, Beijing, https://english.gov.cn/archive/white_paper/2015/05/27/content_281475115610833.htm.

19 C4ISR: Command, Control, Communications, Computers, Intelligence, Surveillance and Reconnaissance.

20 As per the satellite database compiled at the Union of Concerned Scientists, https://www.ucsusa.org/nuclear-weapons/space-weapons/satellite-database.

21 "China Adds to Yaogan-30 Reconnaissance Constellation via Successful Long March 2C Launch," *Spaceflight101*, January 25, 2018, http://spaceflight101.com/yaogan-30-04-launch/

22 Zhao Lei, "China Launches Pair of High-resolution Remote-sensing Satellites," *China Daily Website*, January 09, 2018, http://www.chinadaily.co.cn/a/201801/09/WS5a547ee0a31008cf16da60af.html.

23 Chang Guang Satellite, https://www.cgsatellite.com/about-us/ .

24 Andrew Jones, "First Hongyan Internet Satellite to Launch Saturday," *GBTIMES*, December 27, 2018, https://gbtimes.com/china-to-launch-first-satellite-for-hongyan-global-internet-satellite-constellation-on-saturday.

25 Sputnik, "China Launches First Hongyun Project Satellite," *Space Daily*, December 24, 2018, http://www.spacedaily.com/reports/china_launches_first_Hongyun_project_statelite_999.html

26 Antoine Cordseman and Steven Colley, Chinese Strategy and Military Modernization in 2015, (Washington: Center for Strategic and International Studies, 2015), p. 37.

27 Todd Harrison, Kaitlyn Johnson, and Thomas G. Roberts, Space Threat Assessment 2019, (London: Centre for Strategic and International Studies, 2019), https://csis-prod.s3.amazonaws.com/s3fs-public/publication/190404 spaceTreatAssessment interior.pdf.

28 Peter Dockrill, "China And Russia Have Run Controversial Experiments That Modified Earth's Atmosphere," *ScienceAlert*, December 19, 2018, https://www.sciencealeat.com/china-and-russia-conducted-controversial-experiments-that-modified-earth-s-atmosphere.

29 Brendon Hong, "China Looming Land Grab in Outer Space," *The Daily Beast*, June 22, 2018, http://www.thedailybeast.com/chinas-llming-land-grab-in-outer-space.

30 Cislunar Space is the region or area between the earth and the orbit of the moon.

31 Astropolitics is defined by Everett C. Dolman in his book Astropolitik (Strategy and History) as the "Study of the relationship between outer space relationship between outer space terrain and technology and the development of political and military policy and strategy".

32 Halford Mackinder in his article 'The Geographical Pivot of History' (1904) and book 'Democratic Ideals and Reality: A study in the Politics of Reconstruction' (1919) propounded the Heartland Theory.

33 Everett C. Dolman, Astroplitik: Classical Geopolitics in the Space Age (London: Routledge, 2005).

34 Paul D. Spudis, The Value of the Moon: How to Explore, Live, and Prosper in Space Using the Moon's Resources (New York: Smithsonian Institution, 2016), p. 119.

35 Ibid.

36 China Daily, "Full text of white paper on China's space activities in 2016," *The State Council the People's Republic of China*, December 28, 2016, http://english.gov.con/archive/white_paper/2016/12/28/content_281475572159496.htm.

37 Namrata Goswami, "Walking Up to China's Space Dream," *The Diplomat*, October 15, 2018, http://thediplomat.com/2018/10/waking-up-to-chinas-space-dream/.

38 People's Daily, "China's Space Station will Serve all Mankind: Expert", *People's Daily Online*, September 18, 2017, http://en.people.cn/n3/2017/0918/c90000-9270409.html

39 Shou Xiaosong, ed., The Science of Military Strategy, Military Science Press, 2013, pp. 142-143. Translation from Chase, Michael S., and Arthur Chan. China's Evolving Approach to "Integrated Strategic Deterrence", (Santa Monica: Rand Corporation, 2016), p. 19. https://www.rand.org/content/dam/rand/pubs/research_reports/RR1300/RR1366/RAND_RR1366.pdf.

40 Manya Koetse, "On 'Sharp Power' & the China Threat 3.0: 'The West Is Mentally Stuck in Cold War Era'." *What's on Weibo*, March 05, 2018, https://www.whatsonweibo.com/on-sharp-power-the-china-threat-3-0-the-west-is-mentally-stuck-in-cold-war-era/.

41 "Xi Jinping's Report at 19th CPC National Congress, Secure a Decisive Victory in Building a Moderately Prosperous Society in All Respects and Strive for the Great Success of Socialism with Chinese Characteristics for a New Era." *Beijing, China: Xinhuanet Media Company*, October 18, 2018, http://www.xinhuanet.com/english/download/Xi_Jinping's_report_at_19th_CPC_National_Congress.pdf

42 "CSIS Report Warns of Chinese Interference in New Zealand," *The Globe and Mail*, May 31, 2018, https://www.theglobeandmail.com/politics/article-csis-report-warns-of-chinese-interference-in-new-zealand/.

43 As a consequence of 2008 financial crisis, China turned into a major investor in Greece. China Overseas Shipping Group Co (COSCO) and China signed a thirty-year contract to operate two terminals of Piraeus Port for $570 million. Subsequently in 2007, COSCO purchased 67 per cent of Piraeus Port Authority and today Piraeus port is a major linchpin in the BRI. Moreover, China acquired 51 per cent state in Greece's power grid operator.

44 Tamas Matura, Richard Q. Turcsanyi, and Matej Šimalèík, "Central Europe for Sale: The Politics of China's Influence." Association for International Affairs (AMO) Policy Paper, 3 April 2018, p. 5. https://www.academia.edu/38210836/Central_Europe_for_Sale_ The_Politics_of_Chinas_Influence.

45 Mercy A. Kuo, "China's United Front Work: Propaganda As Policy," *The Diplomat*, February 14, 2018, https://thediplomat.com/2018/02/chinas-united-front-work-propaganda-as-policy/.

46 There are about 60 million 'Overseas Chinese' who mainly (about 70 per cent) reside in South East Asia. Out of the total 60 million Chinese, 15 million (nearly a quarter) left China when the reforms began in 1978.

47 A total of 800,000 Chinese students studied in universities abroad in 2018.

48 There are over 150 chapters of the Chinese Students and Scholars Associations (CSSAs) all over the world. The established task of the CSSAs is to support Chinese students to settle down abroad even though it is tongue-tied on its funding.

49 Following the decision by the Lotte Corporation of South Korea in December 2017 to permit an American THAAD missile defence system to be based on land it owns near Seoul, Chinese state-owned enterprises led a mass consumer boycott of Lotte department stores, forcing the company to sell its assets in China. Beijing also directed Chinese travel agents to cancel tours to South Korea from their offerings, resulting in number of Chinese tourists visiting parts of South Korea falling by 80 per cent. Moreover, in February 2018 US airlines began to encounter reprisal for Cataloging Taiwan as an independent country.

50 The major infrastructure projects undertaken by China in Sri Lanka are; Mattala Rajapaksa International Airport, Hambantota Magampura Mahindra Rajapaksa port, a power plant, expansion of Colombo port and construction on reclaimed land in Colombo for an International Financial Centre.

51 In 2011, ASEAN, chaired by Cambodia failed to forge a consensus on the wording of a joint communique to keep any mention of South China Sea after the faceoff between China and Philippines over Scarborough Shoal. In 2016, ASEAN group members again could not reach consensus due to Cambodia's insistence to remove the mention of the Arbitration ruling by the International Court between China and Philippines in the joint communique.

52 October 2017, China canceled $90 million of Cambodia's debt, only to secure major new contracts.

53 China's major purchases in the core of Europe are Swiss Pesticide maker Sygenta AG, "German technology companies such as industrial robot maker Kuka AG, Scandinavian carmakers like Volvo Personvagnar AB, Switzerland's Addax Petroleum, UK's Hinkley Point C nuclear power station, a mall outside Paris with French supermarket chain Auchan Holding SA. Greece's largest port, in Piraeus, building nuclear reactors in Romania and Bulgaria, buying a Croatian container terminal, taking over Czech vehicle maker Skoda Transportation AS and a Budapest-Belgrade rail link. Moreover, China partially or wholly own at least four airports, six seaports, wind farms in at least nine countries and 13 professional soccer teams". Andre Tartar, Mira Rojanasakul, and Jeremy S. Diamond, "How China Is Buying Its Way Into Europe," Boyden Executive Search, April 23, 2018, https://www.boyden.com/media/how-china-is-buying-its-way-into-europe-4817000/index.html.

54 China used its financial arm twisting Spain on when in "November 2013, a Spanish court issued arrest warrants for former Chinese President Jiang Zemin, former Prime Minister Li Peng, and three other retired top Communist officials consequent to a law suit filed by two Tibetan support groups based in Spain and a Tibetan exile with Spanish nationality, ostensibly for 'crimes against humanity'. Within days, China responded by advising Spanish authorities 'not [to] do things that harm the Chinese side and the relationship between China and Spain'. Besides the cancellation of PM Mariano Rajoy's visit to China, Spain was worried that Beijing may unleash an economic crisis by selling almost 20 per cent of its government bonds bought by China during the financial crisis in the early 2000s. The court order was revoked". Diego Torres, "Why the West Treats China with Kid Gloves," *Politico*, June 22, 2017, https://www.politico.eu/article/china-europe-trade-why-the-west-treats-with-kid-gloves/.

55 Professor Huang Jing was the director of the Centre on Asia and Globalisation and a Professor at the Lee Kuan Yew School of Public Policy, Singapore.

56 Anastasya Lloyd-Damnjanovic, "A Preliminary Study of PRC Political Influence and Interference Activities in American Higher Education," *Wilson Center*, September 11, 2018, https://www.wilsoncenter.org/publication/preliminary-study-prc-political-influence-and-interference-activities-american-higher.

57 Liu Xiaoming, "Confucius Is Key to China-UK Friendship. False Accusations Shouldn't Distract from That," *The Telegraph*, June 07, 2018, https://www.telegraph.co.uk/news/2018/06/07/confucius-key-china-uk-friendship-false-accusations-shouldnt/.

58 Clive Hamilton, "Australian Book on China's 'Silent Invasion' Withdrawn At Last Minute Amid Legal Threats," *Radio Free Asia*, November 13, 2017, https://www.rfa.org/english/news/china/book-11132017110421.html.

59 Mandip Singh, "From Smart Power to Sharp Power: How China Promotes her National Interests," *Journal of Defence Studies* 12, no. 3 (2018), p. 14, https://idsa.in/jds/jds-12-3-2018-from-smart-power-to-sharp-power-msingh

60 Terry Flood, "A Panda on my Veranda-Poem," *PoetrySoup*, December 3, 2018, https://www.poerysoup.com/poem/a_papnda_on_my_veranda_1091503.

61 Mohan Malik, "America and China's Dangerous Game of Geopolitical Poker," *The National Interest,* June 17, 2014, https://nationalinterest.org/feature/america-chinas-dangerous-game-geopolitical-poker-10690.

62 The Northern Sea Route will be 20 days faster than the time-honored route between Asia and Europe through the Suez Canal.

63 Russia has upgraded seven military bases along the route, deploying advanced radar and missile defence systems. Moreover, Russia has pushed for legislation to increase its control over managing access to NSR, claiming the underwater ridges (Mendeleev Rise and the Lomonosov Ridge) in the UN Commission on the Limits of the Continental Shelf and conducting its largest military exercise for a decade with its Northern Fleet in 2018.

64 Presently, the Chinese hold nearly 29.9 per cent ownership stake in the Yamal LNG project with China National Petroleum Corporation (CNPC) holding 20 per cent and Silk Road Fund (SRF) holding 9.9 percent of the ownership stakes.

65 Full Text: China's Arctic Policy, (The State Council Information Office of the People's Republic of China, 2018), http://english.gov.cn/archive/white_paper/2018/01/26/content_281476026660336.htm.

66 The white paper states: "The Arctic situation now goes beyond its original inter-Arctic States or regional nature, having a vital bearing on the interests of states outside the region and the interests of the international community as a whole, as well as on the survival, the development, and the shared future for mankind."

67 "The Arctic Corridor is a global economic region as well as a transport and development corridor. It connects Finland and Europe to the deep-water ports of the Arctic Ocean, large production areas of oil and gas and the western end of the Northern Sea Route." https://arcticcorridor.fi

68 Tillman, Yang, and Nielsson, "The Polar Silk Road," pp. 356-357.

69 Global Construction Review, Denmark "deeply concerned" over Chinese bids to build Greenland airports, March 26, 2018, http://www.globalconstructionreview.com/news/denmark-deeply-concerned-over-chinese-bids-build-g/.

70 Reuters, Greenland shortlists Chinese company for airport construction despite Denmark's concerns, March 27, 2018, https://www.reuters.com/article/china-arctic-greenland/greenland-shortlists-chinese-company-for-airport-construction-despite-denmarks-concerns-idUSL8N1R96F6.

71 Over The Circle, Greenland's Airports: A Balance between China and Denmark?, June 15, 2018, https://overthecircle.com/2018/06/15/greenlands-airports-a-balance-between-china-and-denmark/.

72 Reuters, China central bank signs 3.5 billion yuan currency swap deal with Iceland, September 30, 2013, https://www.reuters.com/article/us-china-cenbank-iceland/china-central-bank-signs-3-5-billion-yuan-currency-swap-deal-with-iceland-idUSBRE98T09F20130930

73 Thorkell Erlingsson, Thorleikur Johannesson, Eldur Olafsson and Gudni Axelsson, Proceedings World Geothermal Congress 2010, Geothermal District Heating System in XianYang, Shaanxi, China, April 25-29, 2010, https://www.geothermal-energy.org/pdf/IGAstandard/WGC/2010/3412.pdf

74 Diki Sherpa, "Sino-Nepalese Engagements in the Himalayan Borderland," *Institute of Chinese Studies,* March 2014, https://www.icsin.org/publications/sino-nepalese-engagements-in-the-himalayan-borderland.

75 "China Hands over Araniko Highway to Nepal After Repair," *My Republica*, March 4, 2017, https://myrepublica.nagariknetwork.com/news/15855/.

76 Government of Nepal, "Joint Press Statement Between the People's Republic of China and Nepal - Ministry of Foreign Affairs Nepal MOFA," Ministry of Foreign Affairs Nepal MOFA Kathmandu Nepal, March 23, 2016, https://mofa.gov.np/joint-press-statement/.

77 Embassy of Nepal, Beijing, "Press Release Regarding Agreement Between Government of Nepal and the Government of People's Republic of China - Ministry of Foreign Affairs Nepal MOFA," Ministry of Foreign Affairs Nepal MOFA Kathmandu Nepal, December 29, 2016, https://mofa.gov.np/press-release-regarding-agreement-government-nepal-government-peoples-republic-china/.

78 Government of Nepal, "Joint Press Statement Between the People's Republic of China and Nepal - Ministry of Foreign Affairs Nepal MOFA," Ministry of Foreign Affairs Nepal MOFA Kathmandu Nepal, March 23, 2016, https://mofa.gov.np/joint-press-statement/.

79 Anup Ojha, "2 Chinese Firms Show Interest in Outer Ring Road Project," *The Kathmandu Post*, February 3, 2018, http://kathmandupost.ekantipur.com/news/2018-03-02/2-chinese-firms-show-interest-in-outer-ring-road-project.html.

80 K J M Varma, "China Nepal Sign Protocol to Operationalise Key Transit Treaty to Access Chinese Ports," *The Week*, April 30, 2019, https://www.theweek.in/wire-updates/business/2019/04/30/fgn24-china-nepal-tta.html.

81 "China's Belt and Road Meet Ends, Affirms Respect for Sovereignty and Territorial Integrity," *The Hindu Business Line*, April 27, 2019, https://www.thehindubusinessline.com/news/world/chinas-belt-and-road-meet-ends-affirms-respect-intergrity/article26968087.ece.

82 Rastriya Samachar Samiti, "Two Chinese Aircraft Handed to Nepal Airlines," *The Himalayan Times*, April 18, 2018, https://thehimalayantimes.com/nepal/two-chinese-aircraft-handed-to-nepal-airlines/.

83 The Kathmandu Post, "Pokhara Int'l Airport Construction Set to Begin from Thursday," *ekantipur.com*, Jun 26, 2017, https://kathmandupost.ekantipur.com/news/2017-06-26/pokhara-intl-airport-construction-set-to-begin-from-thursday.html.

84 The Kathmandu Post, "Gautam Buddha Airport Likely to Be Ready in 2019," *ekantipur.com*, June 3, 2017, https://kathmandupost.ekantipur.com/news/2017-06-03/gautam-buddha-airport-likely-to-be-ready-in-2019.html

85 Nihar Nayak, *Strategic Himalayas: Republican Nepal and External Powers* (Pentagon Press, 2014).

86 Gopal Sharma, "With New Chinese Link, Nepal Ends India's Internet Monopoly," *Reuters*, January 12, 2018, https://www.reuters.com/article/us-nepal-china-internet/with-new-chinese-link-nepal-ends-indias-internet-monopoly-idUSKBN1F11JP.

87 Nayak, Strategic Himalayas: Republican Nepal and External Powers, p. 92.

88 Binod Ghimire, "China Pledges Rs 3b Support to Nepal Army," *The Kathmandu Post*, March 24, 2017, https://kathmandupost.ekantipur.com/news/2017-03-24/china-pledges-rs-3b-support-to-nepal-army.html.

89 Yubaraj Ghimire, "China Set to Supply Heavy Equipment to Nepal Army," *The Indian Express*, March 24, 2017, https://indianexpress.com/article/world/china-set-to-supply-heavy-equipment-to-nepal-army/.

90 Xinhua, "Chinese-built Armed Police Academy Handed over to Nepal," *Global Times*, July 1, 2017, http://www.globaltimes.cn/content/1054420.shtml.

91 The Kathmandu Post Report, "10-day Nepal, China Joint Army Drill Starts Today," *ekantipur.com*, April 16, 2017, http://kathmandupost.ekantipur.com/news/20170416/10-day-nepal-china-joint-army-drill-starts-today.html.

92 Ugo Armanini, "Upgrade in Panama-China Relations: Win-Win for Both Countries?", *CogitASIA CSIS Asia Policy Blog,* August 20, 2018, https://www.cogitasia.com/upgrade-in-panama-china-relations-win-win-for-both-countries/.

93 Armanini, "Upgrade in Panama-China Relations".

94 Álvaro Méndez, "Panama Could Soon Become China's Gateway to Latin America Thanks to an Imminent Free Trade Agreement," LSE Latin America and Caribbean, December 18, 2018, https://blogs.lse.ac.uk/latamcaribbean/2018/12/05/panama-could-soon-become-chinas-gateway-to-latin-america-thanks-to-an-imminent-free-trade-agreement/

95 Yun Sun, "Djibouti: What Europe Should Understand of China's Approach to Military Expansion," *Euractiv.com*, April 24, 2019, https://www.euractiv.com/section/defence-and-security/opinion/djibouti-what-europe-should-understand-of-chinas-approach-to-military-expansion/.

96 Jon Connars, "Djibouti the Latest to Fall Victim to China's 'debt Trap Diplomacy?", *Asia Times*, March 27, 2018, https://www.asiatimes.com/2018/03/opinion/djibouti-latest-fall-victim-chinas-debt-trap-diplomacy/.

97 Justina Crabtree, "The Island Paradise That Could Be China's Next Strategic Transport Hub," *CNBC,* January 17, 2018, https://www.cnbc.com/2018/01/17/china-transport-hub-could-be-the-african-island-of-sao-tome.html.

98 Crabtree, "The Island Paradise That Could Be China's Next Strategic Transport Hub."

99 Lt. General P.C. Katoch (Retd), "China's Military Base in Maldives," *SP's Naval Forces,* January 19, 2018, http://www.spsnavalforces.com/experts-speak/?id=214&h=China-s-military-base-in-Maldives.

100 Xinhua News Agency, "Xi Jinping Arrives in Male, Starting His State Visit to Maldives," September 14, 2014, https://www.fmprc.gov.cn/mfa_eng/topics_665678/zjpcxshzzcygyslshds schybdtjkstmedfsllkydjxgsfw/t1191505.shtml.

101 Samatha Mallempati, "The visit of President of Maldives to China (6-9 December 2017)," Indian Council of World Affairs, January 12, 2018, https://icwa.in/pdfs/vp/2014/visitprezmalchnvp12012018.pdf.

102 Saibal Dasgupta, "Maldives, China Sign 12 Agreeements to Promote OBOR," *The Times of India*, December 8, 2017, https://timesofindia.indiatimes.com/world/china/maldives-china-sign-12-agreeements-to-promote-obor/articleshow/61987083.cms.

103 Gateway House, "China Projects Worth More Than 40% of Maldives GDP," *Maldives Independent*, March 26, 2018, https://maldivesindependent.com/business/china-projects-worth-more-than-40-of-maldives-gdp-136824.

104 Ahmed Naish, "Defence Minister Signs Military Aid Agreement with China," *Minivan News*, December 16, 2012, https://minivannewsarchive.com/politics/defence-minister-signs-military-aid-agreement-with-china-49018.

105 Maldives Monetary Authority, "Maldives Tourist Arrivals," *Trading Economics*, 2018, https://tradingeconomics.com/maldives/tourist-arrivals.

106 The coalition consisted of Progressive Party of Maldives (PPM) led by Abdulla Yameen, Jumhoorce Party (JP) led by Qasim Ibrahim and People's National Congress (PNC) led by Abdul Raheem Abdulla.

107 Daniel R. Russel, "Strengthening Relations with 'Large Ocean Nations,'" *U.S. Embassy in Samoa*, March 3, 2016, *https://ws.usembassy.gov/strengthening-relations-with-large-ocean-nations/*

108 "China Encroaches on Australia's Backyard," Stratfor, April 23, 2019, https://worldview.stratfor.com/article/china-encroaches-australias-backyard.

109 Kathrin Hille, "Pacific Islands: a New Arena of Rivalry Between China and the US Search," *The Financial Times*, April 8, 2019, https://www.ft.com/content/bdbb8ada-59dc-11e9-939a-341f5ada9d40.
110 Halford J. Mackinder, Democratic Ideals and Reality: With Additional Papers (Norton, 1962), p. 150.
111 Elsa Kania, "The PLA's Latest Strategic Thinking on the Three Warfares," *Center for International Maritime Security*, August 25, 2016, http://cimsec.org/plas-latest-strategic-thinking-three-warfares/27468.
112 Abhijit Singh, "China's 'Three Warfares' and India," *Journal of Defence Studies* 7, no. 4 (2013): p. 30, https://idsa.in/system/files/jds_7_4_AbhijitSingh.pdf.
113 Elsa Kania, "The PLA's Latest Strategic Thinking on the Three Warfares," *Jamestown*, August 22, 2016, https://jamestown.org/program/the-plas-latest-strategic-thinking-on-the-three-warfares/.
114 Ministry of External Affairs, India, "Rajya Sabha Unstarred Question No. 2726 Protection of Boundaries of Arunachal Pradesh," Ministry of External Affairs, Government of India, August 10, 2017, https://www.mea.gov.in/rajya-sabha.htm?dtl/28844/QUESTION+NO2726+PROTECTION+OF+BOUNDARIES+OF+ARUNACHAL+PRADESH
115 Suhasini Haider, "Renaming act does not make illegal occupation legal, India tells China," *The Hindu*, April 20, 2017, http://www.thehindu.com/news/national/india-objects-to-china-renaming-six-places-in-arunachal/article18154281.ece.
116 "Defense ministry confirms Indian army crossed border in standoff", *Global Times*, June 26, 2017, http://www.globaltimes.cn/content/1053568.shtml.
117 Xinhua, "China urges India to withdraw border guards crossing the boundary", *People's Daily*, June 27, 2017, http://en.people.cn/n3/2017/0627/c90000-9233537.html
118 Xinhua News Agency, "*The Spark: 7 Sins of India*, Xinhua", August 16, 2017, http://www.xinhuanet.com/english/2017-08/16/c_136531175.htm.
119 Larry M. Wortzel, "The Chinese People's Liberation Army and Information Warfare", Strategic Studies Institute and US Army War College Press, March 5, 2014, p. 45, https://ssi.armywarcollege.edu/pubs/display.cfm?pubID=1191.

6

Dialoguing China

Dialogue between communities, individuals, institutions and even creatures defines the very success of existence of earthlings today and tomorrow. Dialogue exchange has the ability to store and transmit valuable data and insights; it is a valuable tool in both good times and crises. "Dialogue enables inquiry into, and understanding of, the sorts of processes that fragment and interfere with real communication."[1] A dialogue needs to be positively managed to deliver on its potential benefits. With the right kind of dialogue development, transmission and regular monitoring, an expertly crafted and managed dialogue system can lay the foundation for a community and nation's continued success. However, due to its inherent volatility and susceptibility to human biases, a mismanaged dialogue can spark a damaging revolution with widespread public distress and riots. Thus, dialogue creation and management requires ongoing a certain sensitivity, multichannel technological finesse, outcomes-consistency, and strategic intent of the highest order. Managing multiple dialogues across cultures, businesses, governments and time diversities necessitates development of expertise and technological mechanisms that are data driven and are global, national and local in their content-intent, apart from being technologically advanced and aligned to a nation's political, environmental and social priorities.

As the multicultural and geographically dispersed Chinese society evolves into different and diverse communities, it gives rise to multiple urban-rural diversities, namely, the working and living conditions, employment opportunities, communication/dialogue patterns and personal/public identity choices. These business and cultural differences also manifest themselves in economically developed coastal regions as well as the impoverished western regions in China. This has given rise to highly divergent views, identities and interests amongst the people and communities which in turn has led to varied perceptions about the desired socio-eco-politico order prevailing in the country. The same has ultimately led to a split in public opinion, multiple-differences and perceptive-distinctions in the manner Chinese citizens perceive their surroundings and political order. Thanks to modern communication and public interaction tools, especially the web and social media platforms connecting people, different parts of the world are in constant and instant contact with one another. However, despite these global 'instant-communication-linkages', there is an overbearing perception amongst the Chinese public that this interconnected communication 'web' is crumbling under strict state control and censorship. It is our inability to fully comprehend and grasp the larger picture which has brought us all to the threshold of major communication crisis notwithstanding multiple communication clusters and thought leaders in this arena. To be able to differentiate and discern one from the other, it would require comprehension and foresight which is clearly conspicuous by its absence.

With this as the evolving basis, theorists use the approach of complexity-theory to analyse uncertainty and non-linearity to understand and share with laypeople the compelling reasons behind the systems' behaviour that is created by the interaction amongst the large groups of simpler constituents. These individual constituents of societal-systems often act freely to mutually interact with each other. When they share data and merge opinions, typical systemic responses/behaviours are formed which in turn gives rise to an emergent future that cannot be fully comprehended proactively. Experts in the field of Complexity Theory have highlighted the significance of history where the 'path dependency' denotes that constituent parts constantly engage with each other to create positive and negative feedback loops. This further supports the concept of a non-linear emergent future. While this concept embraces the disorder of the real world messiness and binds it with real-life challenges to support multiple analyses by appreciating the fact that boundaries can shift or get permeable in future with their systems steadily evolving.

This Complexity Theory enables people to enhance their understanding of their evolving strategic surroundings and thereby visualise how different elements interact with each other, namely, the virtual, physical, and psychological. Navigating numerous complex interactions across many open systems needs people to accept the reality that it is critical to have flexibility, relationships and willingness to challenge the status quo.

For fully analysing the complex dynamics behind the prevailing contemporary China-based 'dialogues', we need to undertake a multifaceted, multidimensional approach and methodology that identifies 10 fundamental Chinese thoughts relevant to the present scenario. Bereft of negative misinformation, these help experts establish fundamental linkages in ensuing dialogues that are collective in nature. These linkages are threefold—firstly, aligning rationale, content and goals to prevailing CCP guidelines shared in official documents and speeches; secondly, deep domain analysis of people and business attitude, preferences and thoughts shared on different online media, namely, the data culled from top six social media platforms; thirdly, past five years research on vernacular print media to allow systematic profiling of key recurrent dialogue clusters.

Post analysis, the 10 most prevalent dialogue issues that came up comprise five external and five internal issues. The dominant internal dialogue issues are—ecological civilisation, food, regulations rigour supervision, socialist rule of law, and prosperity & well-being. The five key external dialogues are—Beijing consensus, Taiwan, Hong Kong, Japan, and World Order.

INTERNAL DIALOGUES

Ecological Civilisation

'We do not inherit the earth from our ancestors; we borrow it from our children.'

The enormity of the huge gap between China's fragile and endangered ecological ecosystem and its aspiration of 'beautiful-China'[2] has given rise to aggressive efforts to build an environmentally aware and ecological sensitive society—an ecological civilisation. To elaborate, this purported ecological civilisation conceptually combines ecology as a natural phenomenon and civilisation as its human element. It traces its environmental consciousness to the Confucian ideology of respecting nature as a guiding beacon for human beings. To achieve this goal, the great thought leader Mencius recommended thoughtful practices to preserve ecological ecosystems. Its reflections are found in Wen Tao documents published during the time of 'Warring States' wherein they criticised ruling leaders for 'ecologically degrading idyllic mountainous regions thereby inflicting great damage through great floods caused by run-off waters not checked due to the absence of trees to hold back the water and soil'. The positive bent of mind and an urge to cultivate a symbiotic relationship with nature has been part of the Chinese thinking since ancient times.

However, in the contemporary era, China's leaders erroneously emphasised on taming nature instead of preserving it. They were of the opinion that wilderness was devoid of anything that had an intrinsic value as it housed wild creatures. After the creation of People's Republic of China, the supreme communist leader Mao focussed on conquering nature. He proclaimed that "Man must leverage modern science to better understand nature, conquer and transform nature to suit the needs of humans."[3] Premier Jiang Zemin supported these views. In 1997, to mark the developmental milestone of building the huge Three Gorges Dam across the mighty Yangtze River, he proudly proclaimed, "Since the dawn of Chinese history, our great nation has succeeded in its wow feats of conquering, developing, and exploiting nature. The mythical bird Jingwei's legend narrates her determination to fill sea with pebbles, while the Foolish Old Man was committed to move mountains obstructing in his path, and the tale of the Great Yu who successfully harnessed the 'Great Floods'. These are few of the examples of the Chinese citizen's strong conviction and indomitable spirit to successfully conquer mother-nature."[4]

With China becoming the most preferred location for top global manufacturers, it had to strive hard to overcome serious challenges as a result of extensive industrialisation and urbanisation. Hence, guarding the long-neglected nature is now considered a top government priority. This has inspired volunteers to lead policy formulations changes from conquering and changing nature to respecting and protecting nature and building human-oriented sustainable ecological development.

On 18 October 2017, Xi Jinping presented a report to the leaders of 19th National Congress that emphasised on building and sustaining long-term harmony between economic development and environmental preservation. Thus, the word 'environment' was repeated 89 times as compared to the word 'economy' which occurred 70 times in Xi's progress report to the 19th congress. This heralded as the strongest environmental preservation directive from a top political leader since the days of Premier Li Keqiang's "War-on-Pollution"[5] declaration in March 2014. China's economic development guidance incorporates 14 environment protection principles. These principles are part of a chapter in his report named—'Speeding up system-reform for creating and sustaining an ecological-civilization for a beautiful China'. This unique title of the report in itself showcases multiple environmental issues. Firstly, there is no chapter that announces 'reform-speeding up' as its unique focus. This clarifies the top priority given to ecological protection and the related policy reforms. The vision of an ecological civilisation is a positive one that calls for a thorough integration of numerous environmental preservation initiatives into different aspects of governance of politics, economy, society, and culture. Moreover, the overriding clarion call of building and preserving the 'beautiful China' positions environmental protection policies as part of the overall national pride. Lastly, the report liberally uses the word 'building' to denote environmental protection as a long-term Chinese reform project.

Initial content of this report accurately portrays the risks facing China, and boldly shares the overarching economic principles embedded with environmentalism guiding the nation. It thus proclaims, "Man and nature form a contiguous-community of life. And that all human beings, must always respect nature and its wow-ways and always endeavour to consistently protect it. Only by adhering to nature's laws can humankind avoid costly errors of its wanton exploitation. Any harm inflicted on fragile nature would ultimately come back to harm and haunt all humankind. Thus it's an inescapable reality we all need to comprehend. Along with the focus on creation of more material and cultural wealth for fulfilling people's ever-growing better-life needs, we all also should focus on providing more quality ecologically-friendly items to meet everyone's desire for a beautiful world and environment. Hence we all need to act upon the principles of resources-prioritization, environmental-conservation and its continued protection, thereby allowing mother-nature to restore itself. In order to achieve this the nation would need to build spatial layouts, industrialisation plans, and ways of working and living in ways that aid conservation of limited natural resources and environmental-protection. Thus the nation can restore its required environmental serenity, human-nature, harmony and beauty."[6] Reports such as these indicate and reveal an extremely interesting and nuanced aspect of the Chinese behaviour—that is do not make it your priority, unless it becomes an exigency. Concerns regarding environment have found there place but the efforts in that direction seem to be too little and too late.

'Five Reforms' for a Beautiful China Living In Harmony with Nature

This emphasises of the report is on five key reforms—Green development, water conservation, institutional reforms, global climate change, and ecological governance. Green Development is an essential paradigm for the much needed ecological civilisation. This includes many things—recycling, using clean technologies, and energy-water conservation. In addition to the pollution of water, air and soil, few newer areas of emphasis have been added, namely, the conservation of offshore areas, river-basin management, agricultural water utilisation, and checking of wasteful water run-off. There is a huge emphasis on promoting consistent public participation and engagement of NGOs to speed up China's continued march towards sustainable development. This indicates the government's urgency for ushering in this new ecological civilisation phase. Additionally, Green Development has been effectively promoted on-ground through the 'dual Control' mechanism of energy utilisation. This means creating an upper limit on the total amount and intensity of resources utilised per GDP-unit. This supply-side structural reform would significantly reduce reliance on the consumption of resources. The focus would then be on increased conservation leading to overall environmentally friendly economic development.

Water is no Longer Everywhere

Water is pivotal to deciphering China' thoughts on environmentalism. The pervasive relevance of water is very apparent in matters where China has created it as a philosophical-cultural motif and leveraged it as a necessity for preserving 'political legitimacy'. There are today two key Chinese issues with water conservation—"there is not enough of it to go round, and it is often so foul that no one can use it anyway".[7] The Chinese government accepts this harmful imbalance and has enforced numerous measures to rectify this glaring issue—"China would concertedly adopt a holistic approach to the conservation of its rivers, mountains, forests, lakes, farmlands and grasslands. It would thus implement strictest measures for environment protection, development of ecological friendly growth models and ways of life. He (Xi) emphasised on the urgent need to hasten prevention of water pollution by taking concrete steps to improve river-basins and offshore water bearing areas."[8] China thus envisages reduction in its water consumption and minimising water pollution while increasing its GDP. In accordance with this objective, water usage in China and the resultant wastewater discharge per GDP-unit has seen a steady decline. By the year 2020, water usage per GDP-unit is expected to decline by over 27 per cent from its 2018 levels. Overall, pollution levels too need to fall to achieve the pre-decided target of water quality to ensure better ecological and environmental health. Representing a mammoth 42 per cent of China's GDP and population, its only logical that the central government is focussed on the Yangtze River Economic Belt (YREB). As part of Xi's '14 Points', the government is facilitating sustainable development of YREB through the "promotion of expertly-coordinated environment-conservation and avoidance of excessive development."[9] In order to ensure optimum economic development using sustainable means, China is planning to setup eco-friendly industries in YREB. The significance of arresting widespread water pollution at the earliest is clearly explained in Xi's report wherein he has given equal importance to the "prevention of water pollution with superior conservation and control" as to critical issues like poverty alleviation.

Today guardianship of the environment in China is split amongst different government ministries. At times either there are ambiguous divisions of work responsibilities or they suffer from inbuilt conflicts of interest. Xi's new model, as shared in his report, aims to establish regulatory agencies to effectively manage natural resources that are state-owned and regulated while monitoring all of China's key ecosystems with the aim of continuous improvement of the administration of environment. "These government agencies will, in multiple unified ways, discharge conservation duties as the owner of government owned natural resource-assets and tasks of regulating usage of territorial spaces while restoring and protecting fragile natural ecosystems."[10] The monitoring duties to check the discharge of all harmful pollutants in both rural and urban areas are happening through the mechanism of effective administrative law enforcements and control. The Ministry of Ecological Protection (MEP) has been created which possesses legal ownership of all government-owned natural resources, for example, mountains, forests, lakes, nature reserves, and different public lands. This powerful ministry can take any company to the court of law if it defaults in environmental conservation and preservation matters.

The emission of greenhouse gases due to different human activities is the primary reason of climate change today. China emits the highest level of greenhouse gases in the world. Since 2004 China has the world's largest carbon footprint. It was also responsible for 20 per cent of international carbon dioxide (CO_2) emissions in 2018. As the world's largest greenhouse gase emitter, China faces a lot of criticism from other nations. China is also facing increasing domestic pressure to mitigate environment issues while sustaining its galloping economic march. In recent times, Beijing has taken more active steps to reduce its greenhouse gas emissions at the global level. Starting with its contribution in the non-binding 2009 Copenhagen Ecology Protection Accord, and striving for global ratification of 2016 Paris Agreement, China aims to be the leader in environmental preservation. However, with US withdrawal from the Paris Agreement, China has clearly positioned itself to spearhead the movement for reversing climate change. President Xi's 19th congress report clearly states that "...taking a leadership role in international 'climate change reversal-cooperation' is a key goal of the nation. China is thus a key participant, contributor and leader in world's endeavour for a better, saner ecological civilization."[11] Xi has consistently assured the world community that China would keep its commitment to lead in all climate reform actions. From reducing coal usage overcapacity (lesser by 150 million tons in 2018), to increased renewable energy investments, creation and extension of green bonds to increasing use of electric vehicles, China is serious about showcasing its leadership role in matters of environmental conservation. China has already achieved its 2020 Copenhagen emission reduction targets by reducing carbon emissions by 40–45 per cent and increased non-fossil fuel share by over 15 per cent. Since China has a localised carbon trading system, its energy sector's efforts in establishing national emissions trade system needs to be hastened at all costs. Its criticality is apparent thanks to the massive Chinese investments in other nations and its growing clout in various global agreements on conserving biodiversity and controlling climate change.

Xi's report stresses on the urgent requirement to strengthen different law-based governance initiatives with an entire chapter devoted to China's ambitious reforms. This is critical for environmental protection as multiple Chinese environmental malpractices are caused by poor enforcement and implementation of environmental laws. The report clearly lays down the role of the judiciary in these matters. It also got reflected in 2018 when environmental protection bodies issued more than 200,000 punishments to pollution law violators with fines totalling a massive figure of ¥8.63 billion representing a hefty 25–40 per cent increase as compared to previous year's figures. The report further states that in order to make polluting businesses more accountable, the government is taking steps for improving the systems of credibility assessment with the mandatory release of data on key environmental parameters. Each firm is given an exclusive 18 code number which acts as an identity number for the business to check any pollution violations that might occur as per the 'Credit China platform'. With environmental conservation being a major priority in China year after year, this law enforcement work will continue to pick up pace. In 2017–2018 the Ministry of Environmental Protection (MEP) and the Central Disciplinary Commission carried out far reaching provincial inspections, which exposed many environmental violators. More than two-third of the industries were found to be exceeding their permissible pollution benchmarks. In the same time frame, many state prosecutors brought thousands of pollution-violation cases against different government departments. Thus a rigorous approach to 'ecological civilisation' is now well established in CCP's constitution. Recent environmental governance developments clearly show that China means business when it comes to environmental conservation. Its intentions are backed by different legal reforms with an increasing focus on strong enforcements. However, the world should be realistic in its expectations—even though environmental protection is accorded a top priority, these ecological reforms are extremely challenging and will take time to be fully implemented.[12]

On 14 August 2017, Xi called all party workers as well as the public to participate in environmental preservation efforts in the spirit of 'saihanban'[13] wherein people converted a wasteland into a wooded forest. He thus tells his people to consider "green hills and clear waters to be as precious as gold and silver."

Food

Often ridiculed for its long history of regular drought- and flood-induced famines, China has failed to ensure food security for its citizens. A multitude of famines across the years has caused unimaginable public suffering and stress and social instability. "No other civilization has had such a continuous tradition of thinking about famine, and no other nation's modern history has been so influenced by hunger and famine, in at least one of its districts, every year from 108 BC to 1911 AD."[14] In modern times (1920–1921), approximately 500,000 out of a population of 48.8 million in Five Provinces have died from widespread famine and over 19.8 million have been rendered destitute. Then again in 1943, about 3 million perished in Henan province's famine. Thus, it is this long stretch of famine that has led to the fear of famine haunting the thoughts of leaders and economy planners. China is thus unique in its outlook to give such importance to the nation's food security. Since ancient times, the Chinese people have considered 'food' to be a necessity for everyone. For over 5,000 years in the past, the 'mandate of heaven' given to the ruling dynasties has been linked to the availability and distribution of food items. The traditional worldview of China is that the ruler is solely responsible for having enough food to feed his subjects and providing sufficient and timely relief and support should a famine occur. It is believed that rulers who ignore this paramount responsibility would suffer from losing the 'mandate of heaven'. Thus every ruling regime's continued political and public support and official legitimacy has been based on its efforts to build sustainable food security for its people.

Self-sufficiency in producing grains to feed its growing population masses has gained primacy in politics of China. In the past, on many occasions this food security issue has greatly impacted the political legitimacy of the all-powerful CCP. Dean Gooderham, US Secretary of State in 1949, famously stated that CCP will not be able to feed China's 546 million strong population since none of their predecessors was successful in providing food security adequately. In 1949 Mao, in one of his famous writings, *Bankruptcy of idealist conception of history*, defended his party by stating that CCP had finally discovered the solution to persistent famine crises through its 'revolution plus production' initiative to rid China of its perennial food shortages and acute public suffering during famines. In October 1949, on taking over the reins of power across mainland China, CCP proudly assured everyone that not a single person would ever succumb to death due to hunger. Thus CCP has, from the first day in power, considered this as its primary duty to provide adequate food for all people. It recognises that this is critical to winning and sustaining its political support. But, despite Mao's personal pledge, hunger issues remained unresolved and became endemic as the failure of CCP's ambitious Great Leap Forward campaign led to the devastating 1959–61 famine.

At the end of the 10-year-old Cultural Revolution in the year of 1978, the communist ideology began to lose its charm. Food scarcity hit the masses once again. With most Chinese not having food to feed themselves and their families, "at least 250 million persons out of 800 million rural folks were impoverished."[15] CCP authorities thus faced a very serious crisis of their political legitimacy. To overcome this perilous situation, the Chinese government began rolling out widespread agricultural reforms to boost crop yields to feed its burgeoning and hungry populace. The Household Responsibility System was launched nationwide, along with many more ways of enhanced food production. As a result, crop yields began growing at a phenomenal rate. Thus in 1995, China achieved self-sufficiency with regard to food. In fact, China succeeded in not only achieving this milestone, but also gaining a surplus of crops. In 2001, Zhou Rongji (former premier) proudly proclaimed that CCP had successfully mitigated China's food inadequacy and this marvel to save China could only have been delivered by CCP.

Even though the threat of widespread hunger or famine seems to be unlikely in present-day China, growing inflation induced by growing food prices still carries the risk of political and social instability. Thus, it is important to appreciate the fact that grain price hikes of 1987–1989 were one of the key factors in creating inflation in China. This inflation was, in fact, partially responsible for triggering the mass protests across China that were sustained for history-repository in the spring of 1989. Therefore, every Chinese government tirelessly works for creating and sustaining self-sufficiency in supply of grains to safeguard its power and to shield itself from the highly volatile global food and commodities market.

In addition, China's grain self-sufficiency policy is also an aftermath of its perception of international food system. At the time of the worst famine in China (1959–1961), US imposed a damaging food embargo export of grains to China. These US trade sanctions hit China badly, and thus became an indelible part of China's memory that sowed the seeds of a deep mistrust of Chinese authorities towards nations that export grains globally. Thus, in the present day, the Chinese government is rightfully wary of food being used as a foreign policy weapon. As Prof Morton states (2012), "Concerns over global risk that food can be leveraged as a foreign policy tool to harm China's ambitious march for modernizing itself have largely influenced how food-security is comprehended and vigorously enforced nationwide. In recent times, with the geopolitical concerns over the struggle to address international food security challenges, there is widespread deliberation in China over the possibility of grain wars with U.S."[16]

In 1996, the Chinese government published a white paper on this key issue of food grains. This official document proclaimed that to permanently resolve the issue of food shortage in China, it needed to rely on increasing domestic self-sufficiency and not be dependent on importing grains from other countries. China thus made earnest efforts to boost the production of grains in order to build self-sufficiency under normal conditions. So, it set the target to exceed 95 per cent of its national consumption needs so that its net import rate is 5 per cent or lower than its total consumption level.[17]

This 95 per cent self-sufficiency goal became the cornerstone of China's nationwide food security policy. Thus, in the last two decades China has accomplished this target of sustaining a nationwide self-sufficiency (with regard to grains) at a rate that is always above its target of 95 per cent. When many Western leaders in 2008 blamed China for the ongoing global food crisis, China in rebuttal launched its first national food security plan. This was in many cases, a firm reiteration of its continued commitment to maintain its self-sufficiency. The Chinese government thereafter introduced its plan for achieving a consistent 100 per cent self-sufficiency plan by 2020. [18]

When Xi Jinping gained power, he made it amply clear that food self-sufficiency is and will always be critical to the survival and success of China. In 2013, he reiterated that "history pointed out when big famines do occur, money is rendered useless, and thus to feed its burgeoning 1.3 billion population, China should only rely on itself to achieve its nationwide food security goal."[19] However, saddled with scarce water and land resources, this goal is becoming increasingly more arduous for China as it struggles to feed its growing population. Thus in the recent past, China has undertaken concrete endeavours to revise its food security plans.

China's national food self-sufficiency policy is beginning to threaten sustainability of its large agri-business sector. With extremely limited cultivable land, it is a daunting task to boost crop yields. China's remarkable rise in food production has led to rampant soil degradation thanks to the widespread use of intensive farming techniques, overreliance on heavy usage of fertilisers and pesticides, expansion of irrigated lands, and use of high-seeds. Almost half of its stupendous increase in crop yields from 1980 onwards is attributed to these farming inputs. To further increase the productivity of farmlands, subsidised nitrogen and phosphorus fertilisers are being widely used to grow crops. "Even though China has only 9% of world's arable-land, China is consuming more than 30% of the pesticides and fertilizers. China is thus amongst the world's top chemical fertilizer users per hectare, with most Chinese farmers dependent on highly toxic pesticides and agri-inputs."[20]

The Annual Central Rural Work Conference announced a radical new 'food-grains security plan' in December 2013. This reiterated the China's belief that food security needs to be secured through domestic production supported by moderate imports. This highlighted the central government's continued affirmation of its policy to enhance China's ability of agricultural production, speeding up research and development in breakthrough farming sector, and ensuring better utilisation of its international agricultural assets. Towards the end of January 2014, China issued its national policy—'2014 Number One Document'.[21] This policy gave primacy to the continued improvement of national food security mechanisms and allotted it the top ranking in its 2014 reforms list that is valid for ensuing years too. This document highlights the fact that China should never neglect its domestic agricultural production and needs to consistently adhere to its arable land protection appraisal, accurately nominate available farmlands for production of crops, and continuously intensify the nation's overall agricultural output capacity so as to sustain basic self-sufficiency in its required cereals' supply with absolute self-sufficiency in overall food grains for both human consumption and feeding its livestock animals. It also stressed that China should utilise the global food market and agricultural resources to adequately harmonise and complement domestic availability of grains. This policy also stated that adequate consideration needs to be paid to assure continued safety and superior quality of all agricultural products while striving to sustain higher levels of agricultural productivity.

Some of the key changes that were brought about by this new agricultural policy were:

- The definition and meaning of grain has been expanded to cover many more items—soybean, corn, wheat, coarse grains and root tubers.
- 'Moderate imports' became a policy option and was accepted explicitly for the first time in China's history.
- Chinese authorities placed additional emphasis on sustainability of agricultural development while emphasising the importance of safeguarding its overall food supply.

According to China's 13th five-year plan (2016–2020), there are two main objectives for its agricultural sector—attaining self-sufficiency in production of cereals and maintaining "absolute food-security". For attaining self-sufficiency, the supply and demand of food grains, especially corn, wheat and rice, which provide bulk of calories to most people, needs to be evenly balanced. To meet its national goal of sustaining food security, China needs to import 100 million tonnes of soybeans to be used as animal feed for feeding its farm animals. For achieving its food security goals, numerous steps were undertaken to boost agricultural output—firstly, consolidating smaller farms into a large entity for leveraging economies of scale; secondly, enhancing farming mechanisation with an overall investment of $450 billion; thirdly, strategically acquiring global food corporations like Smithfield Foods and Syngenta; fourthly, expanding overseas farm assets to add to its existing 6.6 million hectares to support increased domestic farm acreage (in some 100 countries with $30 billion investment in 2018). The present overseas farm assets of China consist of large soybean plantations in South America and two dozen strategically positioned Agriculture Technology Demonstration Centres (ATDCS) in low-yielding Sub-Saharan Africa. China has also made major shifts in it's crop-growing strategy (what-grows-where strategy). Rice cultivation has now been moved from urbanised provinces of South Coast to less developed Northeast regions, while cotton is now being produced in Xinjiang, and Inner Mongolia has begun cultivating soybean.

China made news headlines for most of 2018 by blocking a majority of US soybean imports through the imposition of punitive 25 per cent import tariff in response to the trade war unleashed by US President Donald Trump on a range of Chinese products. The targeting of agricultural industry is a strategic move by China as a large majority of US agricultural industry is in Republican-dominated political constituencies. China has thus retaliated by increasing its imports from South America and reducing the soymeal ratio with alternative protein-sources such as cornmeal, rapeseed or cottonseed to be used as animal feed for its farm animals. The gap in Chinese soybean market is pretty large as it imports about 90 per cent of its soybean consumption which is largely used to produce edible oil and animal feed. Back in 2017, Chinese imports totalled 95.53 million tons of soybean—32.58 million tons from US and 50.93 million tons from Brazil. However, in 2018 due to US-China trade war, it imported 84 million tons of soybeans from Brazil. 'China is using agri-imports to help it conserve its land. Importing cotton and soybeans is equivalent to importing land and water resources. This is of great advantage to China's ecological environment.'[22]

Food security is one of the topmost priorities in China's list of development issues. As China is the world's most populated nation, it "feeds 20% of world's population with just 7% of the world's arable lands."[23] Additionally, with agricultural imports of 120 million metric tons of cereals annually, any tweaks in China's food security policy could have a significant impact on global agricultural market. In September 2018, while inspecting Beidahuang agriculture and agricultural machinery centres in the Heilongjiang province, Xi said, "Chinese people should hold the rice bowl in their own hands, and this (food) bowl should contain the food produced ourselves."

Rigors of Regulations: Supervision

In China, corruption investigations and political purges are the new norm. Corruption in China is a major political and social problem since the 1978s implementation of "reform and opening" policies due to the existence of its dual economic systems. Growing public outrage directed at the galloping corruption within CCP organisations and government bodies is a decisive reason for the many student demonstrations of 1989. After 1989 Tiananmen Square students' protests, leaders of China gave priority to increasing the tempo of ongoing anti-corruption work. Committed to ramping the government-sanctioned anti-corruption initiatives, this work has gathered momentum in the recent past. But till date corruption still remains largely alive and is currently considered as the second greatest public concern.

As per the prevailing official terminology, core elements of corruption comprise the notions "of misusing public authority and public resources for private interests" ("Yi Quan Mu Si").[24] This has three main features—first, core corruption element is not "abuse" or "misuse" of public power but frequent "use" of public power for furthering private interests; second, ambiguity of "private interest" terminology in contrast to the words "public interest"; and thirdly, the reason of corruption are not clear. This refers to individual public officials as well as their relatives. Corruption is of prime concern to the Party because not only does corruption impede economic development, it also causes political instability by creating a crisis of licitness for the in-power political regime. With an expanding economic reform, Chinese government reinstituted different anti-corruption agencies that were largely paralysed during the decade-long Cultural Revolution (1966–1976). Since 1978, anti-corruption works had been separated between CCP party and the state. In the Party, discipline was enforced in the nationwide cadres by the Central Commission for Discipline Inspection (CCDI). The tasks of CCDI include enforcing anti-graft measures, enhancing Party loyalty, ensuring ethical ways of work and a frugal lifestyle amongst all Party members who make up 80 per cent of all government officials and 95 per cent of state officials. On the state's side, three agencies carried out anti-corruption tasks—firstly, State Council Ministry of Supervision (MOS) supervises the government officials who are non-CCP members for violations; second, National Bureau of Corruption Prevention (NBCP) formulates the anti-corruption policy and also manages the global anti-corruption synergism; and third, specialized departments of Supreme People's Procuratorate (SPP) are accountable for probing corruption malpractices.

Ever since Xi assumed office as China's President in November 2012, he has waged an aggressive multifaceted war on corruption to ensure that all officials live frugally and work sincerely. According to Xi, public figures, "dare not, cannot and do not want to, be corrupt." In his many official statement broadcasts by Xinhua, Xi announced that it is as critical to proceed against "flies" (low ranking officials) to deal with "tigers" (top officials). Xi has assured the regulation of CCP's current anti-corruption measures and has called for strengthening laws in order to punish and prevent corruption. When Xi launched his famous 'mass line' effort in June 2013 to fight corruption, he told all officials to "gaze into the mirror, straighten their outfits, bathe, and treat their illnesses." Here the "mirror" signified the CCP Constitution.[25] After seven years of concerted anti-corruption campaigns "that investigated more than 2.7 million officials, the government has punished more than 1.5 million and criminally tried 58,000",[26] Xi has aggressively pushed forward for more reforms in the anti-corruption drive to "effectively constrain the power of public servants in a cage of regulations under CCP leadership".[27] Thus Xi's approach to address the problem of corruption has been quite similar to the previous Chinese leaders; however, he has shown unusual vigour and persistence. These valiant efforts are bearing fruit as it has stopped corrupt practices from undermining CCP's political ecosystem and the nation.

The Party has come out in full support of Xi's vigorous anti-corruption drive and has stated that its leaders are in agreement with the ongoing rounds of political purges and anti-graft investigations as the new norm for national governance. "At the Party Congress, Xi highlighted party's plan to institutionalize the anti-corruption campaigns by deepening the national supervision systems and building supervision commissions at both national and sub-national levels."[28] In March 2018, in order to enhance the efficacy of various anti-corruption reforms, China created the National Supervision

Commission (NSC) with a countrywide footprint and institutionalised 'Supervision Law', which has authorised the NSC to have extensive supervisory and investigative powers. These March 2018 measures demonstrate CCP's continued commitment towards strengthening all of its anti-corruption campaigns by putting all 'public power holders'[29] under strict supervision. The NSC reports to the National People's Congress (NPC) and has now been empowered to investigate for possibly corrupt officials and official duties-related crimes from MOS, NBCP and SPP. It thus consolidates different anti-corruption responsibilities and anti-graft drives within one institution. NSC also spearheads local and national level commissions at provincial, city and county level.

Under China's Supervision Law, NSC is responsible to NPC; local supervision commissions are responsible to people's congresses at their own levels and to supervision commissions at higher levels. NSC remains a political body instead of being an administrative body similar to MOS, its predecessor. It is not a judicial body like SPC or even SPP. This signifies that anti-corruption supervision system is effectively exempted from criminal procedure immunity and is not subjected to prevailing structure of administrative laws that would have created substantive and procedural hindrances on different government administrative bodies, namely the state police. Supervision commissions' immunity from any legal accountability or laws "other than Supervision Law does raise concerns whether this new supervision system could seriously undermine Xi's other signature initiatives of Rule of Law."[30]

President Xi's and CCP have consolidated domination over all forms of media. Xi stated that all media "should have Party in their surnames, need to love the Party, forever protect the Party and even serve the Party at all times." Xi had also said that news and public opinion work should always be under "supervision by public opinion." The media in China is state-controlled and monitored with the government being the main force in its supervision by public opinion. But consistent growth of new media channels and a tug of war between the international and domestic media has led to reduced state control, a status that Xi wants to alter.

Another sector where corruption is endemic is People's Liberation Army (PLA) which has arisen due to its involvement in China's economy whereby armed forces were encouraged to do business activities for supplementing state budgets. This grew significantly in early 1990s, as an outcome of post-

Cold War cuts in the military budget. Military-managed businesses thus became key sources of corruption. In 1998, President Jiang Zemin's government ordered PLA's divestment from most business initiatives. However, PLA still retained select business activities such as real estate. It was only in November 2015 that the CCP completely withdrew the PLA from all business-related activities. In July 2015, General Guo Boxing[31] became a victim of PLA's widening anti-corruption investigations. He was summarily expelled from CCP and was convicted in a closed-room trial. In July 2016, he was given life imprisonment for taking bribes of $12.3 million for influencing military promotions.[32] The anti-corruption drive uncovered corruption in every PLA activity and department. Departments especially targeted by anti-corruption sleuths were—General Armaments Department (GAD) charged with weapons' procurements; General Logistics Department (GLD) dealing with PLA finances, fuel, construction, real estate and health; and Political Department which handled appointments and staff promotions. New rules were introduced to curb lavish spending, especially on hospitality and luxury cars for official duties. CMC's Audit office and CMC's Discipline Inspection Commission were established and were charged with sending anti-corruption inspectors to different military units.[33]

A key question being asked in national and global sections of society today is whether this concreted anti-corruption crackdown is a genuine initiative, or simply Xi's new power-play to purge political opponents for strengthening his control over CCP and PLA. While this is a certainty, the ongoing anti-corruption campaigns along with the far-reaching PLA's reorganisation need to be seen as attempts to bring media and the military under CCP's iron-clad control, or in other words under Xi's personal control.[34]

Socialist Rule of Law with Chinese Features

China's first written laws of state governance appeared in Spring, Autumn and Warring States periods of 770–221 BC. Later on, from Han Dynasty (206 BC–AD 220) to Tang Dynasty (618–907 BC), Chinese rulers used fully developed sets of written state laws. In ancient times, these laws were meant to regulate public behaviour and the overall social order. Hence, the main focus was integrating 'rule of law' and 'rule of virtues' amongst every strata of life. These ancient laws were based on realities of social life of those times. These laws were practical and focussed on enriching China's socio-political heritage.

This has been clearly explained in Lord Shang's book, *Shang Jun Shu* where he has said, "In governing a nation, wise rulers establish their governing-laws through observation of popular customs to bring order to their kingdom. When you ignore prevailing customs the fundamentals of the land get neglected. Then its people do fall prey to disorder even if laws are made."

The rule of law's passage in China's contemporary era reflects its national goals and identity which are defined by the ruling CCP. Here, rule of law has been changed to support the country's changing goals—economic development, followed by harmonious society, and finally the 'China Dream'. In the early 1970s, China restructured the prevailing legal system as it moved from the Cultural Revolution's chaos to its years of isolation, later transforming itself to be a significant part of the world's market economy. In the beginning, China effectively bifurcated its legal system as its one track was consistent with global standards to adjudicate on commercial disputes of foreign businesses, and another legal system was aligned to traditional Chinese ideologies for domestic citizen's disputes. Early 1990s witnessed accelerated economic development spurring a greater number of disputes. To further boost its GDP, China deepened its nationwide market reforms and encouraged people to use its law courts. More efforts were made to enhance court reforms with amendments in 1991 to the civil procedure law. The Chinese Civil Procedure Code finely blended dominant Chinese ideologies of Mao, socialism, and its prevailing civil law. This emphasised on conciliation, rather than legal adjudication. In 1997, CCP, at its 15th National Congress emphasised on "its 10-year target for national economic and social development to be achieved with a socialistic strategy of managing state affairs based on prevailing laws of the land to build a socialist nation governed by law."[35] Here the reformers of China encouraged greater use of law and its law-enforcing agencies by its citizens. Thus, China announced to the world that it's "a country ruled by law" and its citizens are encouraged to implement its laws in every sphere of their lives.[36] Economic policies and economic activities have been increasingly embedded into its legal system fabric. In June 1998, Supreme People's Court (SPC) promulgated its famous 'Rules of Civil and Economic Trials' which legally assigned the burden of proof of their acts on the parties concerned, rather than on state's judicial investigators. This system suffered from two main shortcomings—first, as the courts were financed by local governments, courts often faced immense government pressure for biased interventions, often termed as 'local protectionism'; second, "judiciary acted more like bureaucratic officials or civil servants within a tightly CCP-controlled power-hierarchy than behaving like independent and unbiased adjudicators".[37]

By mid-2000s, rising citizen disenchantment with growing economic inequalities due to galloping economic growth led to widespread social unrest with people taking to the streets to express their distress. Litigants flooded courts with a multitude of appeal petitions involving different governmental agencies, even as they spilled out in the streets to vent their anguish. Concerned with growing social unrest and the resultant instability, the central government launched its next level of policy reforms to enhance and sustain 'social harmony'. The legal system responded by resurrecting its historical preference of mediation over adjudication and now the trial reforms blended two ideologies, that is, "stability at all costs"[38] and pragmatic legal solutions to boost social, individual, business efficiencies and accountability. Instead of adjudicating on right from wrong, the Chinese courts were increasingly asked to be the safety valve to an increasing range of complaints filed by people and as well as enterprises. Judges in China were urged to terminate disputes rather than deliberate and adjudicate on them to maintain social harmony. Chinese authorities streamlined mediation processes, and on 28 August 2010, National People's Congress Standing Committee passed its first "People's Mediation Law" (PML) which was implemented from 1 January 2011. Supreme People's Court in 2013 identified completion of "Diversified Dispute Resolution" as its major goal of speeding up the reforms initiated by CCP. Under China's diversified dispute resolutions, courts of law are expected to segregate different tracks with different kinds of legal dispute cases with more emphasis on mediation.

In recent times, China has advocated another national goal—the 'China Dream', an inward turn towards countrywide nationalism with a powerful appeal for renewed patriotism with concerted efforts to recentralise. In the 4th Plenum of 18th Central Committee of the CCP (23 October 2014), a decision to "Comprehensively Promote Governing of China according to the prevailing Law was made."[39] The Plenary session was unique as it was the first time it was completely devoted to decisions on the topic of law. Additionally, the Plenum decision reaffirmed centralising the primacy of the Party's and national government's control as they were the key initiators of the country's law.[40] The Plenum Decision declared that China was primarily a developmental state with shepherding CCP within it. This gave rise to a more potent and self-assured China to follow its own independent development path with its custom legal reforms. The Plenum Decision endorsed that in an instance of major policy change, the matter would need to be referred to the Party's central committee for deliberation, this being the first time the CCP endorsed its role in creation of laws for the country. Furthermore, the Plenum decision clearly stressed on dual structures of the Party-State inherent order that China leverages to govern the country according to its prevailing laws. But when it comes to CCP, the political Party were to be governed by its own set of internal rules.

Many reforms consistent with today's realities seek to recentralise the prevailing court system by redirecting legal authority back to China's central state. Under its proclaimed policy of "eating in different kitchens", local governments are required to cover their costs with their revenues.[41] While funding is scarce, many courts resort to extra-budgetary funding that is often sourced from litigation fees and different judicial fines imposed on litigants. Insufficient court funding also induced many judges to indulge in corrupt profit-making practices such as collecting arbitrary litigation fees and selecting high-fee cases. However, what worried the central government was the fact that local funding made courts more susceptible to pressures from local governments. Thus, in 2017, as part of a judicial reform white paper, China's central government promoted centralised control of personnel, material and financial resources of all local courts below the provincial level as part of its major legal reforms.[42] Concrete steps were taken to unify and set uniform legal outcomes through an elaborate guidance system centrally established by SPC. Its case guidance system allowed the Supreme People's Court to unify and effectively 'rein in' lower provincial courts through different circulars, interpretations and publication of prominent cases. Beginning 2011 when the SPC first published its guiding (leading) cases till 2018, SPC had uploaded close to 95 decisions on its website that local courts at all levels need to refer to while deciding on similar cases. Now all the local courts have begun online posting of their case details. By December 2018, about 32 million lower court cases had been posted on the Internet. The primary reason for posting about the cases of lower court cases is to curb wrongdoings, promote greater transparency, maintain the legal authority of SPC and enhance uniformity and quality of court decisions nationwide.

Finally, from 2014 onwards the SPC has added its own physical presence in local provinces by way of 'circuit courts' to adjudicate on inter-regional issues. These 'circuit courts' are a way to stem increased social instability and the resultant public dissatisfaction with the local legal systems. Moreover, the creation of circuit courts firmly reasserts the central control and curbs extra judicial powers of local courts. It also focuses on lowering the legal centre of gravity by getting more disputes conveniently resolved locally, involving a central authority to resolve local disputes. It also helps to effectively funnel all information back to the central agencies in Beijing.

For the past one year, China has carried out numerous reforms to unify the different applications of its different laws to ensure a more efficient, fairer and centralised legal ecosystem. These measures includes the establishment of Shanghai Financial Court on 20 August 2018, restructuring Supreme People's Procuratorate into 10 new departments, launch of two online e-courts in Beijing and Guang Zhou, reshuffling of judges and prosecutors to mitigate bias, live streaming of over two million court trials, and initiating the process to upload all police enforcement activities as directed by Ministry of Public Security.

Prosperity and Wellbeing

China as a nation is currently enjoying its most stable and prosperous period in modern times. Prior to its 1978 economic reforms, Chinese people suffered from prolonged periods of hardship and suffering. For many years, they were 'subjected to aggression and humiliation',[43] shattered by civil wars and painfully uprooted by numerous class-struggles. During the Cultural Revolution (1966–1976) in particular, launched by Chairman Mao Zedong, millions of Chinese were physically and psychologically tortured and killed. China's socio-political problems and issues with its social security system emanated from two historic events—first, the crumbling of the state-run economy that had for many years sustained urban workers with 'iron rice bowl' viz. food, employment, healthcare, housing, and pension; second, the introduction of the one-child policy in 1980s which meant that parents could not rely on large joint families to care for them when they aged. Hence, as the Chinese economy developed and got liberalised in 1990s, state and social structures supporting workers in their old age, ill-health and during economic hardships gradually disappeared, leaving a huge void to fill. Thus Chinese authorities contemplated a social security system with the responsibility of providing pension, medial, disability due to work and maternity issues by the employers in the form of a contract instead of the state.

With the world's largest number of millionaires (1.09 million), and second largest number of billionaires, China boasts of considerable social affluence. It also has many impressive people-parameters which measure the quality of life—life expectancy (75 years), per capita income ($7,600), literacy rate (96 per cent), population with access to health insurance and primary healthcare (95 per cent), and population with access to telecommunication (95 per cent). Additionally, China has made impressive economic and social strides since it began its 'reform and opening up' programme in 1978. China has succeeded in lifting 700 million rural people out of poverty. However, by the end of 2018, China still struggled with 42 million rural people living below the poverty line.

In its 13th five-year plan (2016–2020), poverty relief goals state that by 2020 all the rural poor will have guaranteed access to fulfil their basic living needs of food, clothing, compulsory education, basic medical care and safe housing. The state thus plans to target all poverty stricken areas to ensure growth rate in rural per capita income to even exceed the national average growth rate. Six major measures have been adopted to eliminate poverty—providing job opportunities with focus on local resources, relocating poverty stricken people living under adverse natural conditions, creating more environment-related jobs to strengthen environmental conservation and restoration, improving basic and vocational education, providing superior healthcare support, and guaranteed social security assistance to families unable to escape poverty through customised business-driven poverty alleviation or employment assistance programmes. As per Corporate Social Responsibility (CSR), projects of private companies are also been fully leveraged, namely the 'Joining Hands to Get Prosperous Action' programme initiated by prosperous provinces in the east to help impoverished counties, and the successful 'Programme of 10,000 Enterprises Helping 10,000 Villages' by the western provinces. All these programmes have greatly supported the Chinese government in its efforts to fulfil its poverty relief goals.

The Chinese government has radically changed the perception of its housing sector from that of a non-productive welfare service to recognising it as a commodity. Thanks to this market-driven approach, the government adopted different measures to stop State-Owned Enterprises (SOEs) from constructing and issuing living accommodations to the workers. Instead, workers were required to win their housing needs by bidding in the competitive open market. Additionally, the Chinese government started a housing fund for helping employees with no housing to enable them to purchase their own home. Widespread urbanisation is a major initiative by the central government of China to fully address the housing needs of its people. At the start of reform era in 1976, only 18 per cent (172 million) people lived in cities and towns; however, today about 54 per cent (731 million) of China's population lives in urban areas. This steady increase was spurred by the coming together of three processes—concerted rural-to-urban population migration, mass construction of new urban infrastructure, and the rezoning of various cities. Premier Li Keqiang unveiled the 'National New Urbanization Plan'[44] in March 2014. This was the country's maiden official urbanisation roadmap, as no other government in China's history had attempted to devise a grand-scale plan that was a complete, well-orchestrated nationwide urbanisation plan. This mass urbanisation blueprint for the nation covered issues like lands and buildings, public-private transportation, people and business communication, public services, environment, finances, labour, food, governance, and other pertinent facets of urban life planning. China is spending about $4,000 billion per annum on constructing buildings in urban areas and over 28 billion square feet of new residential housing buildings. The government aims to have 60 per cent of its people residing in urban cities by 2020, thereby relocating 260 million rural residents through the creation of new jobs for 110 million and by absorbing over 150 million migrants currently living in metropolitan regions. Going further, the Chinese government plans that by the year 2030, over 1 billion Chinese people or 70 per cent will be urbanites.

China currently has five megacities with over a population of over 10 million; 14 cities with a population of over five million; and 41 cities with over two million residents. By 2025, China plans to have at least 46 of the world's 200 largest cities to be Chinese. The Chinese government plans to transform its great Pearl River Delta, including Guangzhou, Shenzhen, and Zhuhai into a huge megacity with over 42 million people,[45] and the Beijing-Tianjin-Hebei triangle-grouping (called *Jing-Jin-Ji* in China) into an even bigger megacity with 82,000 square miles and over 130 million residents.[46] China's latest urbanisation thrust to create megalopolises is a recent policy shift from the past, as earlier governments were developing small and medium cities and towns. China's mega-urbanisation plan are very intriguing as it plans to transform its labour market and unlock huge consumer spending while providing enhanced living and working conditions for over one billion people.

Provisioning more accessible and affordable healthcare in China is its major success story. After three decades of continuous decline during its early reform era when its state supported system steadily shrank, this alarming decline was arrested by the government lead by Hu Jintao-Wen Jiabao which launched a major healthcare reform initiative in 2009. It has earnestly begun to rebuild the cracking system to be able to provide universal and comprehensive healthcare to its entire population by 2020.[47] This has been a hugely successful effort as in a short span of five years, about 95 per cent of Chinese already enjoy comprehensive health insurance coverage. This almost miraculous reversal that took effect in a very short time frame has enabled 80 per cent of its households to benefit[48] from this move. This turnaround in healthcare became possible thanks to the significant central government funding and subsidy contributions. From 2009 to 2011, the Chinese government invested over ¥1.24 trillion to resurrect its ailing healthcare system.[49] The Chinese healthcare spending is estimated to further increase from $357 billion in 2011 to over $1 trillion in 2020.[50] Chinese healthcare system has been revamped to include the construction of numerous local hospitals and neighbourhood clinics. This overhaul of the healthcare system is slated to deliver superior macro-economic benefits for the country. One reason for China's excessively high savings rate is the citizenry's fears about exorbitant healthcare and uncertainties in old age after retirement. Now, with state-funded affordable and accessible healthcare, these unproductive savings are now free to be invested into its economy through various activities.

The Chinese government in 2008 instituted the National Pension Administration to revamp the ill-managed system of retirement pensions by injecting more funds. This positive move resulted in doubling of the enrolments (from 30 per cent in 2009 to 60 per cent in 2012).[51] In 2014, the State Council further improved the pension system by establishing a unified countrywide system for the first time and also covering all "non-working urban and rural residents" resulting in the scheme's coverage to 86 per cent of the population by 2018. However, with large numbers of baby-boomers retiring en-masse, there is likely to be a shortfall of pension funds of about $10.9 trillion in 2033 and $128 trillion by 2050.[52] Hence, while China's pension problems may be eliminated for the time being, it could come under grave financial burden that could plague China for many years to come.

Education remains one of China's main bottlenecks which is holding up its citizens' progress to match global standards. China's universities rank far below other world-class institutions, despite numerous state-led reforms since the mid-1990s and enormous funds being infused in the education sector. Minimal qualitative progress has been made till date in spite of the reforms. Project 211 led the initial wave of reforms that focussed on creating 100 top class universities by the turn of 21st century. While initially it aimed at expanding the breadth (newer courses, more seats), the consequent second phase focused on depth (education quality and intensity). This second phase wave education reforms were triggered by the speech of former president Jiang Zemin's on the occasion of Peking University's 100th anniversary on 4 May 1998. Thus 'Project 985' was launched after Zemin announced that "China must have numerous of world-class universities." Project C-9 plus was launched in order to have high-priority institutions who would be favoured with generous funding and top quality faculty.

Project 211 did not progress as planned since it was dependent on funding by the local government which was cash-strapped and had different priorities. Project 985 delivered better results as many of the C-9 institutions emerged out of it, with three of them gracing the global top-100 ranking.[53] Thanks to this initiative's progress, higher education has been made more accessible to millions who earlier could never think of getting good quality college education. With its students enrolments growing consistently over the last two decades, Chinese higher education institutions received record enrolments of 40 million in 2018.

Chinese pedagogy is still stuck in ancient times as it emphasises on rote memorization with the purported 'correct thoughts'. Excelling in college examinations is thus a mechanical process of merely memorising information. Syllabus includes verbatim memorisation of important CCP principles. Little emphasis is given on student innovation, critical thinking or even independent judgment, or performing better with the possibility of multiple explanations for a particular phenomenon. Students are forced to live with the fact that only one 'right' answer exists and any deviation from this fact would attract severe penalties. With absence of instruction in hypothesis formulation and testing, or sharing the logic that underlies it, teaching pedagogy of China's institutions needs to be urgently revamped. These institutions need to inject more critical and inquiry based learning into their courses and teaching methodologies.

EXTERNAL DIALOGUES

The Beijing Consensus

China's consistent economic growth over many decades with a centralised iron clad socialist control has stumped many Western democratic free-market theorists. The Chinese growth model is diametrically opposite to traditional Western democracies that have held the primacy of free markets and freedom of the populace as the yardstick of building and sustaining success. China, on the other hand, has enjoyed stupendous economic growth thereby creating affluence for its citizenry, enormous money surplus for the nation as well as funded poverty alleviation efforts with rapid urbanisation. While the gleaming megacities of China are great brand ambassadors of the new age China that seeks a superpower status rivalling the US, its very own governance and foreign policy model is unique and has begun to seduce many developing nations who get attracted by its state authoritarianism for rooting out inefficiencies and boosting macro- and micro-economic growth. Joshua Cooper Ramo's Beijing Consensus white paper (2004) compared Chinese economic growth complexities and successes with different economic growth principles in Western world's free economy model espoused by 'Washington Consensus'. Washington Consensus model for economic growth makes it imperative for a country to institutionalise financial reforms, drive economic liberalisation, preserve private rights for citizens, and maintain macroeconomic stability with a liberal-democratic political setup. However, China's very own Beijing Consensus is ideologically neutral and consistently flexible as compared to Washington Consensus' doctrinal rigidity. The Chinese model thus allows pragmatic experimentation and opportunistic innovation to make the best use of existing conditions which resulted in continuously stellar outcomes for the nation for 30 years.

In the beginning of the 21st century, many of the developing countries in Africa, Latin America, and Eastern Europe, along with Russia and India moved away from giving primacy to state-controlled economic socialism. Francis Fukuyama, the celebrated political scientist, famously proclaimed in 1992 the "end of history", that is, the end of humankind's ideological evolution and globalisation of the Western world's liberal democratic model as successful human government's final-structure. However, the 2008 financial meltdown changed this scenario. In the present day, leaders are debating on how much and how long can Beijing Consensus succeed as China actively pursues its goal of projecting its economic and political influence in the world. Chinese reforms have delivered rapid and recurring growth for over 35 years, thereby enabling the country to effectively free millions of its citizens from the clutches of poverty. There are 10 million search hits for *zhong guo mo shi* (Chinese nation-governance model) on the popular Chinese search engine which speaks of its growing popularity (national and international). In recent times, China has become an efficient competitor to the Western world's model of living with a liberal democratic setup. A growing number of nations in the post-communist era's developing world are enamoured by China's 'growth with stability' model. Thus, numerous mid-sized, non-Western countries now prefer China's authoritarian model over West's free markets and democracy model thanks to China's ability to deliver higher growth with consistent stability, superior living standards, and restricted public-expression freedom.[54] There are four parts of this Chinese political and socio-economic model:

- first, the state-driven model
- second, right of way: Infrastructure
- third, sound and dependable governance
- fourth, gradual reform and pragmatic path.

The State-Driven Model

In 1978 when China, led by Deng Xiaoping, embarked on its economic reform journey, people had a hazy notion of what could work. Despite Mao Zedong's achievements in uniting China and significantly improving the health and education of the citizens, the Communist regime had struggled for 30 years with a weak economic track record when compared to its prosperous democratic neighbours—Taiwan and South Korea. Thus, Xiaoping and other communist party leaders closely studied their neighbours to develop a strategy for enhanced economic growth and welfare of the people. Alarmed by the prospects of a looming food crisis, China earnestly began its reformation-drive by splitting farming collectives while empowering small-scale farmers. Linking effort with compensation and rewards spurred productivity and led to accelerated growth in the output. This positive impact created the foundation for further changes in the economy. However, Chinese authorities did not go whole hog by transforming all its agricultural markets as many development agencies of the West had recommended to other developing nations. The Chinese instead developed state policies and governance mechanisms to ensure that all farmers had sufficient theoretical expertise, means and motivation needed to increase farm output. State authorities thus retained firm control over input costs, distribution systems, and fertiliser supplies.[55] With the passage of time, superior infrastructure, better agricultural research and development investments with widespread education and training programmes delivered huge benefits.[56] Once the agricultural sector had been sufficiently strengthened, only then did Chinese leaders embark upon more widespread market liberalisation reforms in 1990s and 2000s.

Multi-fold benefits from reconfiguring 'farm output incentives were dramatic and immediate between 1980 and 1985, resulting in steep decline in rural poverty from 76 per cent to 23 per cent. Thus, millions rose above poverty for the very first time.[57] Increased productivity with better incomes spurred a demand for numerous manufacturing products/services and enhanced people's monetary savings that were channelised into different investments. Moreover, this built a surplus labour at the farms that fed the need for workers in the new factories that had begun to sprout.

Rural industries were key beneficiaries of these positive economic growth developments. Leveraging enhanced access to loans, labour, land and technical assistance by local governmental sponsors, Township and Village Enterprise (TVEs) became the most dynamic constituent of China's economy of 1980s and 1990s. Their GDP share rose from about 6 per cent in 1978 to a healthy 26 per cent by 1996.[58] Competition between localities also boosted business investments and put the entire nation on an accelerated growth trajectory. Today, most of China's successful privately-owned manufacturing units began their journey from the largely underdeveloped and predominantly rural agricultural areas.

Chinese leaders smartly prioritised those sectors and firms that were ascertained to become internationally competitive. They then ensured these entities access to cheaper land, capital, labour and technology with better assistance from regulators. They also used state regulation to protect domestic businesses from preying foreign businesses, thereby diminishing foreigner influence. China smartly used Special Economic Zones (SEZs) to attract enhanced Foreign Direct Investment (FDI) at key moments and sectors of its economy thereby allowing them to play a larger role in transforming its economic setup than most of its neighbouring countries. China's state controlled economic-protectionism has always been strategically selective.[59]

The Chinese government has repeatedly intervened in financial markets to ensure stability and development. Its leaders have thus leveraged public policies to change supply and costs of key inputs and goods in a manner that these lead the market with state-controlled and monitored outcomes deemed as critical by the government.[60] Chinese authorities have thus emphasised key roles of the banking and postal savings' system and prudential policy regulations with predetermined limits of competition in financial markets. By minimising risks and maximising conveniences for small and rural depositors, these measures have significantly enhanced capital accumulation with better savings rates. Households in China save approximately 40 per cent of their earnings which is amongst the world's highest income saving rates. The interest rates have deliberately been kept low to boost the capital demand of businesses. China also tightly managed its currency rate and capital controls to prevent wild currency movements. Thus, even though state operations in China are beset with rampant corruption and inefficiencies, the government continues to play a far more positive developmental role despite the state often being regarded as the greatest speed breaker on the way to progress.

Right of Way: Infrastructure

Chinese government has heavily invested in developing all parts of its nation's infrastructure. It has significantly increased its attractiveness to global and national investors thereby boosting its economic growth. From the 1990s, China's focus on developing global-class transport systems and export facilities has resulted in a highly efficient and well-developed transport system which has integrated vast parts of the huge country to reduce great socio-economic inequalities created by nationwide economic reforms. By empowering its people to travel conveniently and affordably, Chinese rail and road network has woven together this continent-sized nation, thereby integrating its people in a manner that seemed improbable until very recently.[61] Millions have transformed their lives with superior job opportunities, more affordable consumer goods, and better travel options. Regional inequalities were further reduced as more firms invested in inland-regions once their severe remoteness and other infrastructural and transportation disadvantages were removed. Additional state investments increased in residential infrastructure—water, electricity, and telephones—leading to inequalities being further reduced. Thus, majority of people have greatly benefitted from China's redeployment of economic gains in infrastructure investments.

The Chinese government discharged a major part in the nation's inclusive development by aggressively promoting local businesses and thousands of SOEs even as they competed amongst themselves at times. This has created an attractive environment for global investors, even as the nation is beset with a weak legal mechanism and higher corruption levels. With regular micromanagement of financial markets to maintain social stability, it is ensured that business outcomes are aligned to China's national objectives. Irrespective of its authoritarianism, there are three features that have helped China outperform most other developing nations—firstly, administrative skills to make complex laws and ensuring their nationwide application such as providing initial support to businesses by the regional and local authorities and governments to ensure that promising micro-enterprises benefit from easier access to funds when money-supply is scarce, thereby ensuring easier access to bigger markets by way of providing more contacts, superior infrastructure and better resources like land and training; second, participation of the citizens in the country's economic growth for wider and better distribution of its many benefits; and thirdly, consistent adoption of aggressive investment-friendly policies attracting more capital, promoting growth, enhanced exports, and spurred development of human resources and technology. Thus global and local investors have shown more confidence in these initiatives by investing huge sums of money in China's economy.

Sound and Dependable Governance

China's heavy investments in education have created a well-educated labour force with highly skilled experts that have greatly pushed forward its economy. While earlier in 1948 about four-fifths of Chinese were illiterate, less than a tenth are uneducated today.[62] In the 1990s, prior to the start of reforms, there were few students who attended higher education colleges and as less than a tenth of college-age children enrolled for higher studies. Today, more than one-fourth of college-age children opt for higher education. However, these significant gains are not only a by-product of modernisation. As China began to emphasise on public health and education in 1950s, 1960s and 1970s, it effectively equipped its people to take full advantage of Deng's wide-ranging capitalist reforms of late 1970s. China created advanced research and development centres for different fields of study—from agriculture to computers—and even strived to mass-disseminate new technologies and information about production strategies. An 'absorptive state' was thus created that was able to increasingly leverage international knowledge and multi-innovation networks.[63] Business models that were found to function well locally were widely replicated and progressively enhanced. This was a continuous process with consistent upgrades across different parts of the economy, namely, industry, agriculture, infrastructure and services. To further accelerate growth, the proven 'experiment-evaluate-scale up' success methodologies were applied widely and implemented quickly.

The government was able to create a distinctive Chinese nationalist power with a common cultural identity and allegiance for nationalist agendas. This created additional support for its own model of economic development focussed on enhancing the country's overall strength. Now, Chinese leaders are mostly concerned with how Chinese citizens and its economy performs as per world standards. This strengthens the leaders even when the popularity of the Communist ideology has somewhat diminished. China's all powerful CCP promoted officials, to deliver consistent growth, and also mapped its own performance from the way incomes have galloped higher, poverty levels have declined, and public welfare services have improved. "While most developing nations often start from a different point, the China-experience make it crystal clear that social cohesion and organic elites' accountability are vital constituents for continued development."[64]

Gradual and Pragmatic Path

Nations around the world often implement state laws without testing them prior to the implementation, but China has consistently used a well-managed trial-and-error process that is evidence-based to test the impact of its policies before their national rollout. Hence, China's reform progress is done in a piecemeal fashion, thanks to its forward-looking measures. Reformist Deng Xiaoping's echoes this approach in his popular dictum—'Crossing the River While Feeling the Rocks'. This piecemeal approach effectively reduces risk while disarming doubting opponents. All the initial economic reformation successes converted many naysayers to support reforms, sometimes due to lucrative dividends these payoffs offered. Subsequent changes set off a positive chain reaction in a heartening evolutionary fashion. These slow and steady changes created remarkable transformations. Instead of wide-ranging market price introductions, China repeatedly used a custom made dual-pricing system to keep its major commodities somewhat under a state-controlled centralised system. While China introduced many incentives, at the same time it effectively enabled the government to minimise any disruptiveness in the reforms. As production expanded more, and more parts of the Chinese economy became market-oriented.[65] Provincial and local authorities made research laboratories for developing new procedures and aggressively encouraged new and innovative ideas. Even those going against Beijing's traditional orthodox set up got state support; for example, Anhui province's local farmers challenged the old commune system thereby creating a platform for introducing more market-oriented techniques in agriculture, and thereafter in industries nationwide. Guangdong's local officials first proposed measures to attract international investment that led to the creation of Shenzen's special economic zones which soon spread to other parts of the country.

Chinese leaders consciously avoided the Western world's 'big bang reform approach' wherein all prices and market functions are simultaneously freed of centralised state controls. Alternatively, China has focused on 'key issues' like "mobility, incentives, price flexibility, openness and competition".[66] This slow and steady approach works to revamp incentives and remove any stumbling blocks through changes in policy that are just sufficient to unleash accumulated economic energy to actualise widespread development.[67] The underlying idea is that these policy measures create a controlled eco-force for unleashing a newly created impetus to overcome developmental obstacles thereby powering subsequent reforms.[68] With China accurately managing its major socio-economic issues, it overcame its shortcomings of government malfeasance, institutional weakness, absence of democracy and even gross distortions to key markets. Impact of these anomalies in China has mattered far less than those in Western capitalistic-democratic models. China's own state-driven centralised reforms model worked well for its economy as all initiatives at different levels were duly rewarded by the state. Organisations manufacturing inexpensive goods could easily sell them overseas. Workers keen to do long work hours in tough conditions were able to remit money home to their families (amounts that were unimaginable previously). Families with resourceful members could now open shopping centres with this accrued money to further enhance their earnings. Farmers with significantly enhanced agricultural yields profitably sold their produce to further boost their incomes. With the passage of time, markets began playing dominant roles across China's diverse economy, unleashing hyper competition and triggering vast expansions in variety, quality production-quantum affordability, and price-competitiveness of the output.

While an elaborate reform roadmap may be absent in China, it does have a 'deliberate-development-compass'. CCP, however, recently realised that while China introduced different reforms, the existing system's structural defects have surfaced such as the absence of a system of policy checks and balances and state's entangled role with markets. All this has emboldened China to further deepen its comprehensive set of reforms which can now be followed by more developing nations who are grappling with slower economic growth.[69]

China appears to be mostly unaffected by different challenges it encounters while pursuing its unique socio-economic reforms and development model. It has moved ahead by leaps and bounds with many of its signature initiatives garnering global fame for the country, such as the BRI, which has created closer ties with many developing countries in Latin American and African. Xi Jinping forcefully asserted this achievement during his CCP's 19th National Congress. He proclaimed that the new age China has "...blazed a new success-trail and is helping friendly developing countries achieve more with modernization. Thus China is today offering newer options for most of developing nations and its citizens who desire faster and wider development while preserving their sovereign-independence." China today has all resources and experiences, Xi declared, to share "Chinese wisdom with the tried and tested Chinese approach to resolve mankind's varied challenges."[70] Prior to his death in 2012, Ethiopia's Meles Zynawi, who was a leader for 21 long years, often professed his keen desire for emulating China's economic resurrection in Ethiopia. He delineated the market-limits of Ethiopia's free markets and consistently praised CCP's economic stewardship and sought China's help in enhancing Ethiopia's manufacturing and infrastructure base. Hailemariam Desalegn, his successor, was far more earnest in trying out new methods of building newer economic-developmental state-plans modelled on China's initiatives. Ethiopia is not a solitary nation in doing this. Countries like Kazakhstan, Rwanda and Bolivia have tried replicating China's eco-transformation blueprint. High-ranking decision leaders travel to China on policy-learning trips. National planning institutions are issuing ambitious developmental white papers based on China's experience of its eco-reforms.[71]

There are no inherent wrongs in this 'copied approach'. If for some valid reasons some nations prefer adopting China's model of governance and economic procedure that challenges West's free market orthodoxies, there is no justification for politicians of the Western countries to hope that these nations remain trapped in poverty. These envious leaders often insist that only democratic West's traditionally free/liberalised market's path to people and national eco-affluence really works with the central theme of their opinion being that 'only democratic and free markets are right pathways for lasting prosperity and stability'.[72]

These free market idealists miss many important Chinese lessons attributed to its meteoric rise and its attraction for developing nations. Also, having a developmental model as an alternative to what the West proposed is important given the free market model's failure across many nations. Despite receiving aid and free advice from the Western countries, very few developing nations were able to transform economies in their respective countries on a scale even remotely approaching the levels of success showcased by China that has often followed a divergent path.

Every nation experiences circumstances specific to its country that calls for a unique and bespoke governance and developmental roadmap. Thus the best approach assimilates developmental ideas and eco-models from all over the world and factors its own legacy of experiences. Understanding the key points of Chinese model will enable developing nations to build their own growth and national strategies.

Taiwan

The relationship between Beijing-Taipei is like teenage romance—partly passionate and partly rocky. From 2008 to early 2016, the two were on amiable terms. However, with the Democratic Progressive Party and Tsai Ing-wen assuming office in Taiwan (May 2016) and Xi being overtly exhibitionist about his 'One China' policy, relations between the two countries have become tumultuous. The glimmer of hope which the world saw in November 2015 after Xi met Ma Ying-jeou in Singapore died when the Tsai administration refused to agree with 'One China policy' on the grounds that the 1992 Consensus did not hold water any more.

Taiwan as a country is dependent on the forever oscillating US and the temperament of its top brass. Coupled with it is China whose increasingly aggressive presence does not give enough breathing space to Taiwan. A nation sandwiched between the two needs to be malleable in order to survive. While China wants Taiwan to be ductile, US hopes for a stronger ally.

For Taiwan, it is crucial to be have an identity of its own. With its economic prosperity being closely linked to that of China along with ongoing trade tussle between its allies, it has become increasingly difficult for Taiwan to tread a neutral and a non-aligned path. Situations like the present are a test of its loyalty and both the countries would want to extract their pound of flesh given that Taiwan has been on the receiving end of their magnanimity more often than not.

China has made many an attempt to convey to the world that the People's Republic of China is the only representative of China and the Chinese interests and it was this unequivocal message which made the rest of the world 'conveniently forget' the independent existence of Taiwan when it came to extending invitation to the World Health Assembly for two consecutive years. This was further accentuated when China procured recognition from some of Taiwan's diplomatic partners. Given China's aggressive lobbying in this area, today there are only 17 nations in the world which recognise Taiwan as a nucleus in its own right, not an electron of China. It is only when the brother from another mother recognised China and accepts its suzerainty does Beijing extend its generosity by representing Taiwan's interests as those of 'Chinese Taipei'.

China regards Taiwan as a part of its core national interests, and hitherto there has been no ambiguity in that regard by any leader. The ferociousness with which the Dragon protects Taiwanese interests entirely rests on its decibel in the international space, and the two needless to say, are inversely proportional.

Over the years, multiple attempts have been made by Chinese leaders to work towards initiating the process of reunification with Taiwan. However, these attempts have been the most during Xi's tenure as he has aggressively assumed a hawkish position on this Chinese dream. Amidst such ambition, Taiwan's fears are not completely unfounded. Given its military might, the Dragon has already won the psychological war against Taiwan.

When China is desperate, it is known to take desperate measures. Beijing's constant manoeuvres, whether in the form of its carrot and stick policy, or the severe cuts in the travel quotas, are indicative that it will not rest unless Taiwan is firmly in its pocket.

Taiwan on its part has tried to engage independently with other nations.

Its stress on developing economic and people-to-people ties with the Southeast Asian countries is a testament of its intentions to hold on to its sovereignty and independence and not relent to the grand Chinese vision of 'One China'. Taiwan is walking the tight rope of maintaining healthy diplomatic relations with the US on one side and China on the other and while doing so, it is trying to not allow any diminishing of its stature as an independent country.

Beijing would be risking far too much geopolitically by ratcheting up Cross-Strait tensions. Any kind of military action against Taiwan would do incalculable damage to China's international image and could well be met by some form of international response premised on the assessment that China's rise is indeed a threat to global peace and security. For a China that is so economically dependent on positive relations with the wider world, this would be a massive setback and might prove fatal for the Communist Party's grip on power. "Therefore, contemporary Chinese strategy toward Taiwan takes a nuanced, multi-faceted approach that has shifted from a primary focus on securing reunification to preventing independence. China's strategic approach to Taiwan will continue to remain ambiguous, operating in a zone of limited war, shy of overt conflict but susceptible to Beijing's abilities to ratchet up or dial down pressures in a manner that best suits its political objectives."[73]

Hong Kong

When Hong Kong was 'returned' to China in 1997, it was as if two lovers were reuniting after a period of long separation. However, what transpired thereafter has been nothing short of dramatic and the relationship between the two has witnessed its fair share of crests and troughs.

As per the 19 December 1984 Sino-British Joint Declaration, Hong Kong was to be governed as a Special Administrative Region of China. It also established that Hong Kong would have high degree of autonomy except in the areas of foreign relations and defence affairs. Although with Xi coming to power, the position has somewhat altered.

The basic freedoms which are a luxury in China were seen as an indispensable necessity in Hong Kong and Xi's stance on the same has led to a severe downgrading of the basic tenets of the rule of law, freedom of speech and expression, etc. Hong Kong's autonomy has been challenged and attempts have been made in form of crackdowns and increasing control to subvert the region and integrate it fully with China. These destabilising and debilitating measures by the Dragon cannot be read and understood in the light of law given its greyness. The interpretation given to the phrase 'broadly representative nominating committee' has attacked the root of Hong Kong's autonomy leading to a gigantic Occupy Movement of 2014. The interpretation virtually threatens the identity and independence of Hong Kong. It was this interpretation which led to the disqualification of its pro-democracy legislators. In furtherance of its objective, Beijing introduced a diktat that any suggestion of Hong Kong's independence is against the pith and substance of the basic law and shall adversely impact the stability and prosperity of Hong Kong and prove to be against the interests of the people of Hong Kong. The attack on the autonomous status of Hong Kong did not end here. The Hong Kong National Party was banned under the Societies Ordinance on the grounds that it was a threat to the national security. The Occupy Moment of 2014 was repeated on 9 June as well as 16 June 2019 when citizens of Hong Kong held two protest marches with millions in attendance calling for scrapping of an extradition law. As there was no government response, the protests continued on 1 July and 7 July 2019 with 550,000 and 230,000 protestors in attendance, respectively, with some students entering the Legislate Council (LegCo) building on 1 July. On 9 July, Hong Kong Chief Executive Carrie Lam announced that the extradition bill did not exist.

Beijing has viewed Hong Kong as its satellite and therefore, any recognition of its independence is antithetical to Xi's ambition of 'One Country, One System'. To what extent would it tread to fulfil the same, remains to be seen. There is a reason why certain events are best left to time. Hong Kong's fate belongs to that category. Also, PRC wants to completely weaken Hong Kong's democratic institutions as it fears that any respite could lead to a 'diffusion of democracy' in the Pearl River Delta Region. How far will Hong Kong go to protect itself is an answer which cannot be answered today.

Japan

Ego damages human relationships but it destroys the relationship which countries share. When two severely egoistic countries try their hand at normalising their otherwise rocky relations, seldom are they able to make any headway. In such cases, the truancy of history is never overlooked.

The relations between China and Japan can be summed up in three words—'clash of egos'. China will never forget the Nanking massacre and ever since Xi has come to power, efforts have been made to not only to revive the public memory but to keep it alive. Xi's cryogenic approach to the brutal incident has made a seventy-year-old issue an attack on the identity of the country in 2019. Deliberate attempts have been in the recent past such as having three new national holidays, changing the war's origin point and renaming the 'Anti-Japanese War of Resistance' as the 'Fourteen Years War of Resistance'.

Often used by the CCP to seek legitimacy, these measures extol the role played by it in the Chinese resistance against Japan. Thus, through one stone Xi has killed two birds—keeping alive the hatred against Japan and cementing the position of the CCP given the glorious role it has played in the past.

The growing economic, political and military might of China has deepened its need to seek justice for all the wrongs done to it by Japan and it is for this reason that its past with Japan continues to dominate the dynamic the two share today.

What has further attacked their rocky relations is the issue regarding Senkaku Islands which were purchased by Japan in 2012. This issue has escalated to an extent that Beijing has often predicted a territorial conflict over the same and with Xi being the front face of the Chinese politics and diplomacy, Japan has often been projected as a barbaric militarist state. Japan-bashing was taken to another level when the Chinese diplomats openly criticised the former in various international forums. However, the Chinese are known for never losing the sight of the bigger picture. When it came to their ambitious BRI, they not only put the best foot forward to normalise their relations with Japan but also send symbolic messages to project that all is well between the two Asian heavyweights.

The attempts made by the China to normalise its relationship with Japan received further impetus given the strengthening trade war between the US and China. It is in the interest of Beijing to have a powerful ally in Asia with which they can foster greater economic cooperation.

China now wishes to concentrate on defending its interests at a global level which includes acquiring foreign technology and give the much needed push to a weakening economy. For Japan, this 'trade war' is a god-sent opportunity to cement its business relations with China.

What will however determine the quality of their engagement are the defence plans of Japan, and China's reaction to them. The decision of Japanese government to upgrade warship Izumo and Kaya to aircraft carriers and to accommodate up to a dozen F-35 fighter jets are signs of Japan's shifting defence position, from reactive to proactive. Moreover, the latest National Defence Program Guideline (NDPG) is historic in its number of features. First is the increase in spending on defence. Japan plans to splash out $245 billion over the next five years—an 11 per cent rise over the past five years, and then about $49 billion annually. That is less than a quarter of China's defence budget, and only around 1 per cent of Japan's GDP. Second is Japan's acquisition of new offensive capabilities which are stretching the constitution even further. This includes the development of a seaborne strike force, upgradation of electronic warfare equipment and procurement of missile defence systems. But as important is the acquisition of the 'stand-off' munitions with long ranges—'JASSMER', a cruise missile fired from a warplane that can travel more than 900 km, about the distance from Okinawa to Shanghai. Japanese officials insist that the target would not be China's mainland but People's Liberation Army (PLA) ships and troops in Japanese waters or on Japanese soil, should that occur. Third, the NDPG has recognised for the first time that Japan needs to prepare for war in space, cyberspace, and on the electromagnetic spectrum. To that end, the air force is establishing a $240m unit to track threats to satellites, backed by powerful new radars in the south-western city of Sanyo-Onoda. Japan also plans to increase its ranks of cyber-warriors over the next five years, from 150 to 500. These shifts are a response to the rapidly changing security environment. "The new NDPG still takes China as a hypothetical adversary, and if implemented the new plan will help Japan respond more quickly to territorial disputes, as well as placing an emphasis on the survivability of its assets."[74]

The relations between Japan and China, for now, can be termed as 'quid pro quo' where both sides lend support to each other in exchange of putting a strong front against a protectionist US. How far they continue to have each other's back will be seen and evaluated only when the loyalty of the new found friendship and their nobility of intent are tested.

World Order

From 1945 onwards (post-World War II) to the present day, global economic and geopolitical is structured in a manner that US is its preeminent global power. The US controls most international institutions, directly or indirectly, for example, World Bank, United Nations, World Trade Organisation, International Monetary Fund, etc. The US dollar is the world's only dominant currency with about two thirds of international trade being carried out using it. Also over 60 per cent of the monetary reserves of central banks of different countries are maintained in US dollars.[75] The US is able to reinforce this US-tilted global eco-architecture through its strong military capabilities. Its military tie-ups with allies in the West and East Europe, Middle East/Gulf, Asian and Pacific countries like South Korea, Japan, and Australia give it an unparalleled political and economic clout. Its globally dispersed 'blue-ocean' capable navy polices apply to many oceans and work out of a 700-strong international network of dedicated military installations in 42 nations.[76] It also has infrastructure-sharing alliances with many other countries around the world to bolster its global military power projection capabilities. Besides, its military, economic and political clout, the US also is the undisputed global leader in scientific research and development and high-tech innovations. Additionally, with a liberalised democratic political order with a free press/multichannel media, a vibrant and strong judiciary, creative arts and sports primacy, the US often serves as modern civilisation's omnipotent beacon. Thus, the traditional US-driven 'world order' has proven to be powerful and resilient. This open market ecosystem has sustained its global edge despite steady decline of the US in terms of its relative economic wellbeing as compared to the galloping growth in many emerging mid-sized developing nations.

In the two decades after the Cold War ended, the world experienced a unique era shaped by the absence of war and growing worldwide eco-prosperity. The disappearance of serious geopolitical competition created global opportunities for more international interdependence with enmeshed global cooperation amongst different nations rising over individual national ideologies. However, in recent times, many fundamental challenges to this prevailing new order have emerged—the collapse of the fragile state order and rising violence in Middle East, Russia's military challenge to the European security order and growing geopolitical Asian regional tension.

Since the birth of People's Republic of China in 1949, US endured a series of dramatic phases recognised by widely different perceptions of what its national leaders believed to be the new world order. Mao Zedong's ascension to national power in 1949 and Deng Xiaoping's leadership put China on different economic paths. China was primarily a revolutionary power, with its own style of domestic policies or attitude towards the emerging global order. China regarded the prevailing international order of free markets as ineffective. This represented the triumph of strong over the weak nations led by imperialists and colonialists with hegemony of the rich and powerful over their poor victim-countries and of the white race over non-white people. These views led China to the reject the global order and geopolitical actions with a strident call to replace it by a more 'democratic/open' global world order. China has always been keen to join the United Nations, but it was blocked by the US. When China joined the UN in 1971, it made no effort to join UN's other bodies. In addition to UN and its global system, China reserved particular ire towards the US dominated-bodies and global pacts with nations that it regarded with hostility, for example, NATO, the US-Japan alliance, and many other US-led security pacts with different nations with military bases around the world designed to project geopolitical hegemony of the US. In 1972 when US President Nixon told Chairman Mao that he as China's supreme Chairman has changed world order, Mao famously replied back, "No, I've changed just a few things on China's outskirts!" China's other reformist leader, Deng Xiaoping also started a domestic strategy of economic reformation by opening up China's economy to global world. This economic restructuring strategy needed foreign investments, global trade, international knowledge and high-technology with foreign business cooperation. With change of attitude towards the US, China's attitude towards the entire world order changed. During Deng Xiaoping's ruling years, China effectively started on a path towards joining all of key UN organisations that it had once abhorred (World Bank, IMF, Nuclear Non-proliferation Treaty, WTO, International Atomic Energy Agency). During Deng's rule and even afterwards in Jiang Zemin's and Hu Jintao's era, China conveyed a sense of comfort with prevailing global order that it joined and constructively engaged with on specific issues. Its initiatives were neither obstructionist nor were they destructive in content and intent.

President Xi Jinping-led China seeks a global role for itself commensurate with its expanded economic and military clout. At the start of Deng's reform, with the opening up of Chinese economy in 1978, China's GDP (measured in current US dollars) was about $150 billion, while in 2018, it surpassed a whopping $12 trillion. China is today the world's second largest economy by GDP, and largest if measured by its purchasing power parity (PPP). As China's economy gallops, so does its military spending—from $19.3 billion in 1989 to a massive $228 billion in 2018. This is second only to the US's defence budget. China continues to make significant monies available for many global bodies; it is both the second largest contributor to the peacekeeping budget and UN's budget. Thus, China has transformed from being a 'silent watcher' to one that is now agreeable to participating, and even revising and reforming the world order. This dramatic change in China's foreign policies is based on Xi's belief in restoring China's "rightful" honour as a preeminent international power.[77]

Unlike in the past, China now recognises that global rules and institutions provide a stable means for its economic development, and China does not have solid incentives to seriously damage or disrupt existing global socio-economic systems. China thus does not seek a disrupted global order. All it desires is a global order that is more aligned to its own economic and political priorities and interests. This, however, does not mean that China is satisfied with the prevailing global order. Today, more than ever, Chinese leaders are disillusioned with global governance institutions, principles and norms. According to them, the current and future world order needs an urgent update to rightfully reflect international multi-polarity, disruptive internationalism and high-tech changes, while preserving socio-economic and political aspects that are still valid for global peace and prosperity. China's domestic politics cannot exist in isolation, separated from its foreign policy. Authoritarian Chinese leaders are in constant fear of domestic unrest so any outside influence targeted at any change in its regime makes Chinese leaders extra careful about applying global norms that might override the sovereign nations' individual objections.

As Xi consolidates his position in perpetuity, he is making every effort to further strengthen the CCP's determined push to consolidate the internalisation of authority within its party. By centralising more power within his own office, Xi is effectively squeezing out any chance of any kind of dissent, political or otherwise, from challenging his and CCP's absolute power stranglehold. Under Xi's leadership, the places where issues have changed recently is government's absolute centralisation with which Xi is transforming the future of CCP. Xi's policy alterations have greatly watered down the global expectations of liberalisation of Chinese political system aligned with its economic reforms and liberalisation.

China's core foreign policy objective is to reshape the global world order in a manner that protects its domestic CCP-driven political ideology. This calls for resisting the spread of liberal norms and denying support to any form of democratic government, and blocking any international proposal of norms that undermines its sovereignty to determine its own governance rules.

Today China is a significant player which is involved in global issues and regions which were once only parametrical to its interests. China's international behaviour is altering the dynamics of organisations, relationships and perceptions all over the world by efficaciously forging balancing coalitions, advancing unique development models for economic resurrections or incorporating high level military diplomacy. China's international behaviour seeks to work within the system to reduce the influence of established powers and to attract others to create an environment in which China is able to expand its access to markets, resources, investments and technologies.

China acknowledges the liberalised global economic order as the one that has delivered numerous benefits to the nation. Of particular significance is China's ongoing membership of WTO (World Trade Organization) which applauds its remarkable era of stupendous economic growth. China thus wants to strengthen WTO's centrality in all matters of international trade. At the same time, China vociferously deplores that US deploys punitive trade-tariffs to influence their bilateral trade disputes as opposed to using WTO's acknowledged trade dispute management systems. China favours WTO mechanisms over US' unilateralism as WTO mechanisms help enhance the stability of global trade. While still seeking a comprehensive WTO reform, China's emphasises on increasing the say of developing countries over matters affecting global business.

The constitution of China proclaims that "The nation will respect and preserves its citizens' human rights", that its people will enjoy many personal freedoms of speech, of assembly, of press, of association, of demonstration and procession and also "enjoy freedom of practicing individual religious faith" with every "individual's freedom being inviolable." Its stellar economic achievements present a unique kind of progress on the front of human rights. China is currently applying this concept as its way of deflating a valid international criticism of state-controlled throttling of many human rights to preserve its state-governance model. Thus, China is promoting its own brand of alternative global norms for human rights that lead to little or no criticism of the Chinese policy of repressing political and individual liberties. China is trying to increasingly use UN-instituted measures in which it is participating to twist how human rights measures are globally interpreted to suit its own personal agenda. With its clear purpose of undermining principles of universality that are a key to legitimate public functioning of the human rights law, China strives to weaken freedom of speech and the associated rights within the prevailing human rights mechanisms. China sees human rights defenders as subversive people out to destroy China. Deploying strong arm tactics, China subjects such dissidents to vicious and systematic persecutions. In December 2017, Xi hosted the 'South-South Human Rights Forum' in Beijing which Chinese government hailed as a mega achievement since it saw an enthusiastic participation of over 300 delegates from over 70 countries. The forum published its Beijing Declaration, proclaiming that every country should have the freedom to "choose its own human rights developmental path or people-better-life-guarantee model that suits its own socio-eco conditions." Hence, Xi stressed on this global necessity for being equitably recognised and universally respected. He vigorously asserted that all nations, big or small, should have the right to choose what suits their political ideology and freely use their respective resources to enhance national governance and socio-cultural-political-economic development. This represented an alternative human rights vision, different from the existing global thought of universality of people's life, freedoms and their right to principles of natural justice. In the human rights arena, evidence points to the fact that CCP will never reform the global rules-based system but rather will sabotage it, by pushing its own version of alternative human rights that focusses on economic development at the expense of universality of individual political and civil liberties.

In recent times, during the anti-globalisation waves, China portrayed itself as a firm believer of multilateralism and as a free trade advocate, with Xi vociferously espousing economic globalism to be irreversible and inevitable. With US withdrawing support from numerous global institutions and pacts, Xi has spoken against such moves; for example, he opposed Trump's administration's withdrawal from Paris pact for reversing climate change. Xi opposed this on the grounds that such unilateral acts sabotage global cooperation to reduce global warming. Xi was also critical of Trump administration abandoning global efforts to arrive at an amicable Iran nuclear deal. Despite global onslaught of criticism, US left the UN Human Right

Council and UNESCO, effectively removing $1.3 billion from the UN budget and also suspending support towards many refugee relief programmes.

China, in its different diplomatic relations, is emphasising on areas of mutual interest rather than fields of conflict. Thus, contentious issues are mostly shelved in favour of going forward with dialogues in other common interest areas; for example, in Russia, it focuses on their mutuality of interests for preserving an interpretation of the Cold War in the UN system and mutually beneficial trade relations, instead of raking up contentious issues like Chinese immigration in Russia's Far East and Russia's 2008 Georgia military intervention. Similarly, notwithstanding its South China Sea territorial disputes with many neighbouring South East Asian countries regarding overlapping maritime claims, China's relations with ASEAN group of countries focus on trade and investment, thus making China's relations with ASEAN pretty robust. Its Shanghai Cooperation Organization of Central Asia effectively showcases a kind of world order with coexistence as envisaged by Chinese leaders. This China-styled coexistence of different nations calls for policy coordination with conflict resolution by prioritising on different non-offensive means of negotiation and persuasion in place of punitive coercions. This focuses on the government's solidarity with a solid top-down cooperative arrangement as it involves strengthening traditional UN mechanisms with emphasis on absolute national-sovereignty. Additionally, China appears to push forward specialisation and the regional focus of authorities to evaluate and act upon purported dangers to peace and the nation's security. This principle of coexistence system enjoys widespread acceptance in today's developing world and it effectively justifies China's global status of an internationally acclaimed maker of global order instead of a nation that is a mere follower of global order.

As China's global profile grows, in the coming decades China would seek a role as an agenda setter with an aim to play a leading role in setting global norms, rules and institutions. However, at present and in the next few years, China seeks to achieve a status of a peer-competitor of the US and not displace it from its predominant position. The present domestic fragility and insecurity coupled with fear of backlash against diverting resources from internal development has forced China to delay its aspirational of being a superpower for the time being.

This phenomenon of China beginning to challenge existing global order has been appropriately summarised by Huang and Patman in their publication *China and the International System: becoming a world power*. They put forth their views that, "China's relationship with the international system is...often framed in terms of how China will adapt, challenge, or integrate with prevailing international systems, and how such global system will engage, constrain, or even accept China."[78] As for China being aware of its global role in the emergent world order, geopolitical thought leaders Lee and Chan state that "Chinese strive to adjust and learn from outside constraints instead of redesigning or reconstructing existing systems and even less attempt to overthrow it."[79]

Much has been said and written about China. While some have heralded the new decade as the decade of the Dragon, others have written China off on the grounds of it being lucky. To a large extent, both these opinions can be said to be right and wrong on equal measures. Fortune favoured China in the light of an unstable Europe, diminishing US, a struggling India and a rebalancing Russia and needless to say, China made full use of this golden opportunity by ensuring that not even an ounce of it went to waste.

From being fully aware and cognisant of its internal challenges to being the voice that matters on the issues of international importance, China has embraced it all. How far it will be able to tighten this hold is yet to be seen.

NOTES

1 David Bohm, On Dialogue, (London: Routledge, 2013).

2 "Beautiful China where skies are blue, mountains green and water lucid", Xi Jinping at the 41st group study of the Political Bureau of 18th CPC Center Committee.

3 Elizabeth C. Economy, The River Runs Black: The Environmental Challenge to China's Future, (Ithaca: Cornell University Press, 2010), p. 48.

4 Deirdre Chetham, Before the Deluge: The Vanishing World of the Yangtze's Three Gorges, (London: Palgrave Macmillan, 2002) p. 178.

5 On March 5, 2014 Premier Li Keqiang 'declared war on pollution' describing the country's smog problem "as nature's red light warning against inefficient and blind development."

6 Xinhua News Agency, "Full Text of Xi Jinping's Report at 19th CPC National Congress," *China Daily*, November 4, 2017. http://www.chinadaily.com.cn/china/19thcpcnational congress/2017-11/04/content_34115212.htm

7 Philip Ball, The Water Kingdom (New York: Random House, 2016), p. 291.

8 Ministry of Foreign Affairs of the People's Republic of China, "Statement of Ambassador MA Zhaoxu on the High-level Event to Launch the International Decade for Action," Water for Sustainable Development (2018–2028), March 23, 2018, https://www.fmprc.gov.cn/mfa_eng/wjb_663304/zwjg_665342/zwbd_665378/t1545168.shtml.

9 Feng Hu, "What 'Xi's Thought? Means For Water," *China Water Risk*, November 17, 2017, http://www.chinawaterrisk.org/resources/analysis-reviews/what-xis-thought-means-for-water/

10 Xinhua News Agency, "Full Text of Xi Jinping's Report at 19th CPC National Congress," *China Daily*, November 4, 2017. http://www.chinadaily.com.cn/china/19thcpcnationalcongress/2017-11/04/content_34115212.htm

11 Ibid., p. 4.

12 Dimitri D. Boer, "Opinion: What Does 'Xi's Thought? Mean for the Environment?", *Chinadialogue*, November 28, 2017, https://www.chinadialogue.net/article/show/single/en/10235-Opinion-What-does-Xi-s-Thought-mean-for-the-environment.

13 The 'Saihanban Spirit' converted a once barren, ninety four thousand hectares wasteland, 312 kilometers North of Beijing into the world's largest human-made forest. The Saihanban Forest Farm was nominated for the 2017 'Champions of the Earth' award.

14 Lillian M. Li, Fighting Famine in North China: State, Market, and Environmental Decline, 1690s-1990s (Redwood City: Stanford University Press, 2007).

15 Du Runsheng, The Course of China's Rural Reform, (Washington, D.C.: International Food Policy Research Institute, 2006), http://dx.doi.org/10.2499/ChRROC52

16 "How China responds to the global food crisis," *Financial Times*, May 8, 2008, http://www.ftchinese.com/story/001019233?archive

17 White Paper, "The Grain Issue in China", Beijing: Information Office of the State Council, 1996, https://www.iatp.org/sites/default/files/Grain_Issue_in_China_White_Paper_The.htm.

18 "Mid-and Long-term Grain Security Plan (2008–2020) Policy Guideline". Beijing: Information Office of the State Council, 2008.

19 "With grain in hand, one would be vexed", *Xinhua New*, November 20, 2013. http://news.xinhuanet.com/politics/2013-11/28/c_118339303.htm

20 Wu and Zhang, China's Global Quest for Resources, pp. 28-29.

21 People's Networks, "The state council issued the division of work for the implementation of the '2014 Central Document No. 1'," *People.cn*, March 10, 2014, http://politics.people.com.cn/n/2014/0310/c1001-24587218.html

22 CGTN News, "Why does China import so many soybeans?", *China Global Television Network*, April 14, 2019, https://news.cgtn.com/news/3d3d514e3441444d34457a6333566d54/index.html

23 China Ministry of Agriculture, China Agricultural Yearbooks (China Agriculture Press, Beijing, China 1982-2017).

24 Zengke He, "Corruption and anti-corruption in reform China," *Communist and Post-Communist Studies* 33, no. 2 (2000), p. 244, doi:10.1016/s0967-067x(00)00006-4.

25 David Bandurski, "Under Xi, the Media Has Turned from a 'mouthpiece of Masses' to the Party's Parrot," *Hong Kong Free Press*, June 21, 2016, https://www.hongkongfp.com/2016/06/21/under-xi-the-media-has-turned-from-a-mouthpiece-of-masses-to-the-partys-parrot/.

26 Gordon Watts, "China Lays Down the Law in Corruption Clampdown," *Asia Times*, 2018, https://www.asiatimes.com/2018/10/article/china-lays-down-the-law-in-corruption-clampdown/.

27 Jamie P. Horsley, "What's So Controversial About China's New Anti-Corruption Body?", *The Diplomat*, May 30, 2018, https://thediplomat.com/2018/05/whats-so-controversial-about-chinas-new-anti-corruption-body/

28 The 19th Central Committee of the CCP, "China's National Supervision Commission: Mercator Institute for China Studies," *Mercator Institute for China Studies*, January 19, 2019, https://www.merics.org/en/polsys/law-digest/chinas-national-supervision-commission.

29 'Public-power-holders' is a term created by Supervision Law which encompasses varied tasks and offences performed by power holders while discharging public duties. The offences covered under the new term are bribery, abuse of official power for personal gain, duty derelictions, power rent-taking, tunneling interests, practising favoritism and wasting national/local government assets.

30 Jamie P. Horsley, "What's So Controversial About China's New Anti-corruption Body?", *Brookings*, June 14, 2018, https://www.brookings.edu/opinions/whats-so-controversial-about-chinas-new-anti-corruption-body/.

31 General Guo Boxiong was during 2002-2012 one of two vice-chairs of CCP's Central Military Commission (CMC).

32 "Former top China military official 'took huge bribes,'" *BBC News*, April 5, 2016, http://www.bbc.com/news/world-asia-china-35970863; and "Former Chinese military leader sentenced for life in corruption case," Deutsche Welle, July 25, 2016, http://www.dw.com/en/former-chinese-military-leader-sentenced-for-life-in-corruption-case/a-19425788

33 Jon Grevatt, "China's PLA introduces spending regulations," *Jane's Defence Industry*, July 7, 2015; Ben Lowsen, "China's military commission digs deep to root out corruption," *The Diplomat*, February 19, 2016, http://thediplomat.com/2016/02/china-military-commission-digs-deep-to-root-out-corruption/; and David Finkelstein, "Initial thoughts on the reorganization and reform of the PLA," *CNA China Studies*, January 15, 2016, https://www.cna.org/cna_files/pdf/DOP-2016-U-012560-Final.pdf.

34 Derek Grossman and Michael S. Chase, "Why Xi is purging the Chinese military," *The National Interest*, April 15, 2016, http://nationalinterest.org/feature/why-xi-purging-the-chinese-military-15795.

35 Jiang Zemin, "16th National Congress of the Communist Party of China, 2002," *China.org.cn*, http://www.china.org.cn/english/features/45607.htm.

36 Margaret Y. Woo, and Mary E. Gallagher, Chinese Justice: Civil Dispute Resolution in Contemporary China, (Cambridge: Cambridge University Press, 2011), p. 25.

37 Kenneth W. Dam, The Law Growth Nexus: Rule of Law And Economic Development (Brookings Institute 2007), p. 250.

38 Joseph Kahn, Deep Flaws and Little Justice, in China's Court System, *N.Y. TIMES*, September 21, 2005, http://www.nytimes.com/2005/09/21/world/asia/deep-flaws-and-little-justice-in-chinas-court-system.html

39 Randall Peerenboom, "Fly High the Banner of Socialist Rule of Law with Chinese Characteristics! What Does the 4th Plenum Decision Mean for Legal Reforms in China?", *SSRN Electronic Journal*, November 2014, doi:10.2139/ssrn.2519917.

40 Jeremy Daum, "CCP Central Committee Decision Concerning Some Major Questions in Comprehensively Moving Governing the Country According to the Law Forward," *China Copyright and Media*, October 28, 2014, https://chinacopyrightandmedia.wordpress.com/2014/10/28/ccp-central-committee-decision-concerning-some-major-questions-in-comprehensively-moving-governing-the-country-according-to-the-law-forward/

41 Chunli Shen, "Fiscal Decentralization in China: History, Impact, Challenges and Next Steps," 13 ANNALS ECON. & FIN. 1, 10.2012, pp. 1-5.

42 China Daily Group, "China Issues White Paper on Judicial Reform of Chinese Courts," *China Daily*, February 27, 2017, http://www.chinadaily.com.cn/china/2017-02/27/content_28361584.htm

43 X.P. Deeng, "Building a Socialism With a Specifically Chinese Character," *The Selected Works of Deng Xiaoping*, June 8, 2013, https://dengxiaopingworks.wordpress.com/2013/03/08/building-a-socialism-with-a-specifically-chinese-character/.

44 Jon R. Taylor, "The China Dream is an Urban Dream: Assessing the CPC's National New-Type Urbanization Plan," *Journal of Chinese Political Science* 20 (2015), pp. 107-20.

45 Moore, Malcoalm, and Peter Foster. "China to Create Largest Mega City in the World with 42 Million People," *Telegraph.co.uk*, January 24, 2011. https://www.telegraph.co.uk/news/worldnews/asia/china/8278315/China-to-create-largest-mega-city-in-the-world-with-42-million-people.html.

46 Ian Johnson, "As Beijing Becomes a Super city, the Rapid Growth Brings Pains," *New York Times*, July 19, 2015.

47 Qian Jiwei, "Reinventing China's Health System," in Wang Gungwu and Zheng Yongnian (eds.), China: Development and Government, (Singapore: World Scientific Publishing, 2013).

48 Baozhen Luo, "China Will Get Rich Before It Grows Old" (Foreign Affairs, October 30, 2015), p. 22.

49 Information Office of the State Council, White Paper on Progress in China's Human Rights in 2014, in China Daily, June 9, 2015.

50 Shirley S. Wang, "Hospital Attempts Cultural Shift in China", *Wall Street Journal*, September 12-13, 2015.

51 Luo, "China Will Get Rich Before It Grows Old", p. 22.

52 Ibid., p. 23.

53 The Core-9 Universities are: "Peking University, Tsinghua University, University of Science and Technology of China, Nanjing University, Fudan University, Shanghai Jiaoton University, Zhejiang University, Xian Jiaotong University, Harbin Institute of Technology".

54 Stefan Halper, The Beijing Consensus: How China's Authoritarian Model Will Dominate the Twenty-First Century, (New York: Basic Books, 2010).

55 Brandt and Rawski, "China's Great Economic Transformation," pp. 9-10.

56 Hauke Brankamp and Tobias Reichert, "China's Agricultural Development: Lessons for Africa?", Worldwatch Institute (Nourishing the Planet blog), June 30, 2010.

57 John Bruce and Zongmin Li, "'Crossing the River While Feeling the Rocks': Incremental Land Reform and Its Impact on Rural Welfare in China," International Food Policy Research Institute Discussion Paper 926 (2009), p. 22.

58 Pranab Bardhan and Awakening Giants, Feet of Clay: Assessing the Economic Rise of China and India (Princeton: Princeton University Press, 2010), pp. 19-21.

59 Brian Wang, "Re-examining the China Economic Miracle," *NextBigFuture.com* – Coverage of Disruptive Science and Technology, February 13, 2018, https://www.nextbigfuture.com/2018/02/re-examining-the-china-economic-miracle.html.

60 World Bank, The East Asian Miracle: Economic Growth and Public Policy (Oxford University Press, 1993).

61 Seth D. Kaplan and Frederik Teufe, "The role of road networks in addressing fragility and building resilience", *Chief Economist Complex*, AEB Vol. 7, Issue 5, 2016, https://www.afdb.org/fileadmin/uploads/afdb/Documents/Publications/AEB_Vol_7_ Issue_5_ The_role_of_road_networks_in_addressing_fragility_and_....pdf

62 People's Republic of China, Ministry of Education, "Historic Achievements: 60 Years of Educational Reform and Development", September 14, 2009.

63 Kirsten Bound, Tom Saunders, James Wilsdon, and Jonathan Adam, *China's Absorptive State: Research, Innovation, and the Prospects for China-UK Collaboration* (Nesta, 2013).

64 Seth D. Kaplan, "Development with Chinese Characteristics: Ten Lessons for Policymakers," *ECDPM*, November 27, 2014, https://ecdpm.org/great-insights/peacebuilding-statebuilding/development-chinese-characteristics-ten-lessons-policymakers/

65 Brandt and Rawski, "China's Great Economic Transformation," p. 10.

66 Ibid., p. 20.

67 Justin Yifu Lin, Fang Cai, and Zhou Li, "The Lessons of China's Transition to a Market Economy," *Cato Journal* (Fall 1996).

68 Dani Rodrik, One Economics, Many Recipes: Globalization, Institutions, and Economic Growth (Princeton: Princeton University Press, 2007).

69 He Li, "The Chinese Model of Development and Its Implications", *World Journal of Social Science Research* 2, no. 2 (2015), 128-138, https://doi.org/10.22158/wjssr.v2n2p128.

70 Yu Tao, "Get Ready for an Even More Assertive China," *The Diplomat*, November 1, 2017, https://thediplomat.com/2017/11/get-ready-for-an-even-more-assertive-china/.

71 Seth D. Kaplan, "Development with Chinese Characteristics," *The American Interest*, April 11, 2018, https://www.the-american-interest.com/2018/01/03/development-chinese-characteristics/.

72 Wang, "Re-examining the China Economic Miracle".

73 Lauren Dickey, "Strategic Theory and Xi Jinping's Taiwan Test," *Journal of British Association for Chinese Studies*, no. 7 (July 2017): pp. 11-12, http://bacsuk.org.uk/wp-content/uploads/2017/07/JBACS-vol-7-July-2017.pdf.

74 Gordon Orr, "What Can We Expect in China in 2019?" McKinsey & Company, December 2018, https://www.mckinsey.com/featured-insights/china/what-can-we-expect-in-china-in-2019.

75 Arthur R. Kroeber, China's Economy: What Everyone Needs to Know (New York: Oxford University Press, 2016), pp. 233-266.

76 US Department of Defense, "Government of USA, Base Structure Report Fiscal Year 2015," https://www.acq.osd.mil/eie/downloads/bsi/base%20structure%20report%20fy15.pdf

77 Dr Yu Jie, "Foreign Affairs Committee: on 'China and the Rules-Based International System'," *Data.parliament.uk*, April 17, 2018, http://data.parliament.uk/writtenevidence/committeeevidence.svc/evidencedocument/foreign-affairs-committee/china-and-the-international-rulesbased-system/written/76381.pdf.

78 Xiaoming Huang and Patman G. Robert, China and the International System: Becoming a World Power (London: Routledge, 2013), p. 1.

79 Huang and Robert, China and the International System, p. 105.

Concluding Remarks

China's growth story is here to stay. The Dragon is here to stay and will continue to exert the influence as it always has. While one may be tempted to predict an endless glory for this nation, one needs to understand the dynamics of this country before predicting anything about it.

China's rise has been slow but steady. While the world was busy being seduced by the stellar growth of the West, China was progressing in its own pace. In the proverbial race of the tortoise and the hare, China was the tortoise which became a hare halfway through it. China emerged faster than imagined and sooner than expected. A country which was struggling till late 1940s to free itself from the Western powers is today ahead of most nations of the world. As one gets mesmerised by its glittering and glamorous growth, one must not forget that the Dragon had no one to lean on. It had to make its own decisions and stand by them. However, what is important here is the manner in which those decisions were made. China only said 'yes' to itself and its interests. Fervently guided by its national interests and funnelled by the ideology and Party loyalty, it sent a clear message that no one should expect China to swallow the bitter fruit that hurts its interests.

What has played in its favour are multiple factors which did not necessarily begin as being favourable. Thus, China's confidence is not unfounded when it comes to its ability to deal with the West, to take positions on territorial disputes or religious fundamentalism, or even fiercely guarding its cyber sovereignty. China has taken a firm stand about all these issues and has been able to leverage its economic and emotional investment to its advantage. While many might paint this as being assertive and manipulative, it is only wise to see it as assertive and moulding because a country like China need not blackmail, it can simply order and others will comply.

The message Beijing intends to send to the world is loud and clear and therefore, to pretend not to hear it is being naïve and foolish.

China is battling with internal issues, especially with Xi being impervious to any sound except his. Constant irritants on the domestic soil, the jittery attitude of the nations around the BRI, risk of an unintended escalation in the South China Sea, the Korean conundrum, the slowdown in growth, etc. are some of the real issues which Xi has on his plate. What seems to be conspicuous by its absence is a direct confrontation with the US in the Indo-Pacific region. China is nothing if not realistic and it is this awareness and realism which has made it steer clear from any kind of military and diplomatic shenanigans in the aforementioned region.

Managing issues is one thing, battling against them is another and living with them is something very different altogether. In relation to social media, China is embroiled in all three. It is managing the ghost of its Christmas past where it had taken a strong position against free media. It is battling against the feeble voices of dissent which are scattered and disintegrated and so, it is living with its legacy of not providing an unfettered freedom of speech and expression. A worried China has an army of online commentators who can pledge their loyalty in the virtual world but for how long can it contain the critique and communication surrounding economy, healthcare, pollution, income disparity. This is something which only time can tell. Legitimacy is like respect it needs to be commanded and not demanded and when the Party demands absolute loyalty from its people, it is clear that not all is well in the Kingdom of Han and Tang.

The leaders in China have always taken a tough, nationalistic stance when it came to defending the interests of China. More often than not, they have worn blinkers when it came to matters of global relevance. Despite much criticism, nor have they altered their position and neither have they relented. One such instance was the repeated exercise of its veto power in the United Nations Security Council when it came to the issue of declaring Masood Azhar as a global terrorist. China was reluctant to exercise its vote against its 'all-weather' ally until it realised that its investment in Pakistan will gain from the permanent shutting down of the terror groups operating on its soil. Beijing is essentially and unapologetically transactional and the world knows about it.

Xi is not afraid of playing any card that suits China but not necessarily the Chinese. He plays the nationalist card when it comes to taking positions on the issue of Xinjiang peninsula under the garb on containing religious fundamentalism; he plays the security card when it comes to expansion in the South China Sea; he plays the peace and mutual non-interference when it comes to cyber space. In essence, China will do whatever it takes to preserve, prevail and propel. The rest of the countries have two options to either be a spectator to the journey of the Dragon or wait to get trampled (read: influenced) or emerge as a power with some meaning and significance to the Dragon's existence.

Index